LODESTARS ANTHOLOGY

PATHWAYS

Edited by Liz Schaffer

When first planning this book I had a moment of panic. I'd agreed to do the project wholeheartedly – and remained excited beyond words – but with it now all laid out before me, how on earth was I to choose 12 soul-lifting pathways from the hundred-odd journeys my team and I had braved?

Lodestars Anthology has complicated my travelling life. For what I deign to call work, I've been allowed to spy scenes that border on the sublime, meet passionate locals who turn holiday destinations into hideaways that could be home, sip tea with artisans redefining their craft, and walk the labyrinth-like side streets of towns untouched by time – all the while sampling more fine fare than could possibly be good for me. When it comes to travel, I've been unashamedly spoilt – and for this reason, the idea of playing favourites seemed like a formidable task indeed.

To make selection easier I added a little order and decided to revisit a single pathway from each of the magazines we had produced (or were at least in the process of producing), along with three locations that, while not yet captured in magazine form, are places I would run away to in a heartbeat. I wanted these pathways to reflect some of the magic that defines the countries they're found within and, in the process, ponder travel's allure. From here, it was simply a case of calling upon a handful of *Lodestars* contributors (crossing paths with photographers, writers and illustrators who adore their professions and produce work that fills you with awe is one of the unparalleled joys of this business) and sending them off on yet another adventure.

The resulting chapters take in everything from England's coastal communities and the calm and creativity they nurture, to Scotland's mythic history and the charms of lesser-known Italy. We explore the flavours of Sweden, the power of Australia's waterways and the unique form of nature worship that has helped shape Japan – and much more besides.

While these journeys may be varied, for me, each was a reminder of travel's potential. For is there anything else that so keenly throws us into the unknown, encourages chance encounters and, more often than not, reminds us of our small yet precious place in this remarkably big world? And so, journeys chosen, travel undertaken and book complete, I can only hope these pathways result in welcome daydreaming and a jaunt or two into the great, wide beyond.

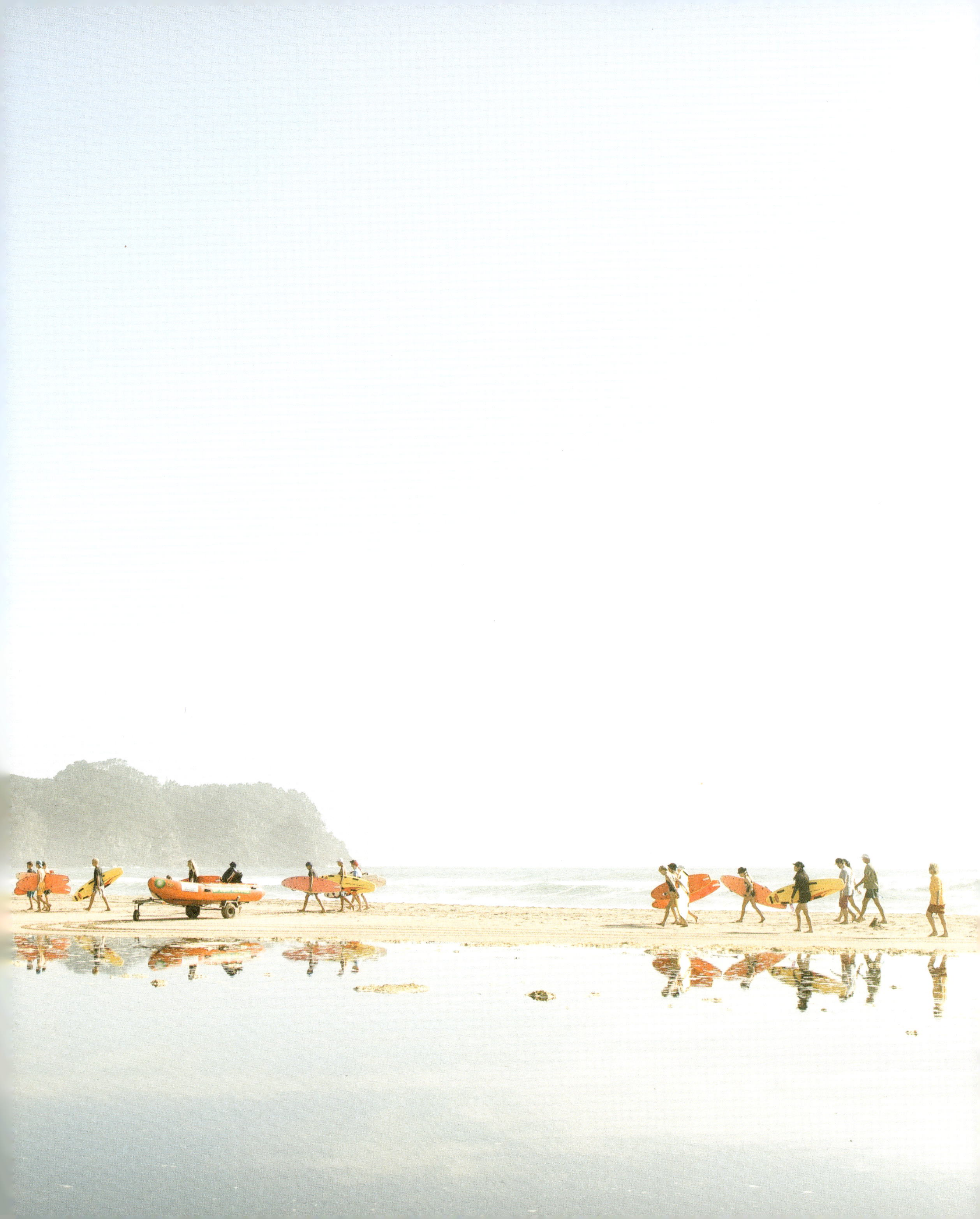

England
6

Scotland
24

Australia
38

Italy
54

Sweden
68

Canada
86

Japan
102

New Zealand
116

France
134

USA
148

Mexico
156

Bermuda
164

ENGLAND

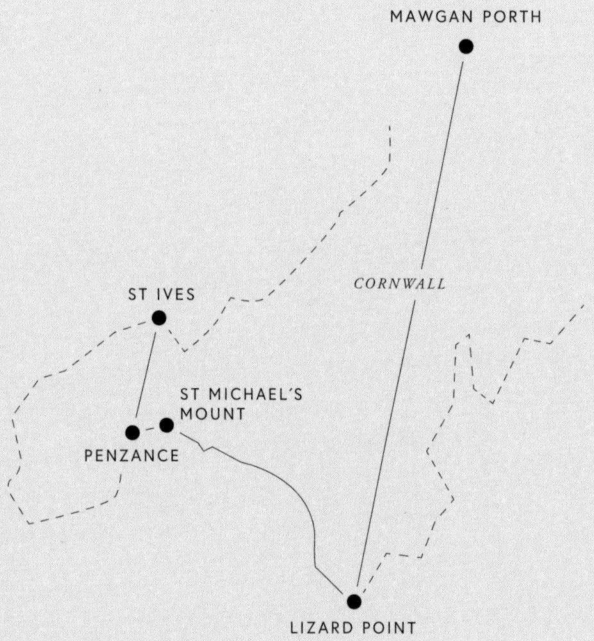

WORDS BY KIEREN TOSCAN

PHOTOGRAPHS BY RENAE SMITH

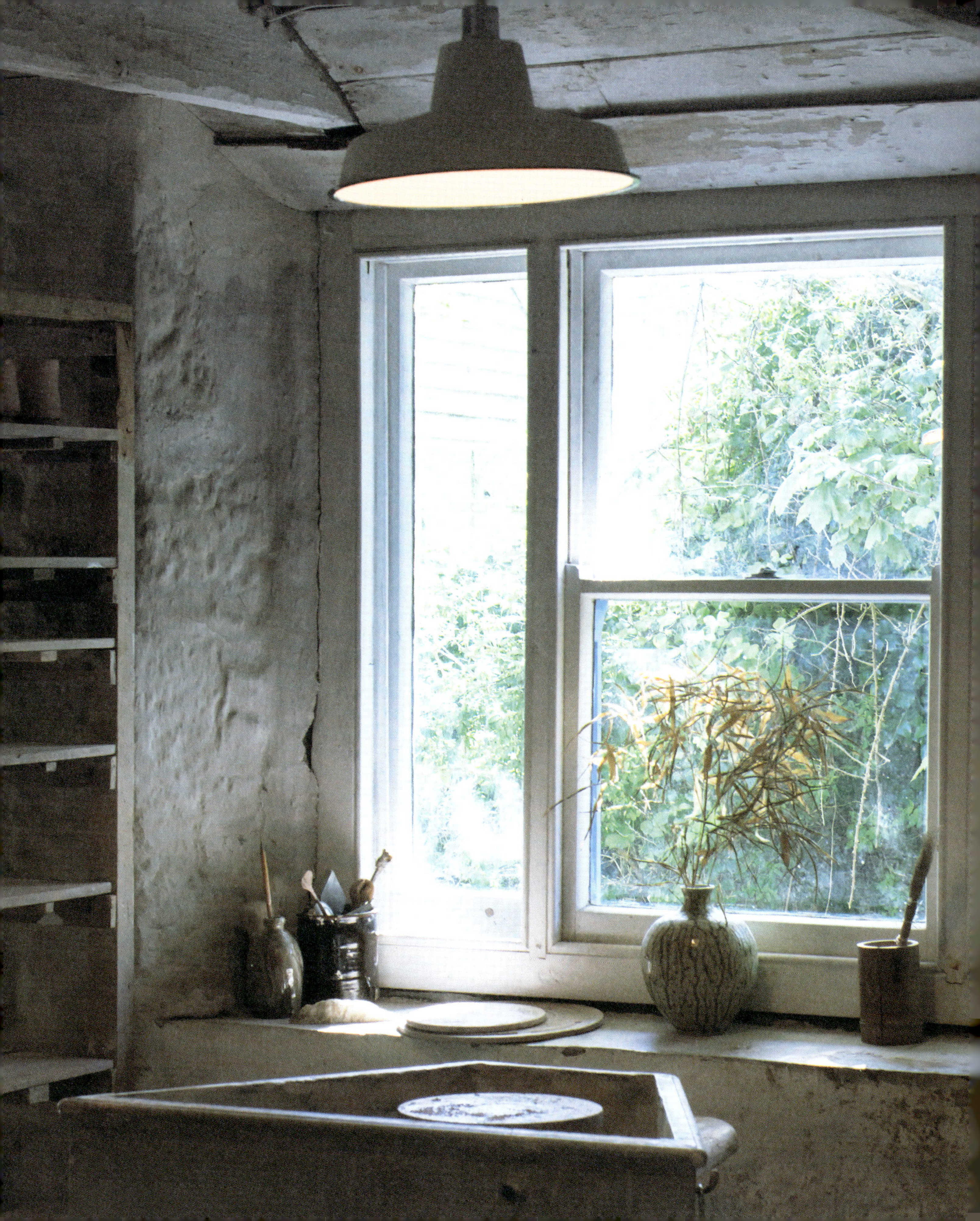

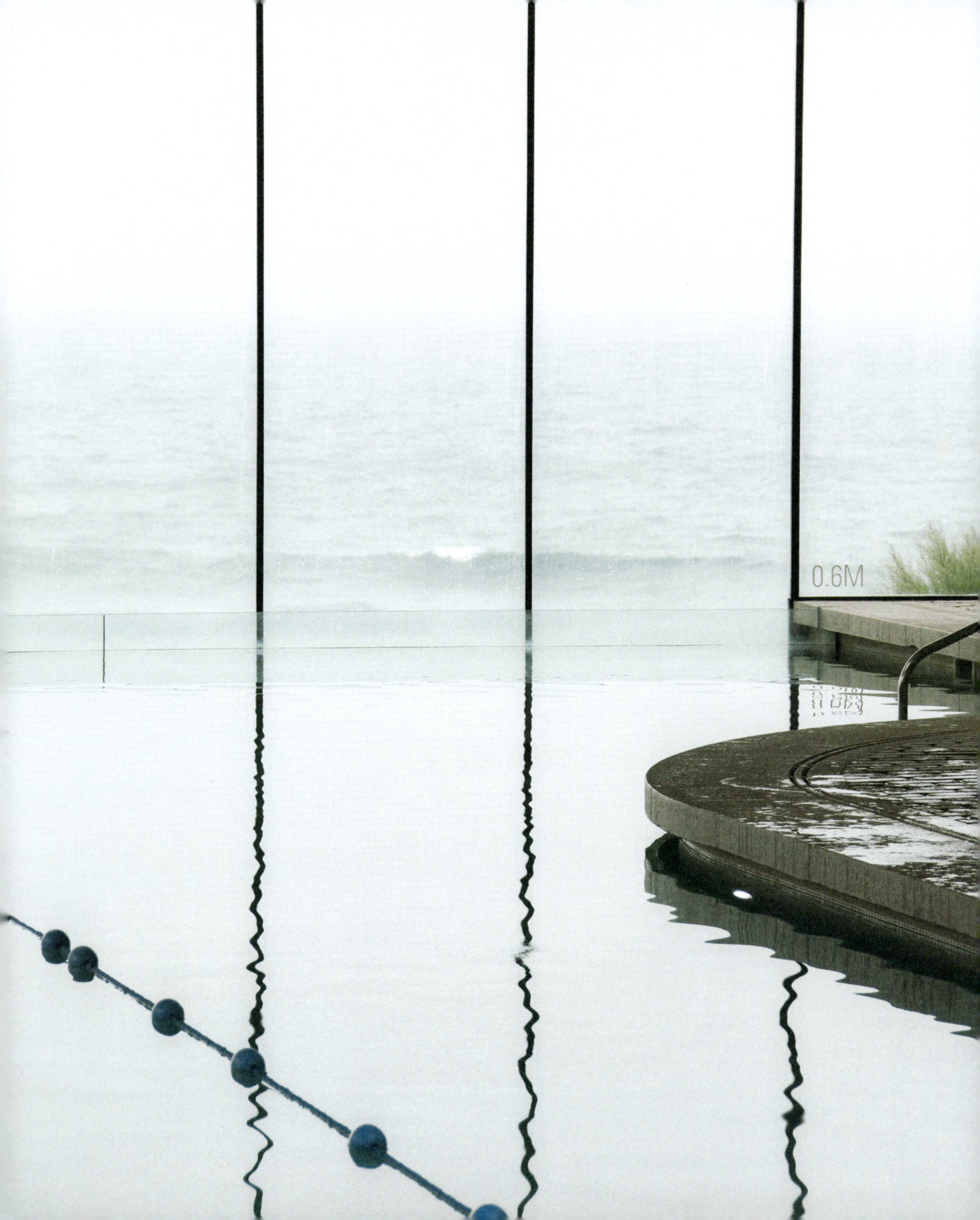
0.6M

Beside the Seaside

I had only been to Cornwall once before, years ago, over an Easter long weekend. It was one of those Easters that fell early, and I recall it being dark, oh so cold, dreary and wet. The type of weather that makes you want to find a spot near the fire, only stirring when it's your turn to procure another bottle of wine. I could count the times I moved that weekend on one hand (but for the wine), and I wasn't sure I would ever come back. But here I was, on a train clattering over the Tamar Bridge, heading towards the coast once more.

I was travelling with my wife, a photographer with a flair for serene scenes, and we arrived late into St Ives, the soft glow of the setting sun giving us the last rays of the light for which the town is famed. The air was cool but carried with it the occasional hint of the coming summer, and as we walked the cobbled streets we found the locals spilling from cafes and pubs, the sound of Friday evening merriment filling the air. It seemed only right to join in, and we did, enjoying lively discussions with new friends – something easily made in the West Country – as, in the growing dark, we watched the tide slowly slip out of the harbour until we could sight the water no more.

Hours later, as the early morning sun rudely burst into our hotel room, I awoke to the question, "shall we venture north or south?" The answer led us to the most southern part of Great Britain, Lizard Point, bounded by the English Channel to the east and Celtic Sea to the south west. It was warm, almost uncomfortably so (an unexpected contrast to what I remembered from all those years ago), inspiring us to walk for hours up, down and along the magnificent South West Coast Path – breaking constantly to marvel at the views and enjoy perhaps one too many cream teas along the way.

Off in the distance, St Michael's Mount beckoned and we arrived just in time to climb to the top and enjoy the devilish pleasure of watching the incoming tide chase late-comers along the causeway below. Some would consider that to be the perfect end to a day, but it was barely past noon, so we chose to follow the sun's growing retreat westward towards Penzance, Mousehole and Land's End beyond.

No trip to the south coast would be complete without a visit to the beautiful open-air Minack Theatre, and soon I was sitting high above the stage, which is perched on a rocky outcrop with a dramatic view over the sea. From here I watched as a fishing boat slowly chugged towards the clear horizon, a trail of hopeful seagulls in its wake ready for whatever spoils the fishermen would soon share. Below, at Porthcurno Beach, with its golden sand and turquoise water, I counted almost a hundred people enjoying the sun and surf.

Had I not known better I might have easily mistaken the scene below for a beach town from back home in Australia. Surely this was an aberration? We were in England after all, and this was not the Cornwall I thought I knew. As I turned in that night (having picked a hotel with a knack for design and particularly comfy beds) I expected to wake the following day to find the weather balance restored – rain, wind and cold. But, yet again, bright sun accompanied us as we sipped coffee and admired the view from the boutique, ocean-inspired Trevose Harbour House early the following morning.

With more to explore, we first headed to Leach Pottery where we were mesmerised by the skill of the artisan potters as they crafted their pieces so effortlessly yet with such care. Then onwards north, where we watched surfers, squeezed into their black steamers, chasing their own form of perfection as we ate a scrumptious lunch on the terrace of the Watergate Bay Hotel. Here the light-filled design perfectly complements the beach scene below, the decor appearing simultaneously modern and rustic. We could have stayed for hours, unwinding in style and putting the huge glass windows of their living space to good use, but couldn't resist the water's allure. Once on the sand we prepared ourselves to dip our toes in the sea – legs spring-loaded and ready to recoil at the slightest chill, only to find that it really wasn't that cold. Emboldened, one of us even ventured into the waves, surfboard in tow, again making it seem just that little bit more like home.

Early that evening at the eco-friendly and refreshingly modern Scarlet Hotel, as I sat high above the village of Mawgan Porth – sipping a beer in their log-fired clifftop hot tub no less – the view suddenly disappeared, enveloped in a thick mist that had come in from the sea. Down below we could hear the laughter of children still playing on the sand and along the water's edge, their ghostly silhouettes briefly appearing and then disappearing again, as a game of tag ensued. And then as quickly as the mist had arrived, it was gone, returning the views it had stolen only ten minutes before.

Finally turning our attention inland over the following days, we lost ourselves on small country lanes with hedgerows that seemed to tower metres over the car, the sun dancing through the leaves. There were days spent stumbling across more hidden beauty – quaint villages with nothing more than a church, pub and unexpected view over the valley beyond – and even a winery. Sitting with the owners of the Trevibban Mill Vineyard and sharing stories over glasses of their delicious wine, I realised once again how first impressions can be deceiving – there was more to Cornwall than I had imagined.

As we waited to reluctantly board the sleeper train back to London, I struck up a conversation with a stranger outside the station. "You sure have had the best of it – the weather has been wonderful. It's never like this," he told me. I suspect that perhaps it was a ploy, something he and others tell tourists. After all, if you had all of this for yourself, would you want to share it? I know for sure now that I'll come back again. For the wine, the sun and, as well I expect, for much, much more. ⋆

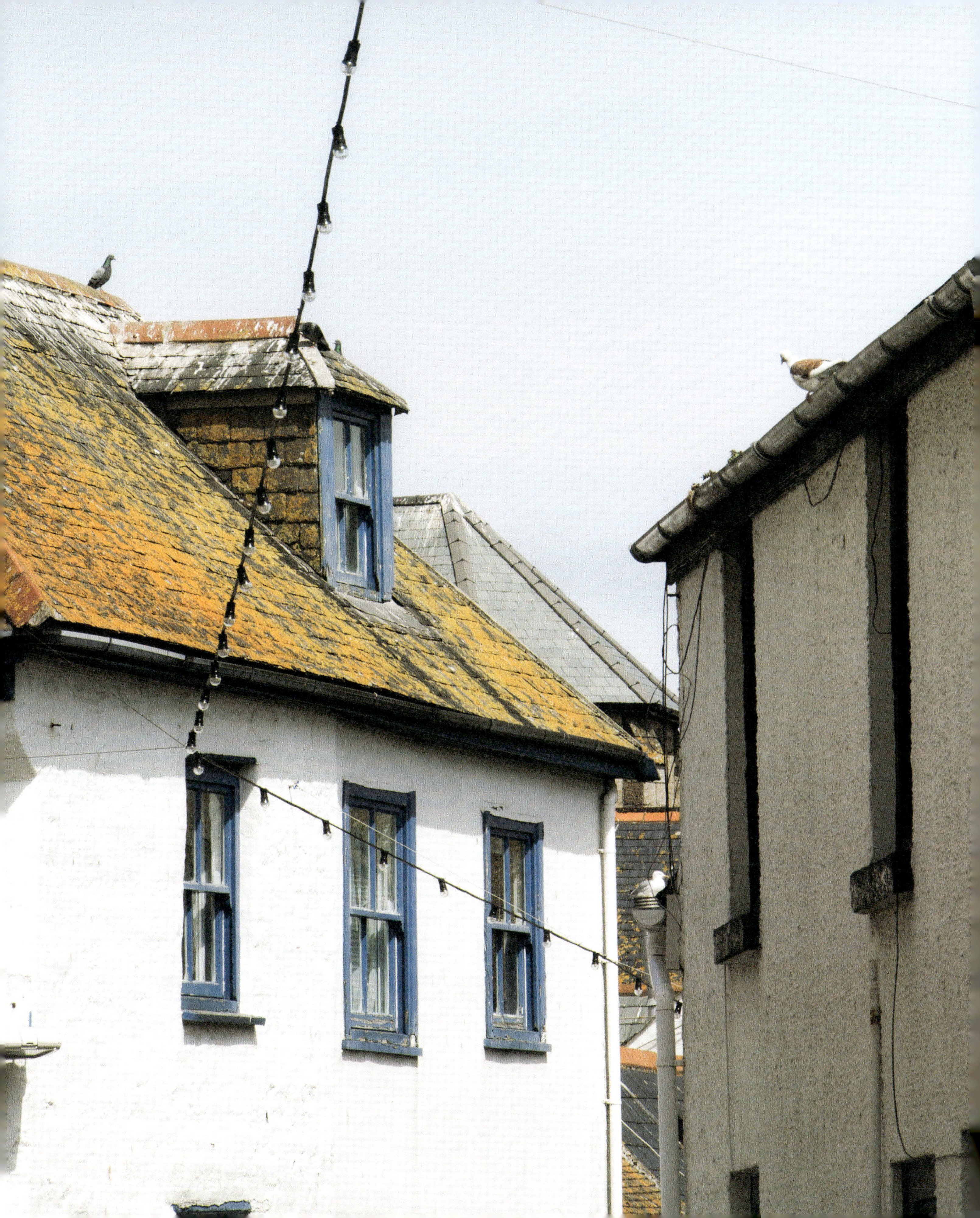

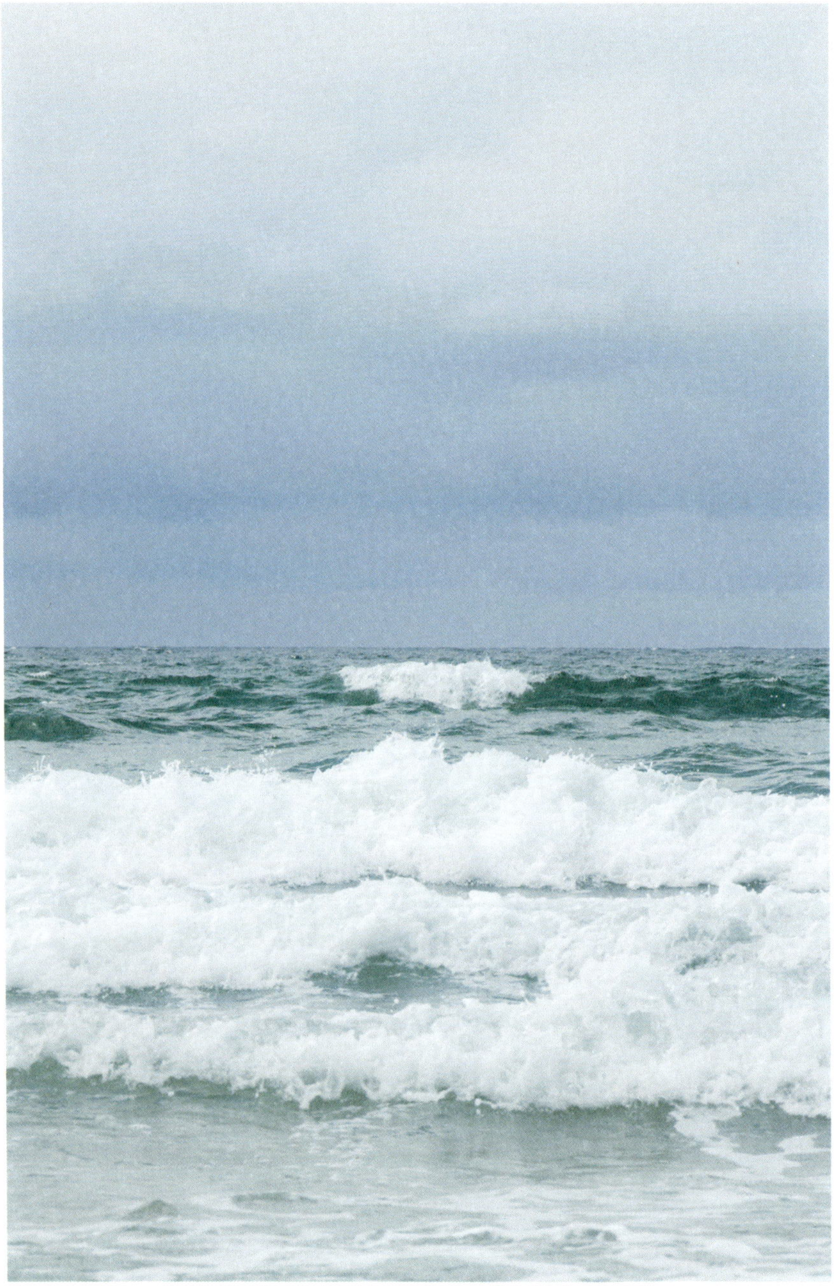

From here I watched as a fishing boat slowly chugged towards the clear horizon, a trail of hopeful seagulls in its wake ready for whatever spoils the fishermen would soon share.

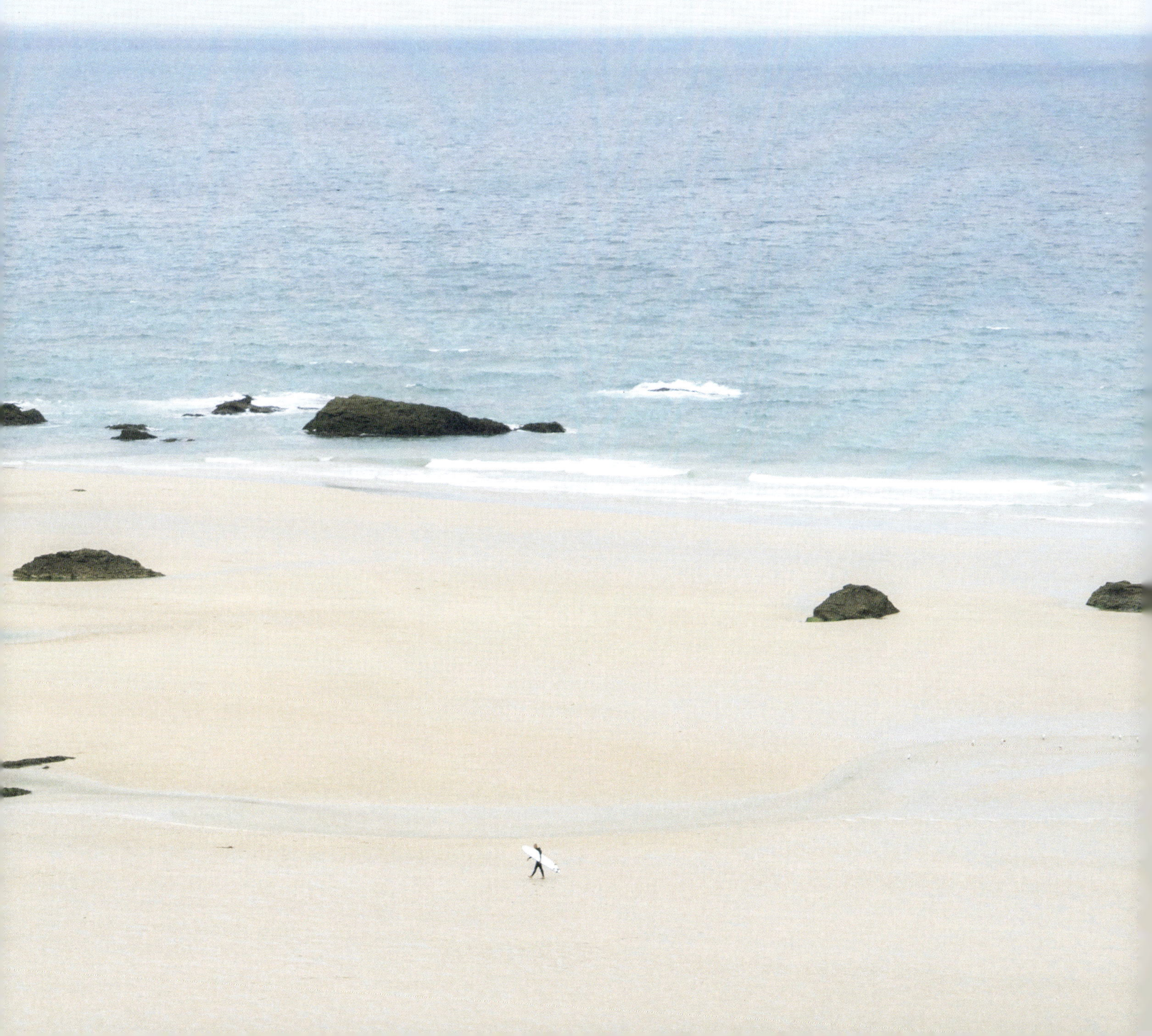

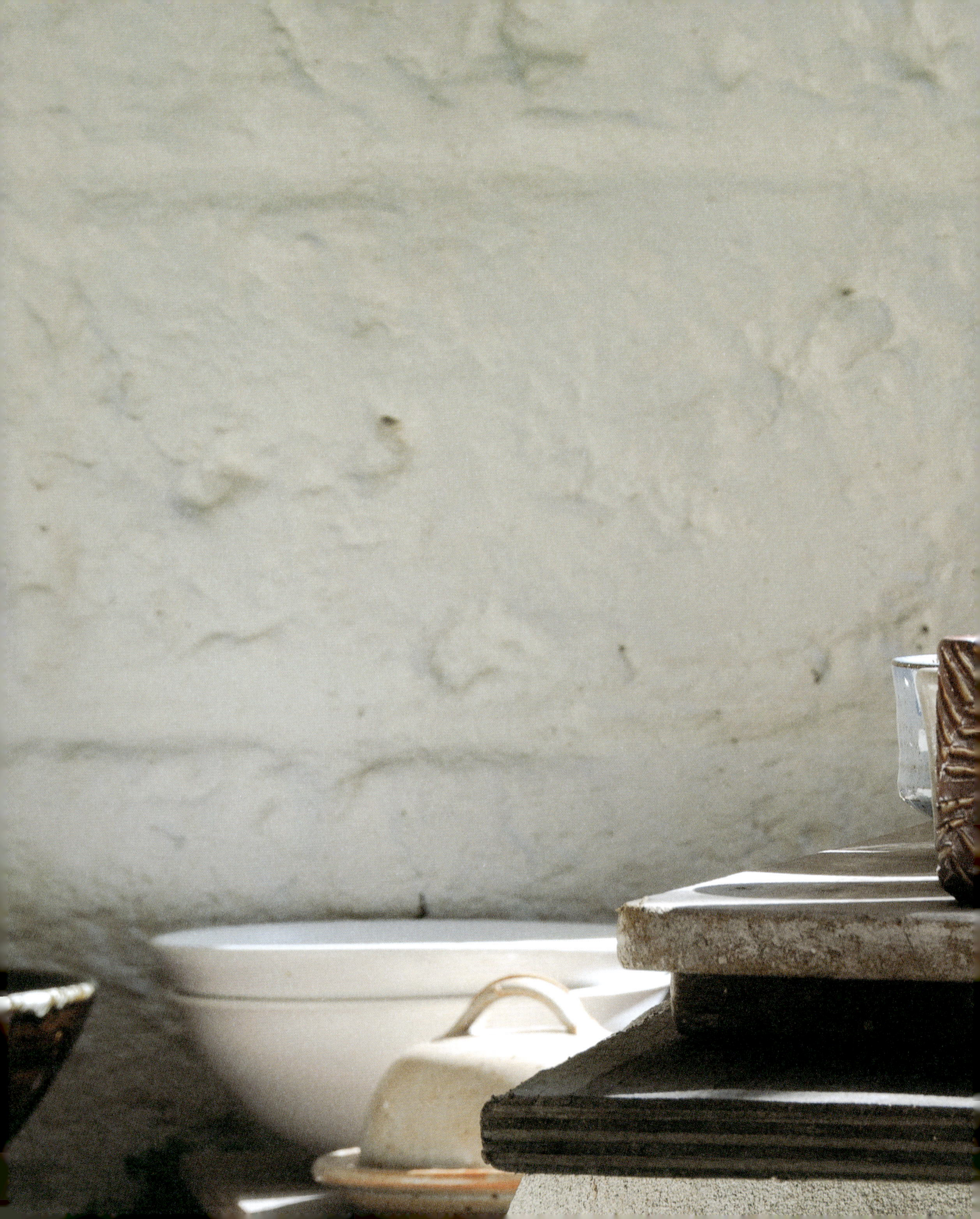

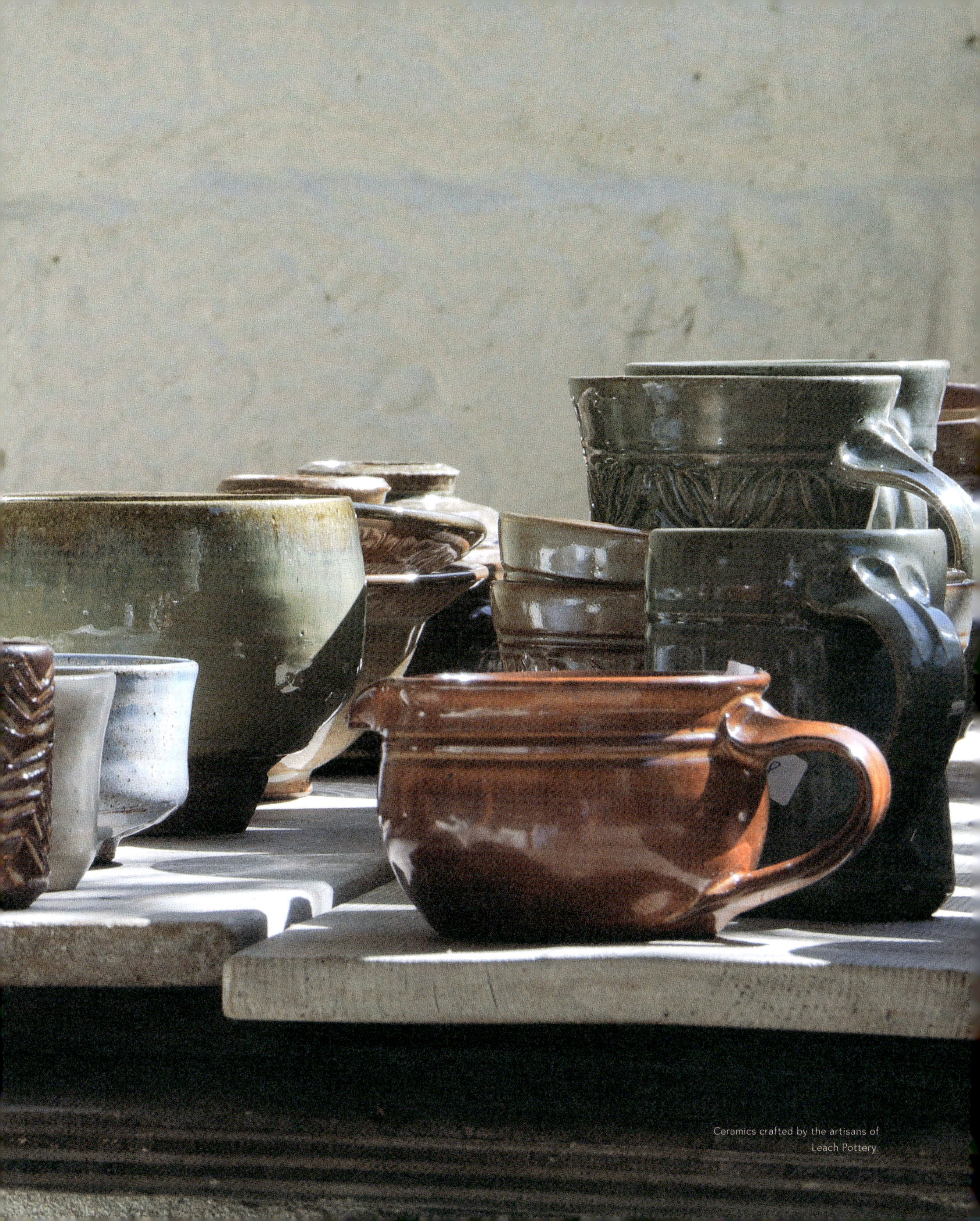

Ceramics crafted by the artisans of Leach Pottery.

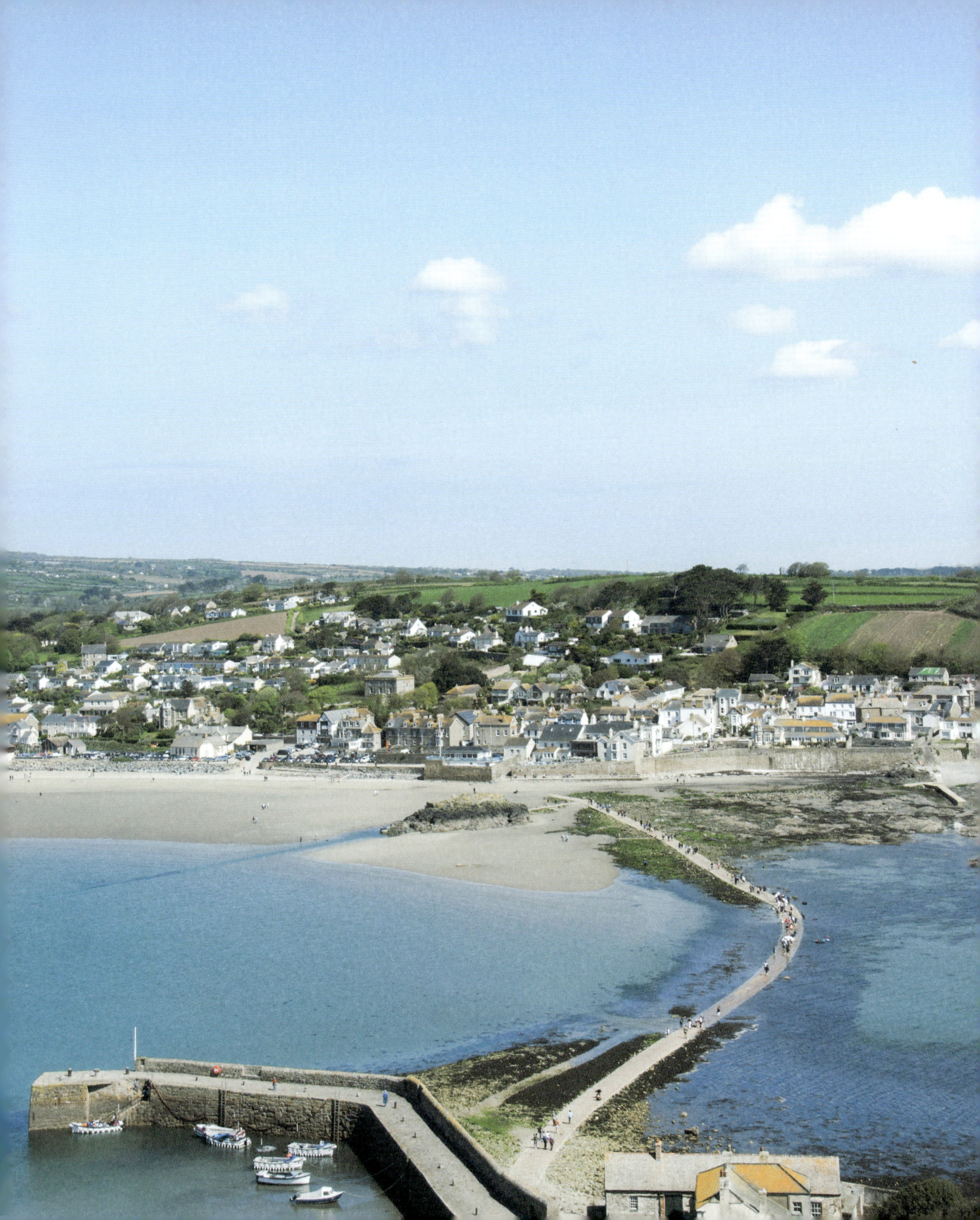

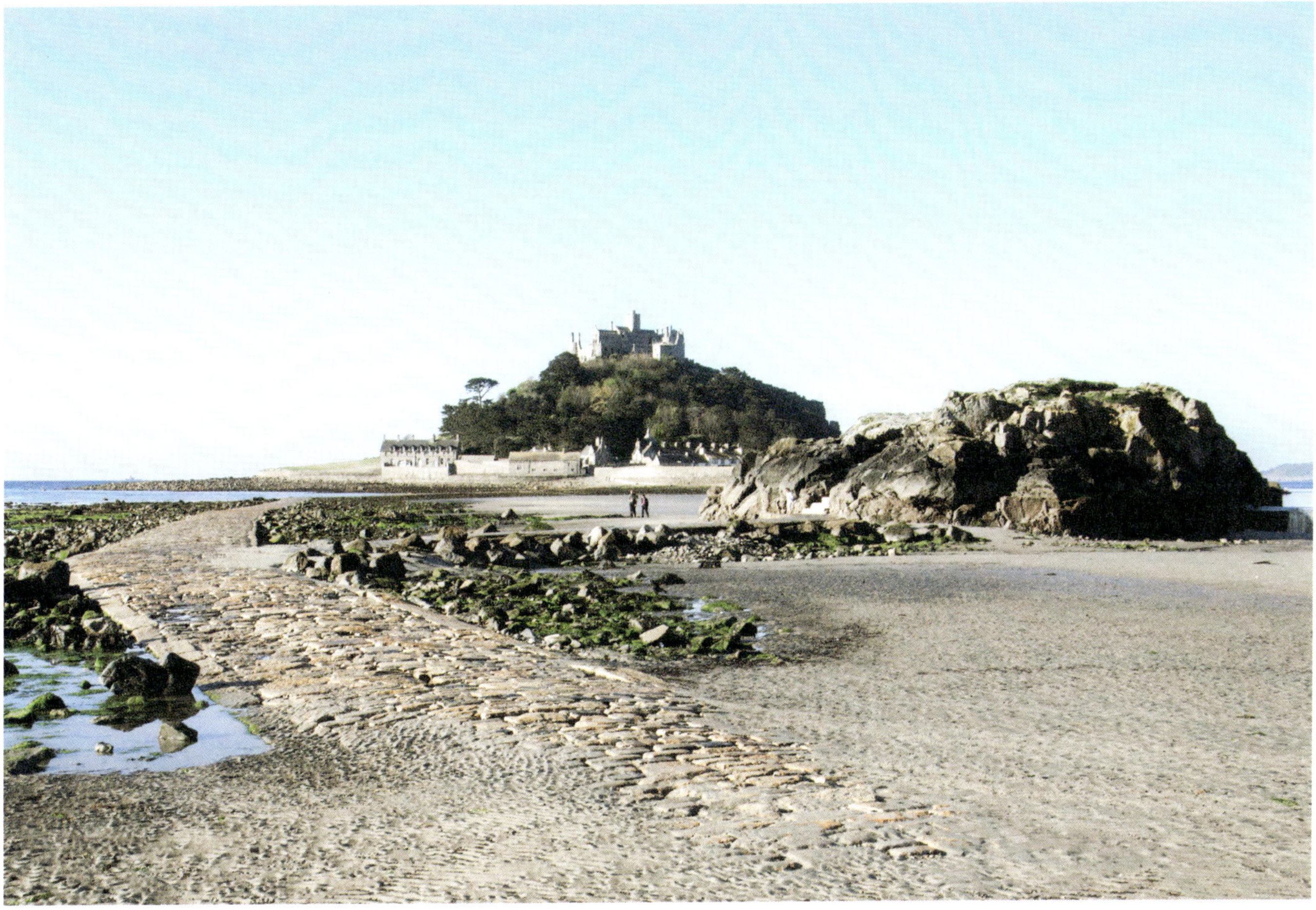

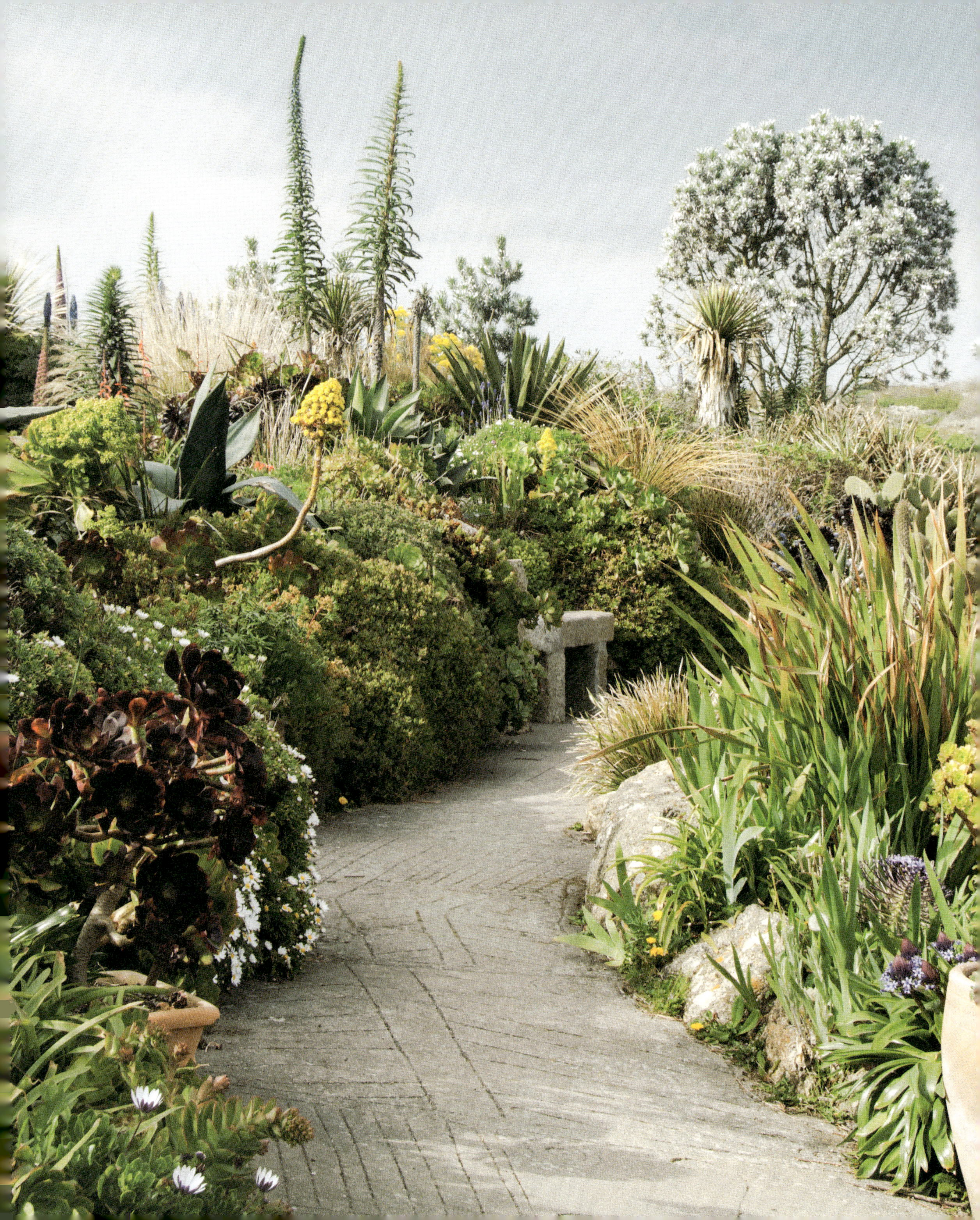

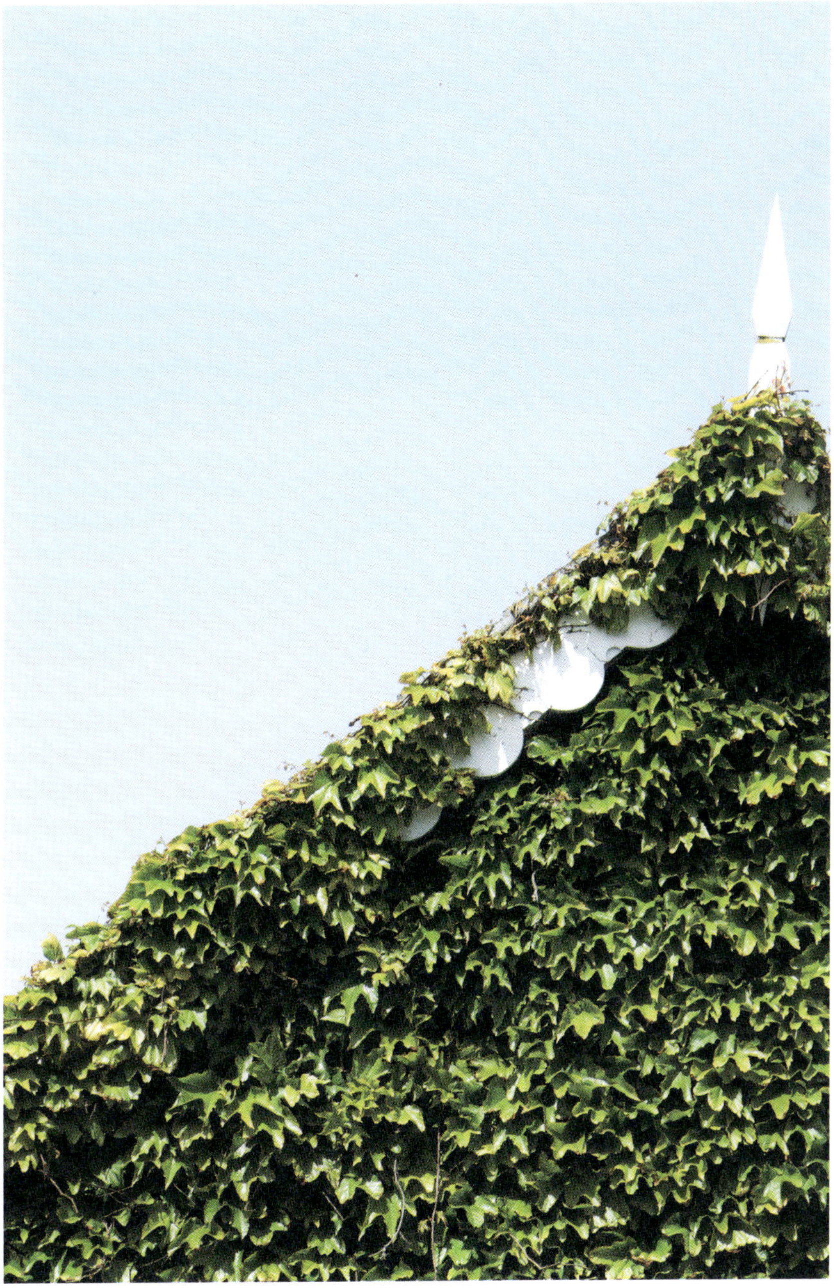

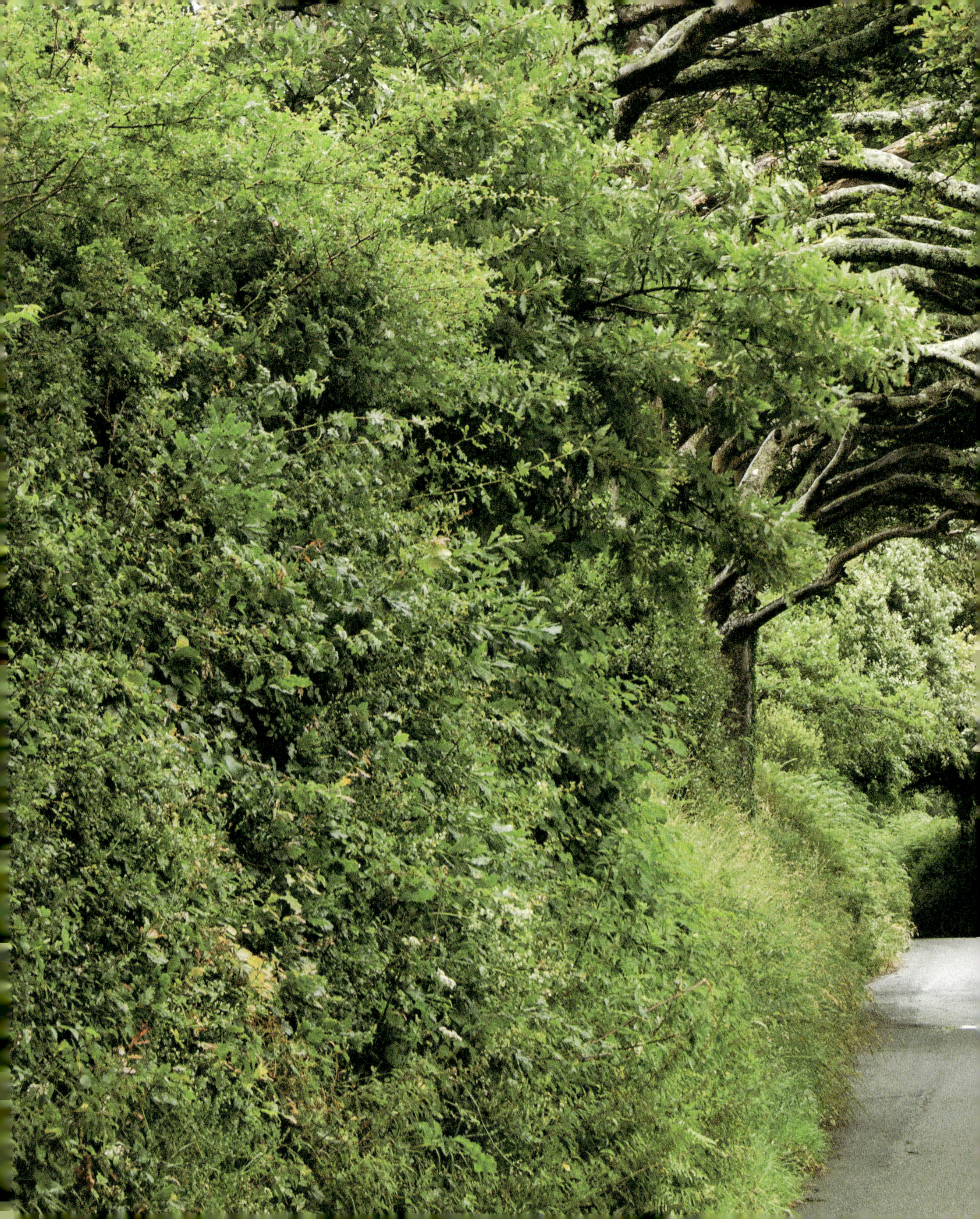

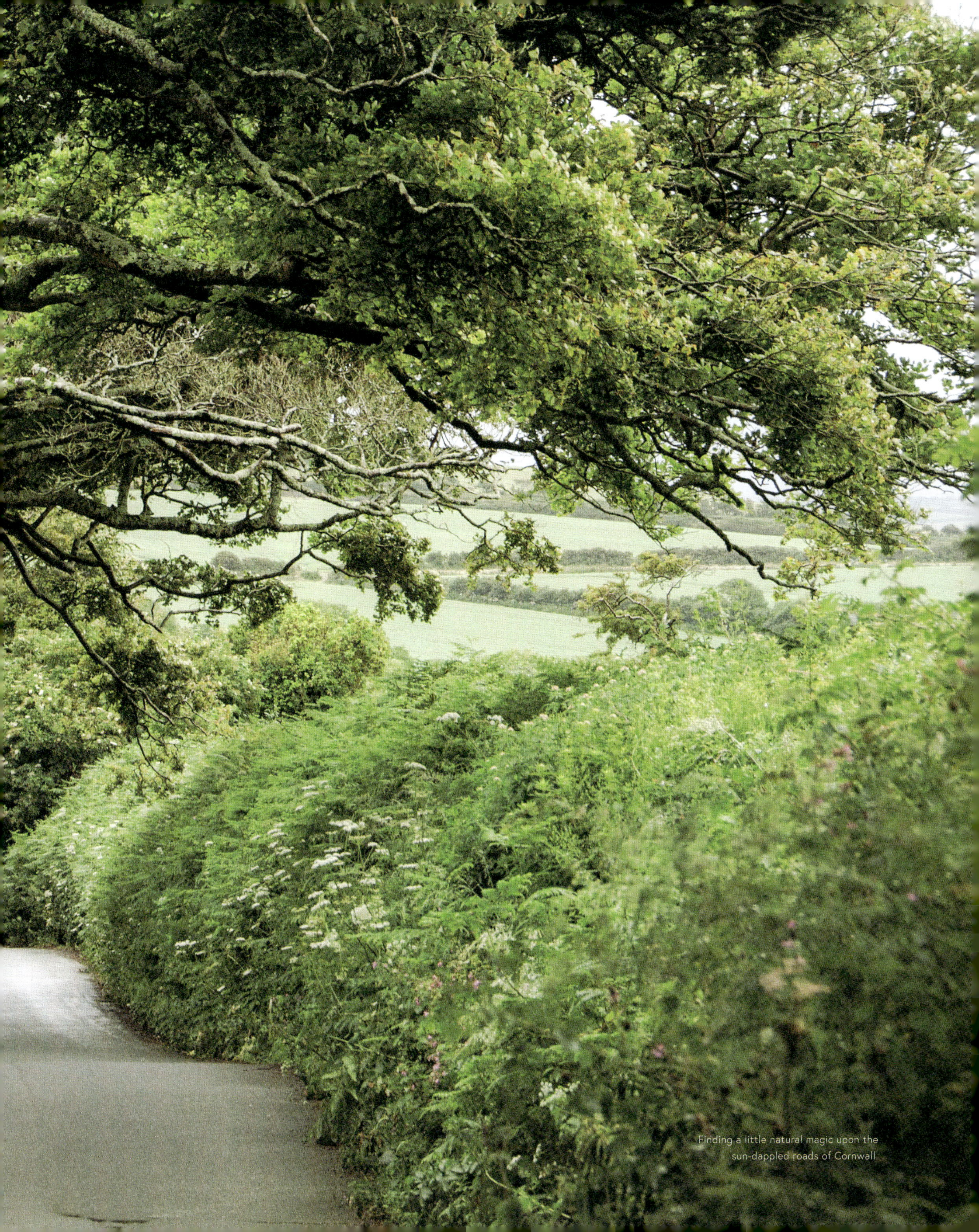

Finding a little natural magic upon the
sun-dappled roads of Cornwall.

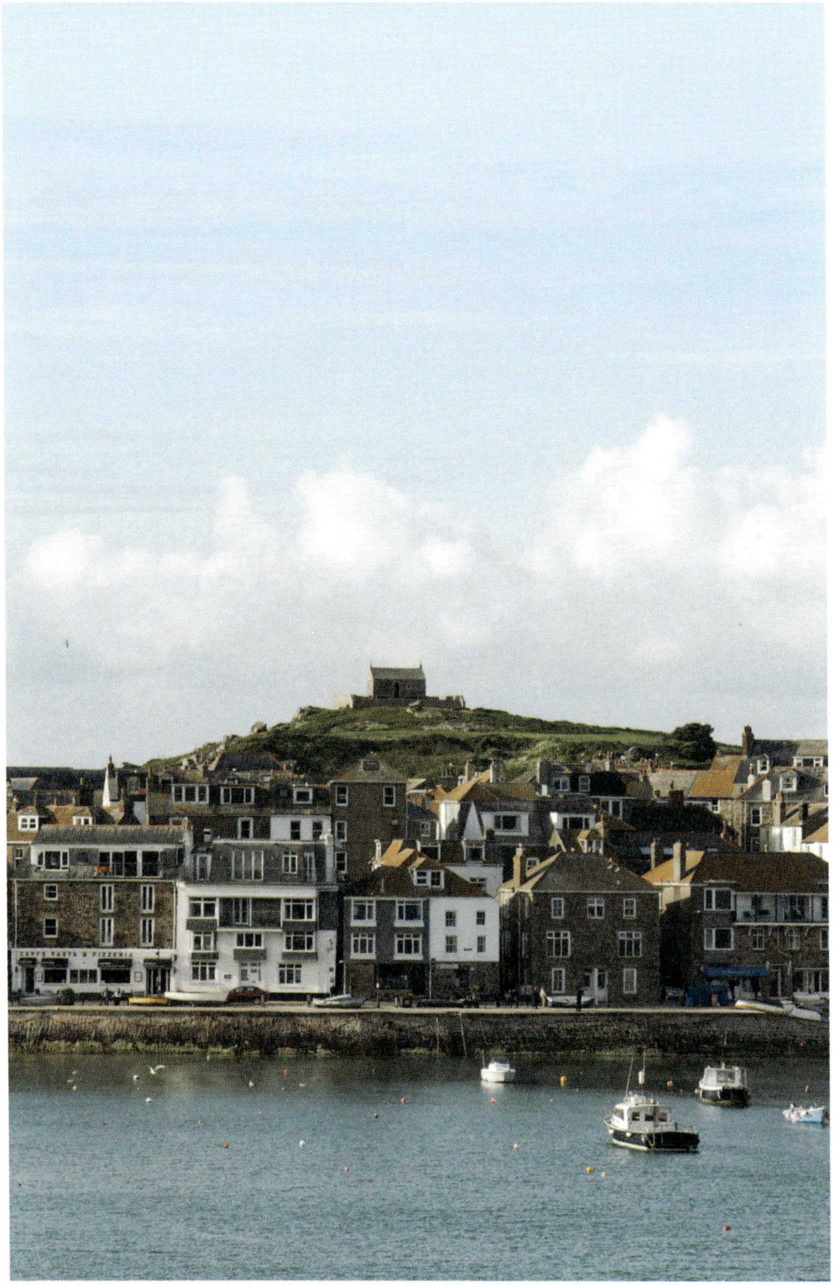

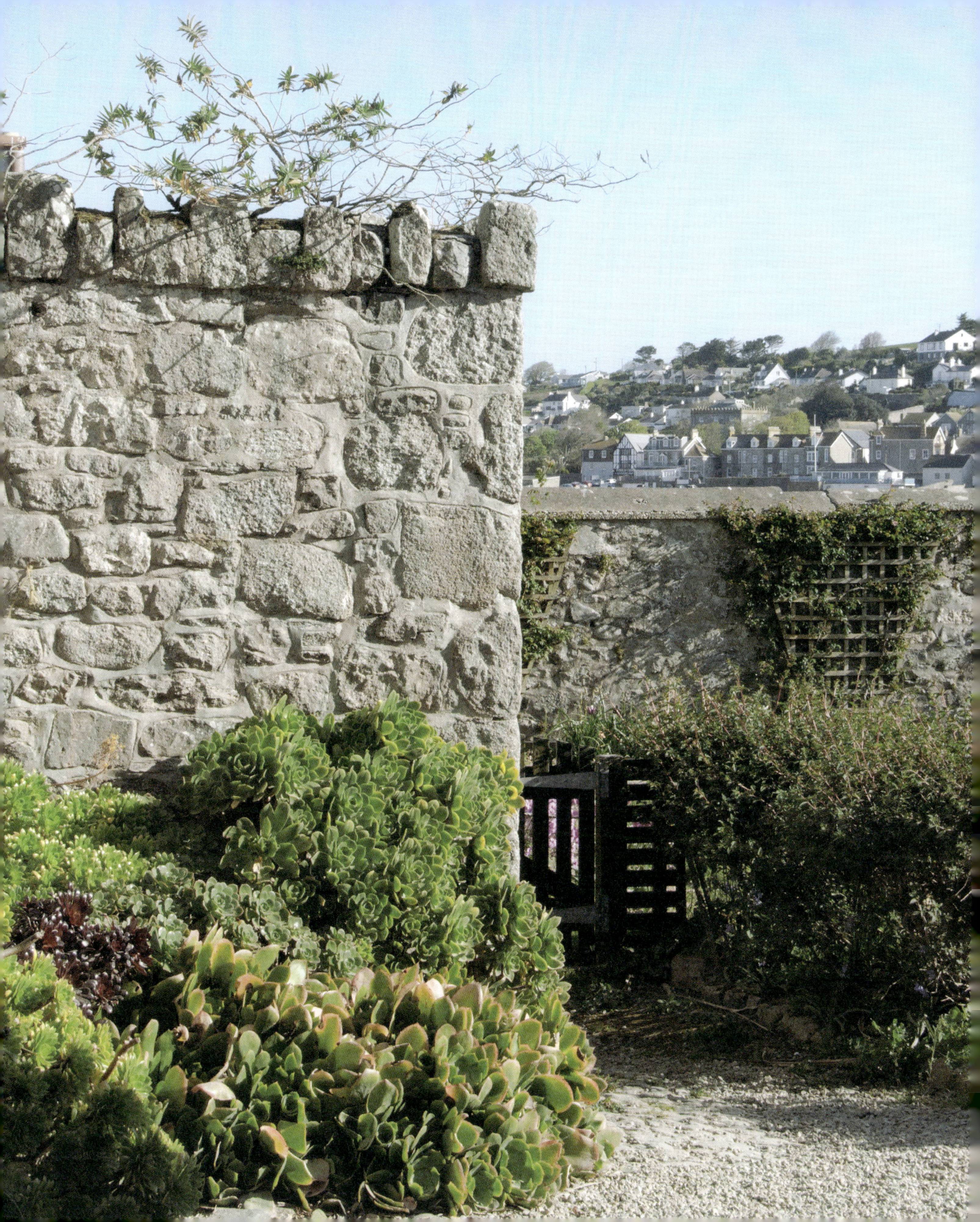

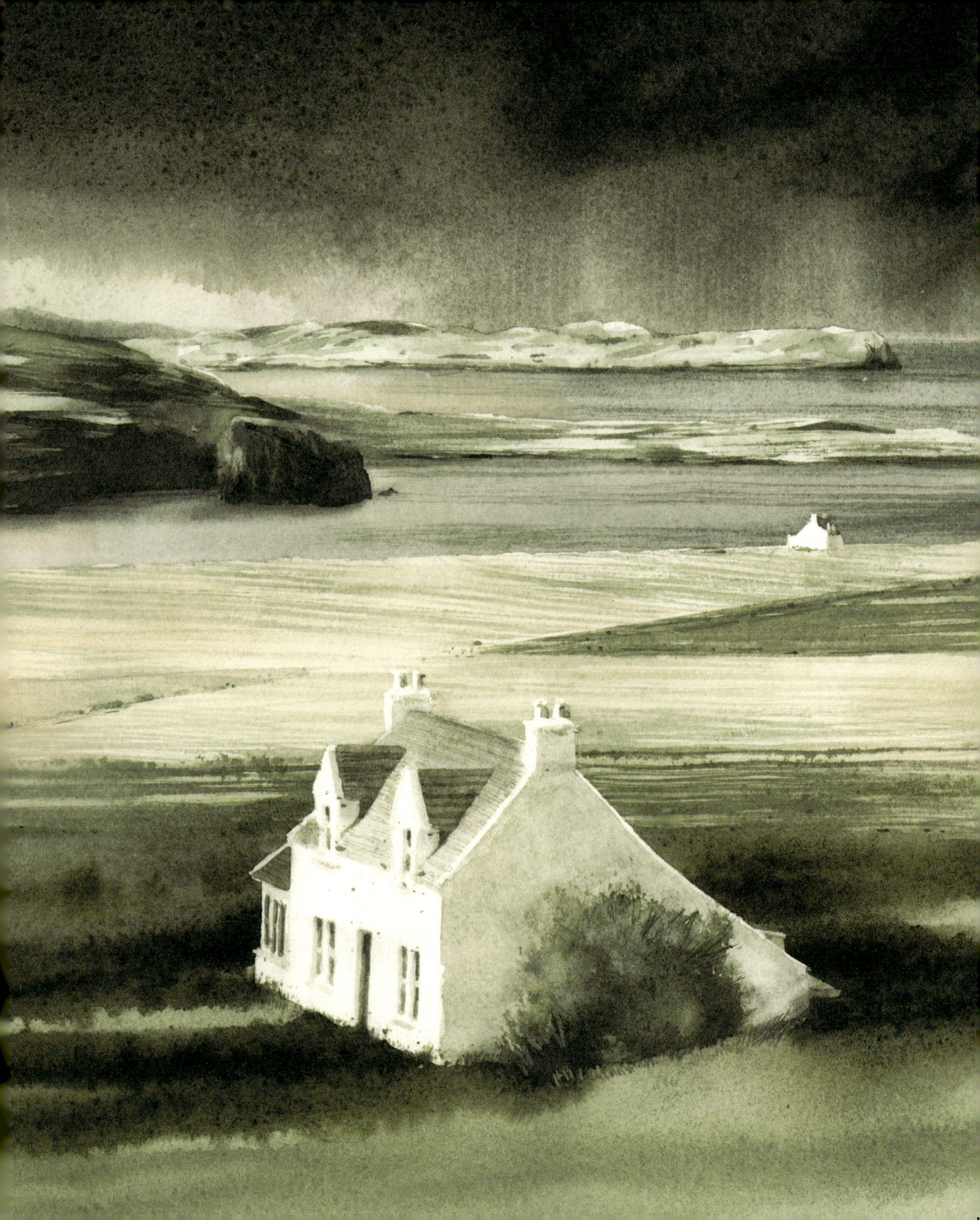

SCOTLAND

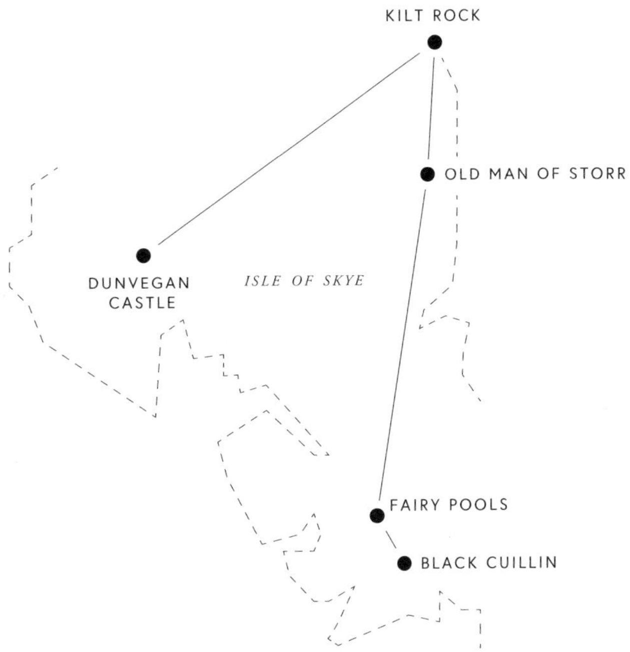

WORDS BY LIZ SCHAFFER

PHOTOGRAPHS BY ANGELA TERRELL

ILLUSTRATIONS BY MARINA MARCOLIN

The Tides of Time

Hugged by the poetically named Little Minch and Sea of the Hebrides, The Misty Isle is imbued with its own special power. Beguiling yet unapologetically fickle, this is the domain of fitful clouds and unseasonable snow – and while you will inevitably encounter fog, sleet and rain, these don't detract from the scene. Instead, they make it something mythical; an otherworldly setting where the elements reign supreme, perspective is altered and visitors bow to nature's might.

There is also a feeling of poetic isolation upon the Isle of Skye. You could be alone here, at ease with your thoughts and absorbed in a landscape that, despite its immensity, carries a sense of calm. You remember the importance of solitude, of having space to think accompanied only by the relics of history.

Known in Norse times as Skýey (Isle of Cloud), this wing-shaped landmass, the largest island of the Inner Hebrides, is an adventurer's dream. Or a poet's for that matter. Rolling sea mist dances over knife-sharp peaks, deer roam the forests, glaciers have left their mark and waterfalls grow and fade with the rain. The Old Man of Storr stands guard over the quaint village of Portree, while the Black Cuillin mountains whisper to climbers – with one of their peaks, Sgùrr Dearg, known as the Inaccessible Pinnacle, how could they not? When night arrives, Skye's narrow roads are illuminated by celestial displays alone, and come spring the land is awash with wildflowers – daffodils, foxglove and thistles claiming the land as their own.

When the sun emerges, which happens frequently and without warning, there are few scenes more glorious; a reminder that this island comes with quieter corners too. Indeed, Skye has been captured in painted form by J. M. W. Turner, inspired the words of Robert Louis Stevenson and remains a place where art flourishes, minds wander and eternal youth may be bestowed upon anyone daring enough to submerge their face in the freezing waters of the Fairy Pools.

But should you forge a pathway across Skye it will be more than a scenic experience. Instead, you will find yourself travelling through history. As tranquil as this island may seem, one must not forget that it was the realm of Vikings and warriors, some with their hearts lost to fairies. This is a place where maidens saved princes, sanctuary was sought, and a battle was waged to avenge the honour of a one-eyed woman.

When I first arrived here, lured by the promise of postcard-worthy landscapes and the space to breathe, I felt something

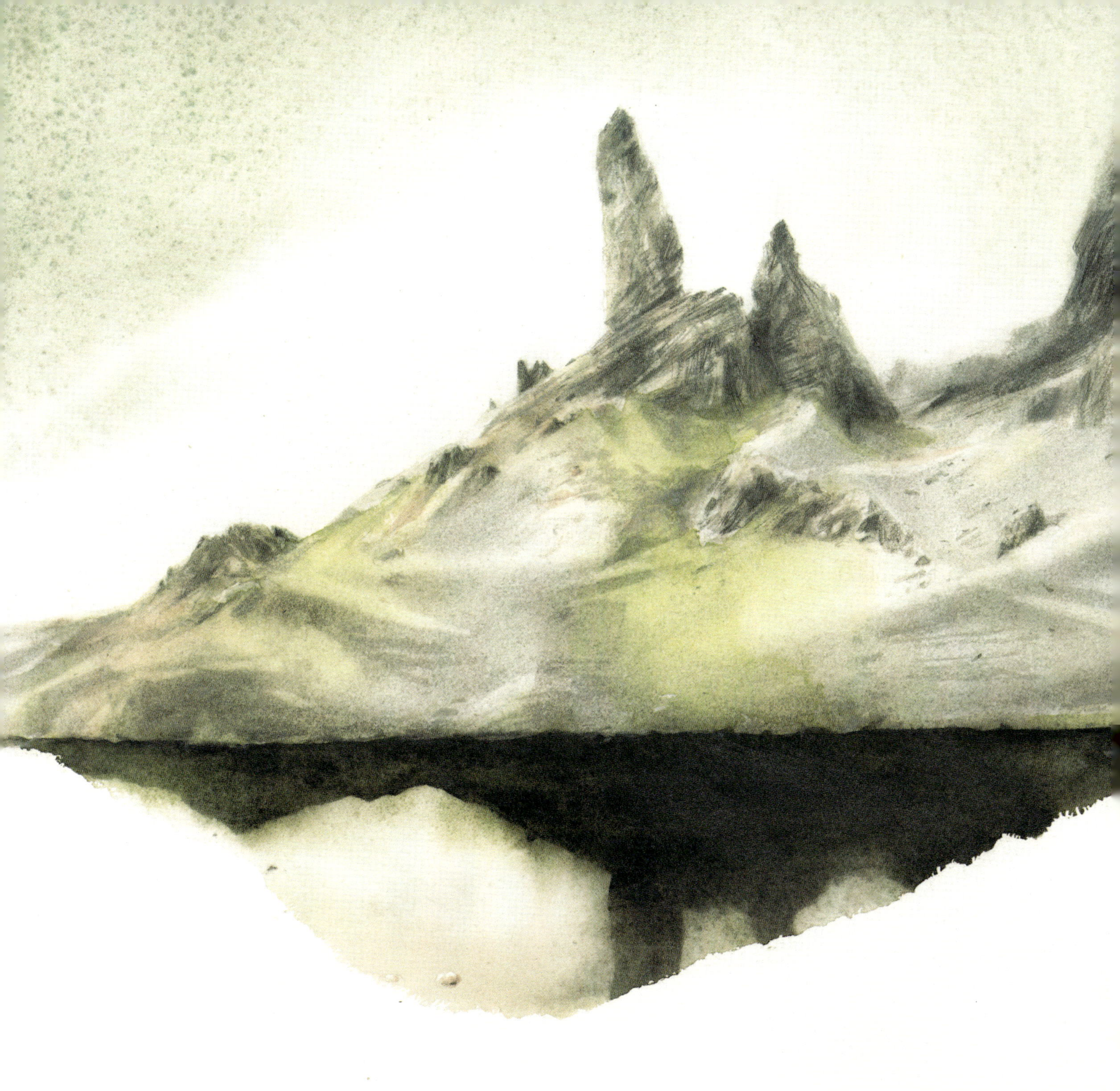

The Old Man of Storr – a stoic icon of the mythic, time-ravaged Isle of Skye.

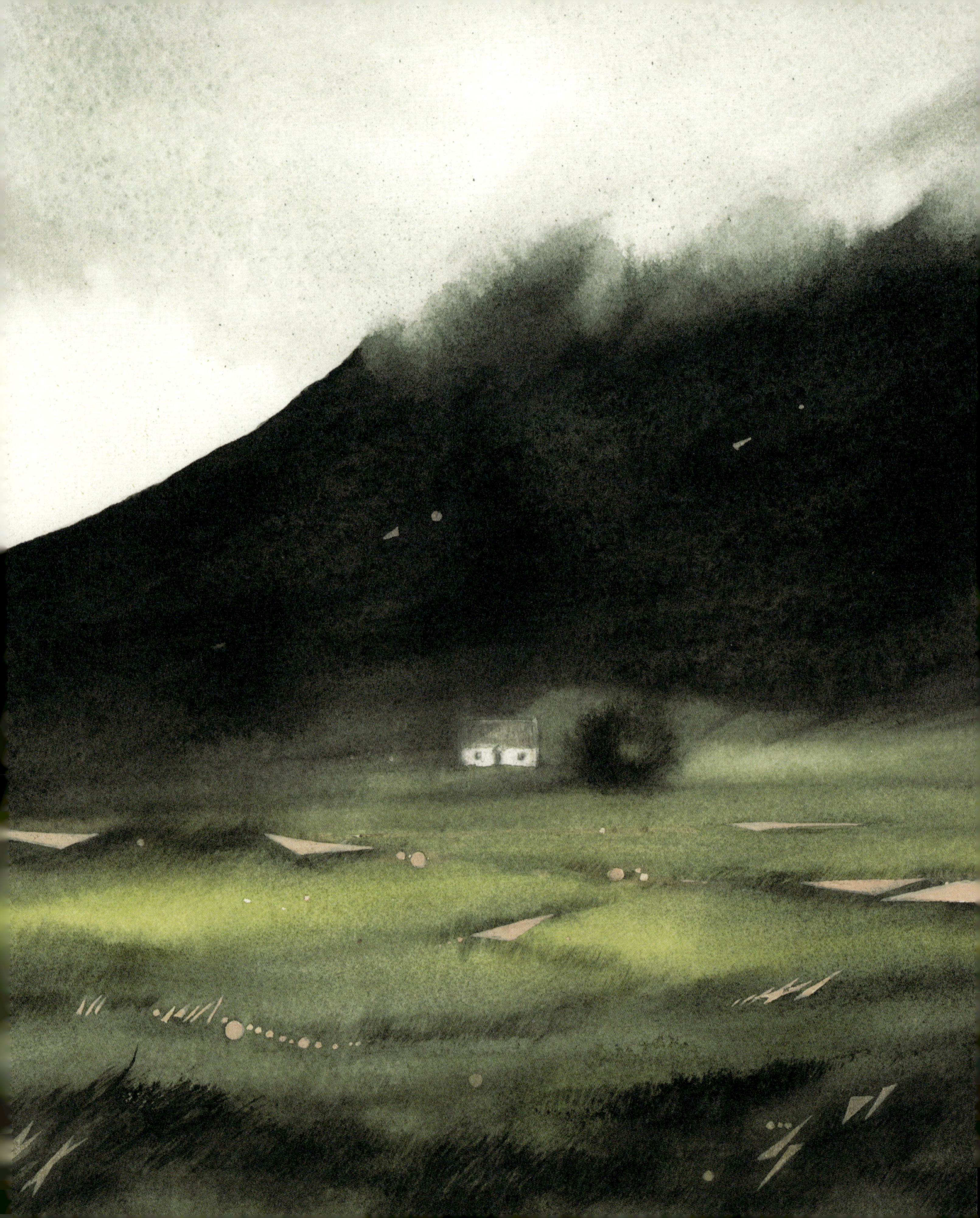

Rolling sea mist dances over knife-sharp peaks, deer roam the forests, glaciers have left their mark and waterfalls grow and fade with the rain.

stir. Yes, there was a sense of adventure – a desire to hike over the Quiraing and along dog-dotted beaches – but I also felt that upon Skye myth wasn't confined to the past. 500 million years of history are written across its time-worn terrain; fortresses are reduced to rubble, churches have crumbled and entire communities have been devoured by the earth. That said, other landmarks stand tall, like Dunvegan Castle on the Waternish Peninsula. The seat of the chief of Clan MacLeod for more than 800 years, it has been visited by the likes of Virginia Woolf and Sir Walter Scott and is home to the Fairy Flag: cloth given by a fairy queen to her MacLeod husband when she was forced to return to fairyland. However, historical analysis suggests it may actually be the 4th century remains of the banner of a Norwegian King or a gift from the Knights Templar. Regardless, should a clan member wave it in a moment of peril, legend has it that help will always be granted.

Beside the nearby ruins of Duntulm Castle, rows of rocks, which could easily be mistaken for primitive dry stone walls, are all that remain of Viking fortifications. And while Vikings made the island their own from around 700 AD until Haakon's defeat in 1263, it was the ill-fated Jacobite Rebellion, fought to return the British crown to the House of Stuart, that cemented Skye's place in history books. Although the most ferocious battles unfolded on the Scottish mainland, it was to Skye that the would-be monarch Bonnie Prince Charlie fled, dressed as Betty Burke, the Irish maid of local Flora MacDonald. Flora's bravery is still admired today, as the epithet on her Kilmuir grave will attest. Penned by Sir Walter Scott, it reads: "Her name will be mentioned in history, and if courage and fidelity be virtuous, mentioned with honour."

The rebellion's failure was followed by a period of cruel subjugation, culminating in The Highland Clearances of the 18th and 19th centuries – mass evictions that decimated the population. With a generation of young men soon lost to the wars of Europe, the farming landscape of Skye was forever changed – craters in the earth being all that remain of entire villages. Once there was a settlement in every glen, and walking past sites like Kilt Rock or the fishing village of Elgol, you realise that a journey around Skye quickly becomes an amble through history. You see masses of lichen-covered rocks for what they were – family homes – and let your mind wander, considering the daily rituals of those who lived there; the tales exchanged, the elements battled and the beauty that enveloped them. Spend time upon Skye and this history will consume you; scenes from the past dancing up with the wind as you expect to hear the chants of warriors long forgotten around every corner.

Some places make you acutely aware that you are simply a visitor – that the antediluvian land you stand upon has been here for eons, and will remain long after you're gone. But that doesn't mean your relatively fleeting moment upon Skye is insignificant. You are instead part of a greater epic, connected to the heroics, dreams and everyday lives of those who came before you. Drink it in, embrace the power of this place and enjoy feeling remarkably small indeed. ⋆

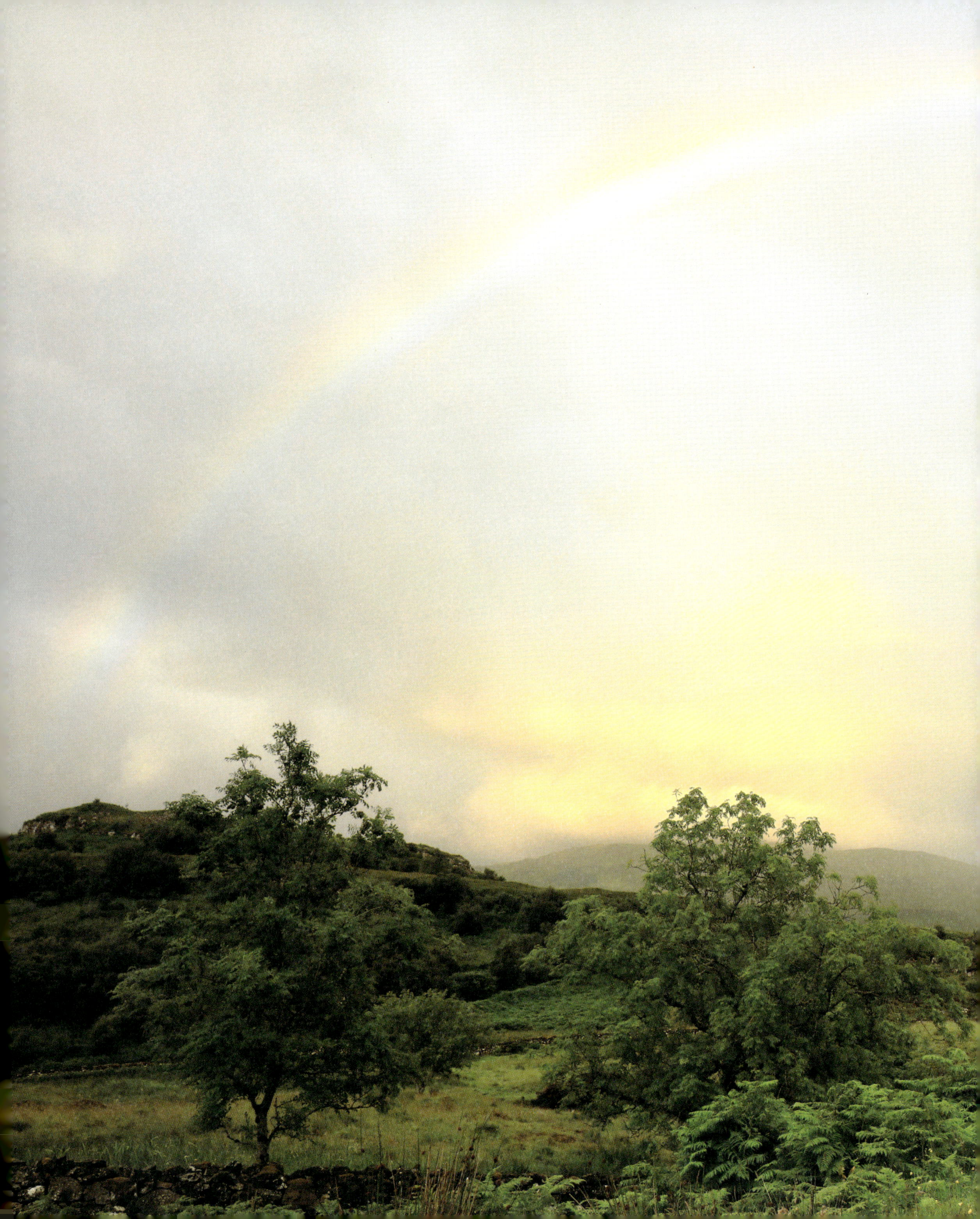

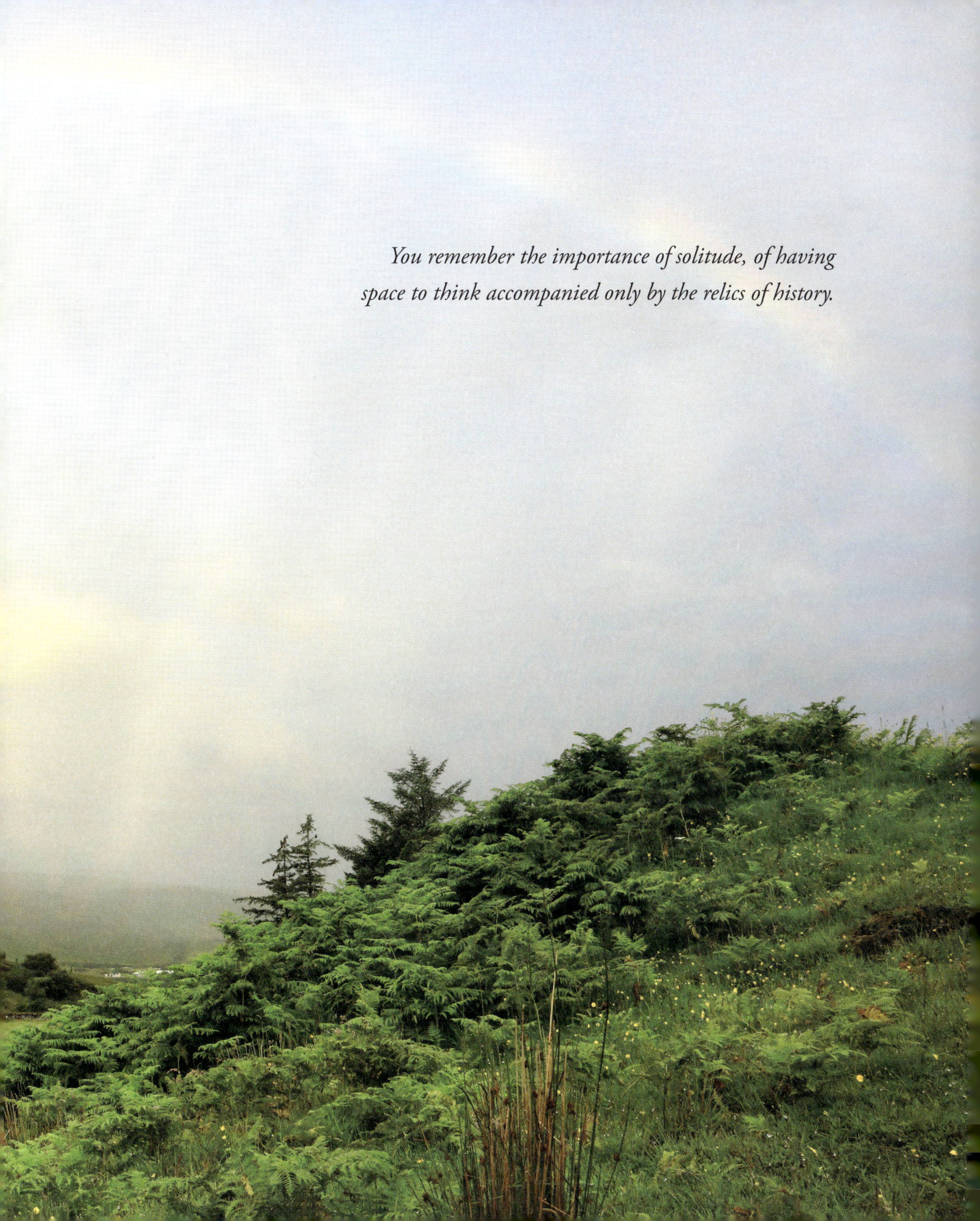

You remember the importance of solitude, of having space to think accompanied only by the relics of history.

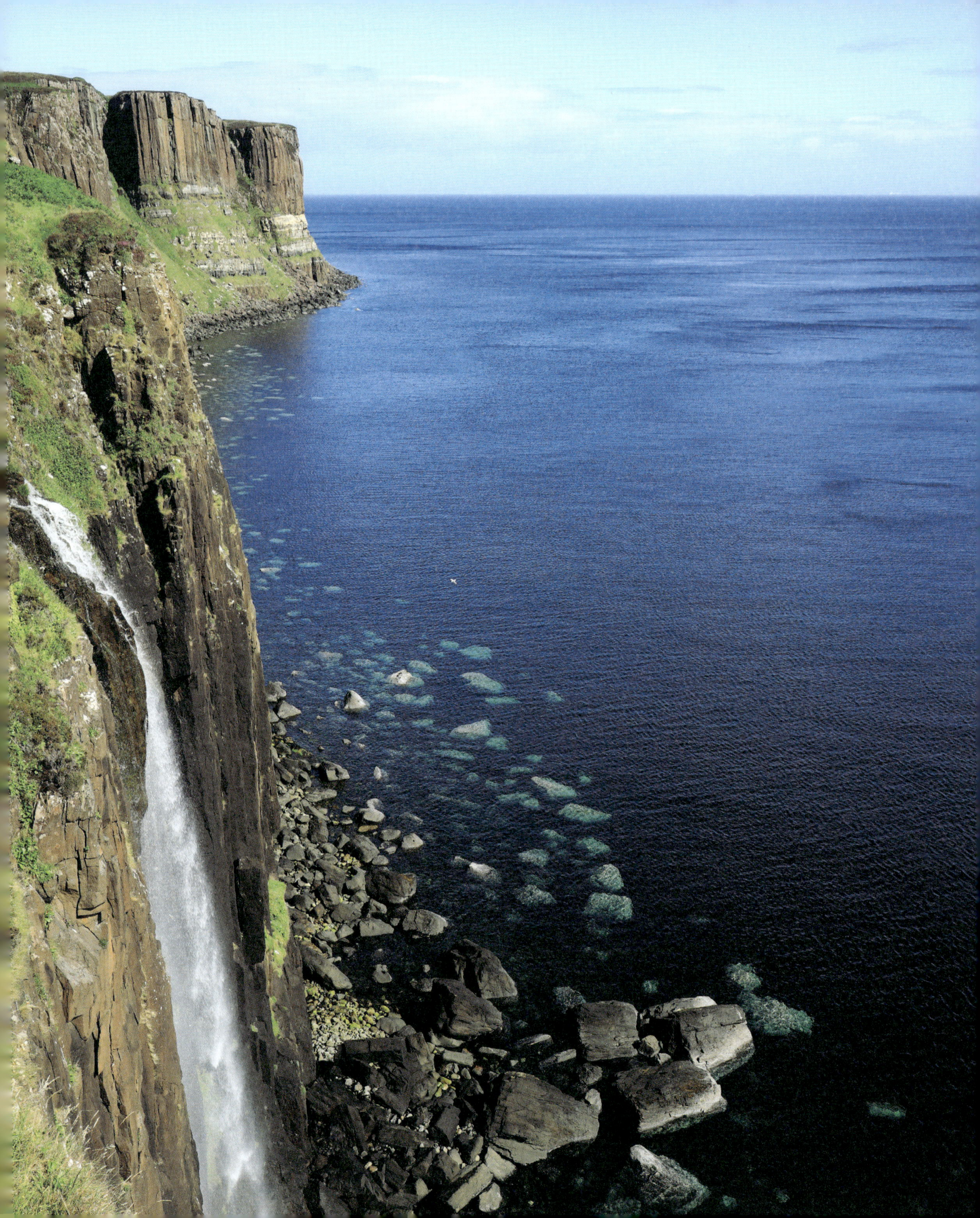

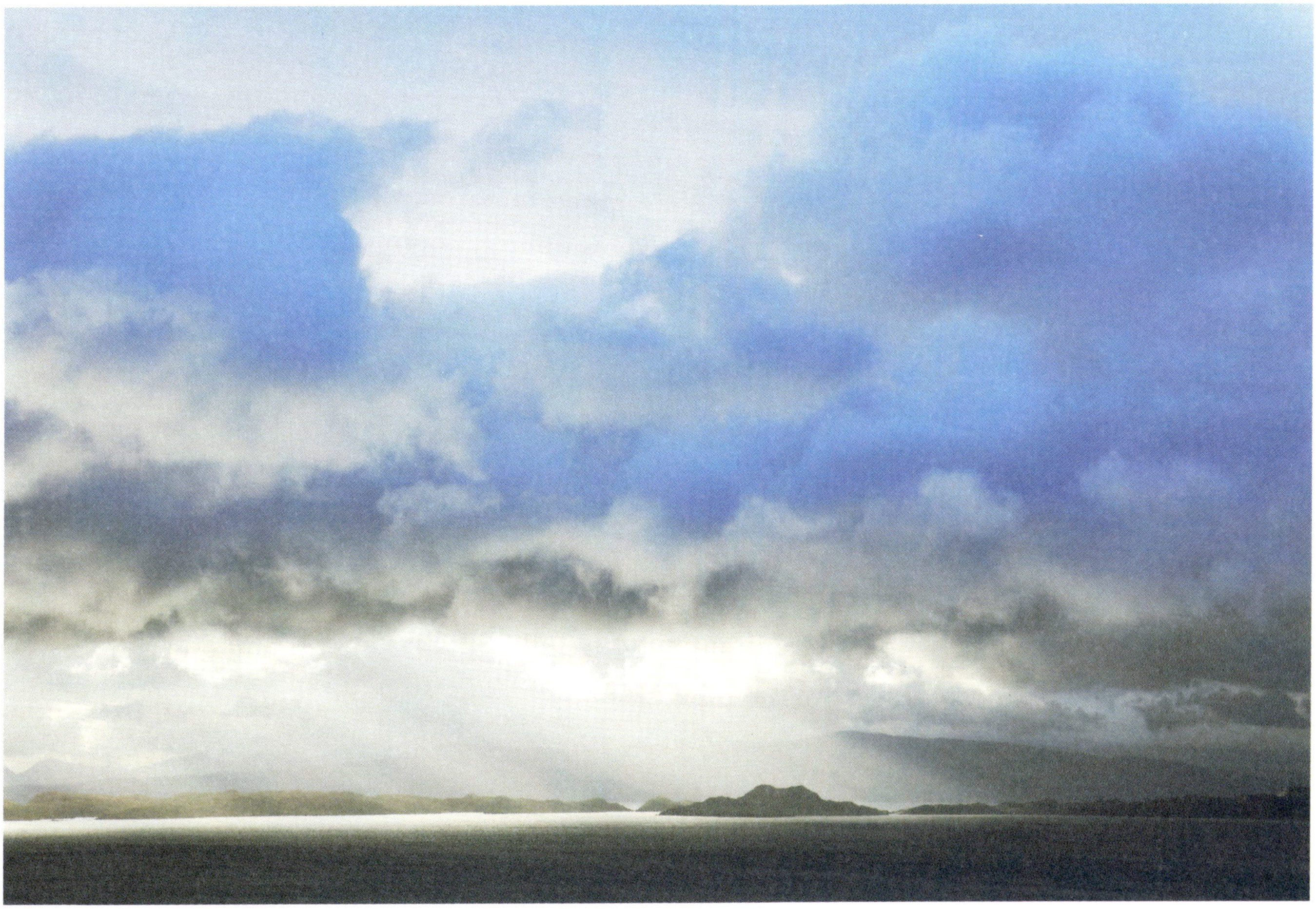

The fickle, hypnotic skies of the Inner Hebrides.

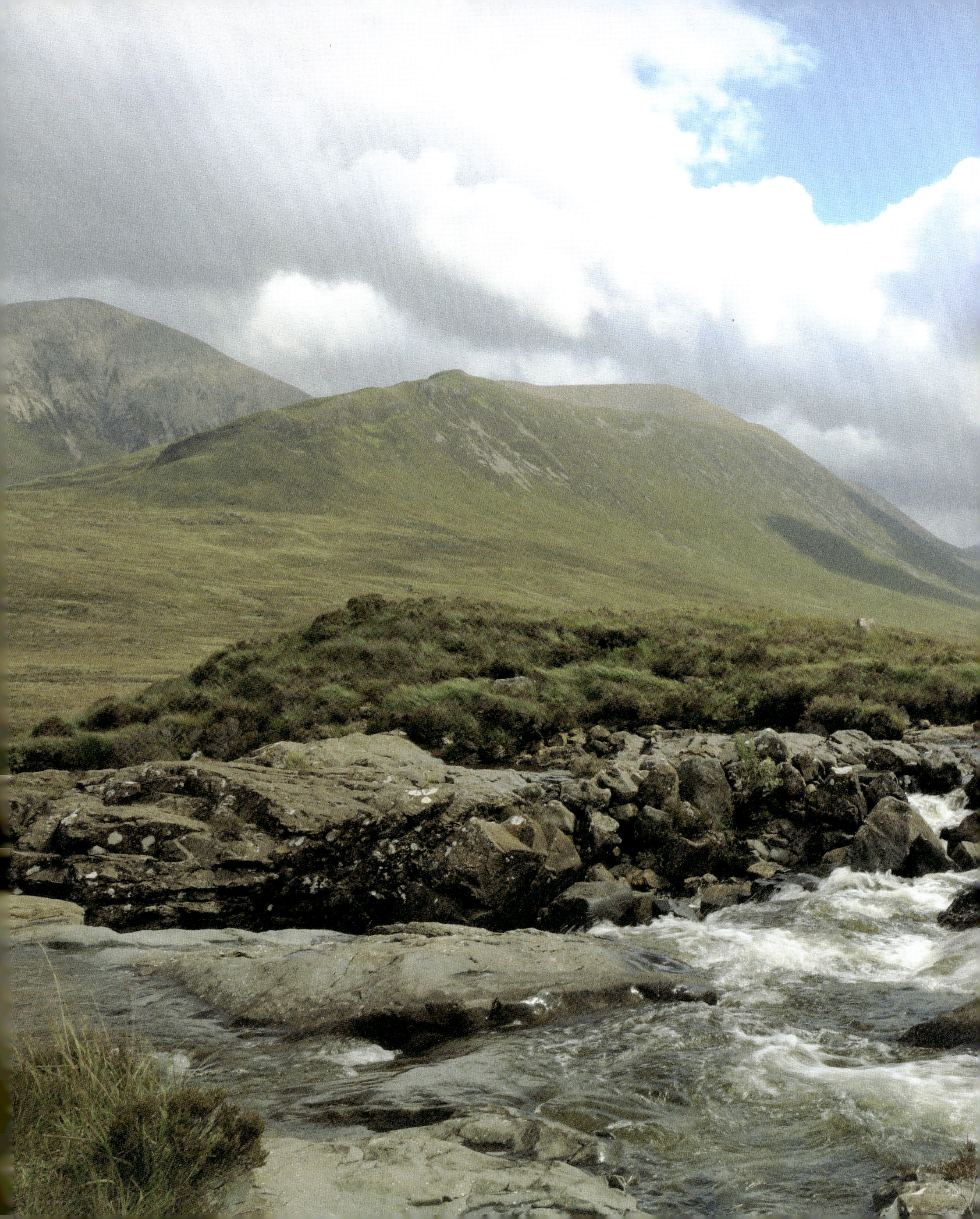

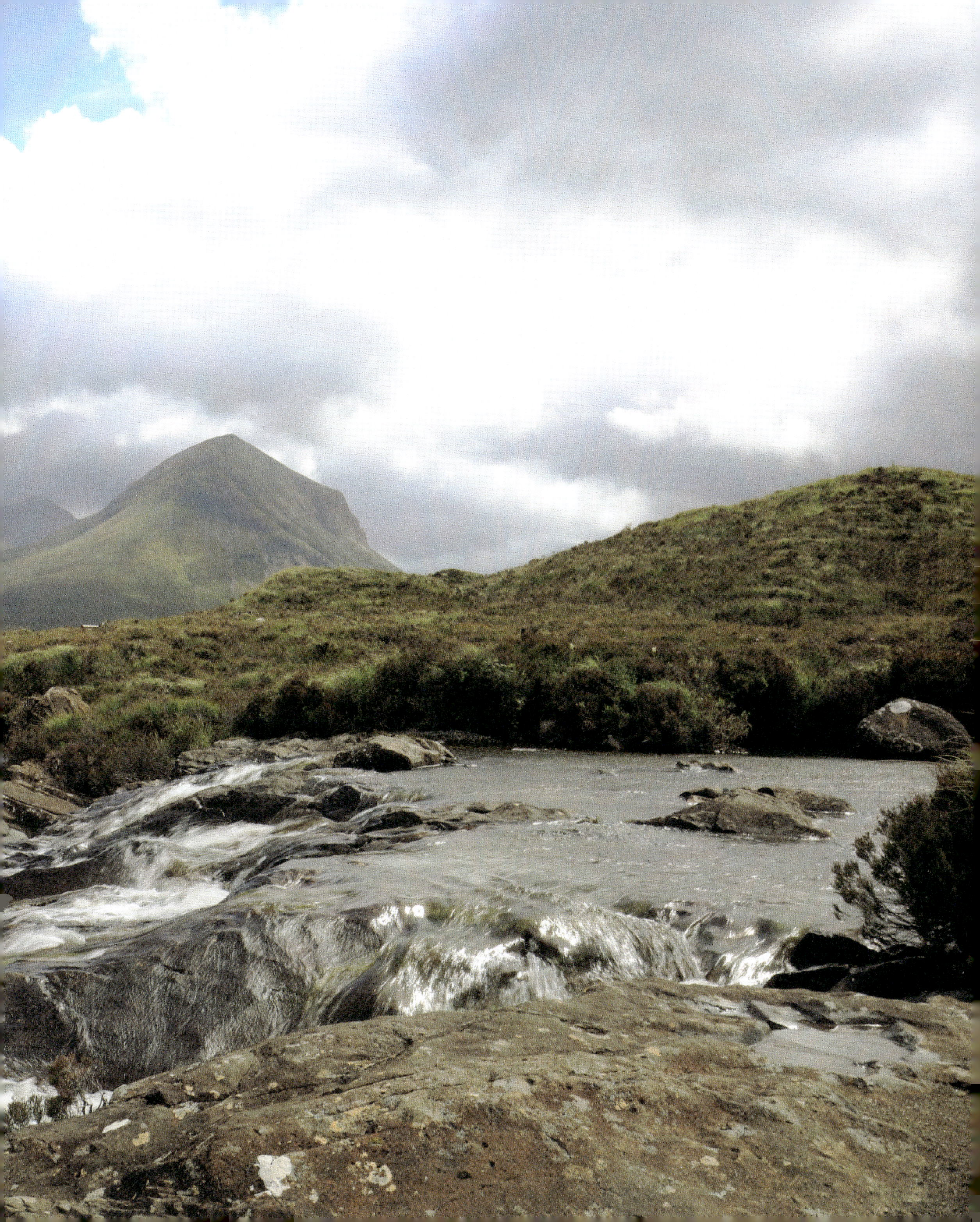

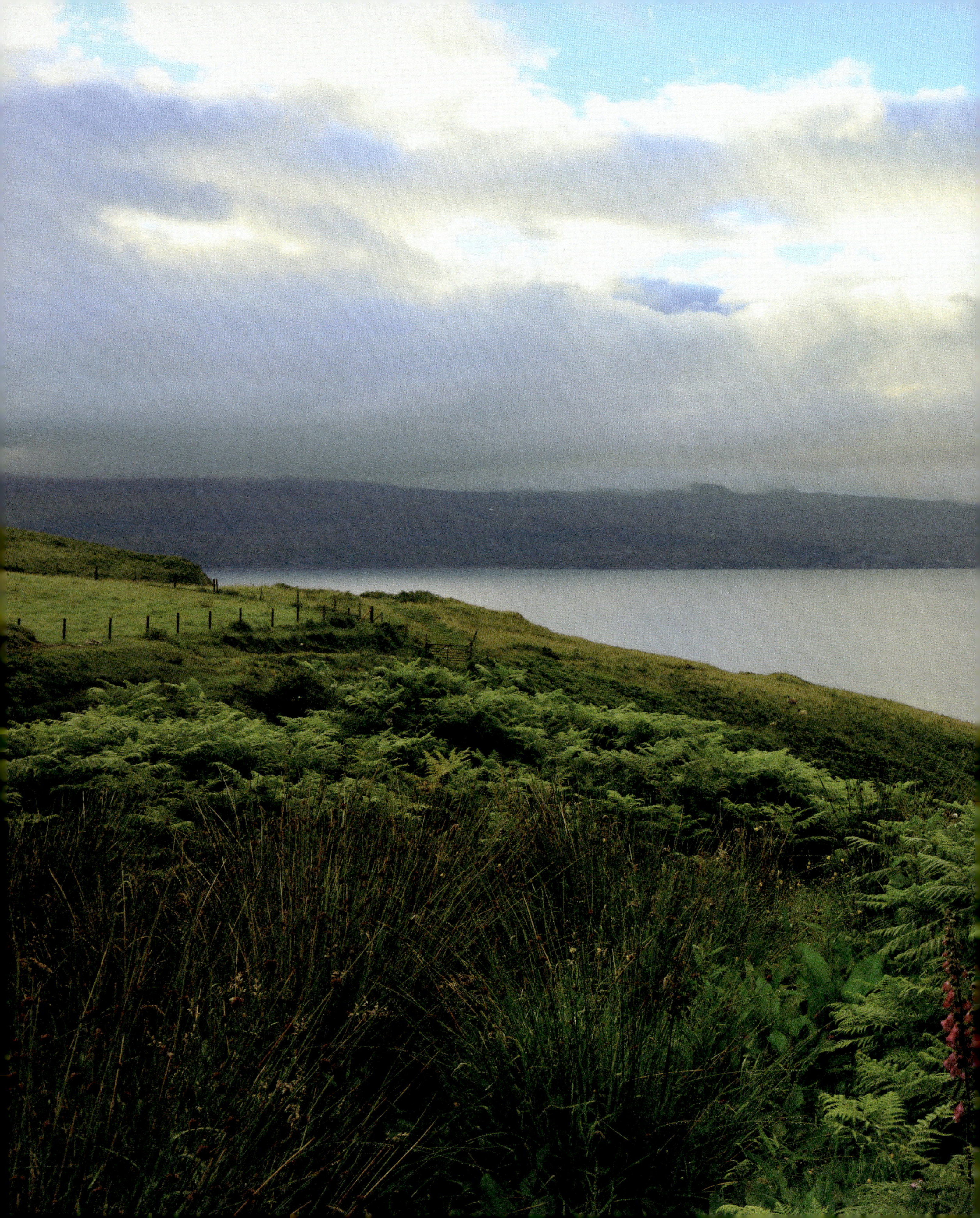

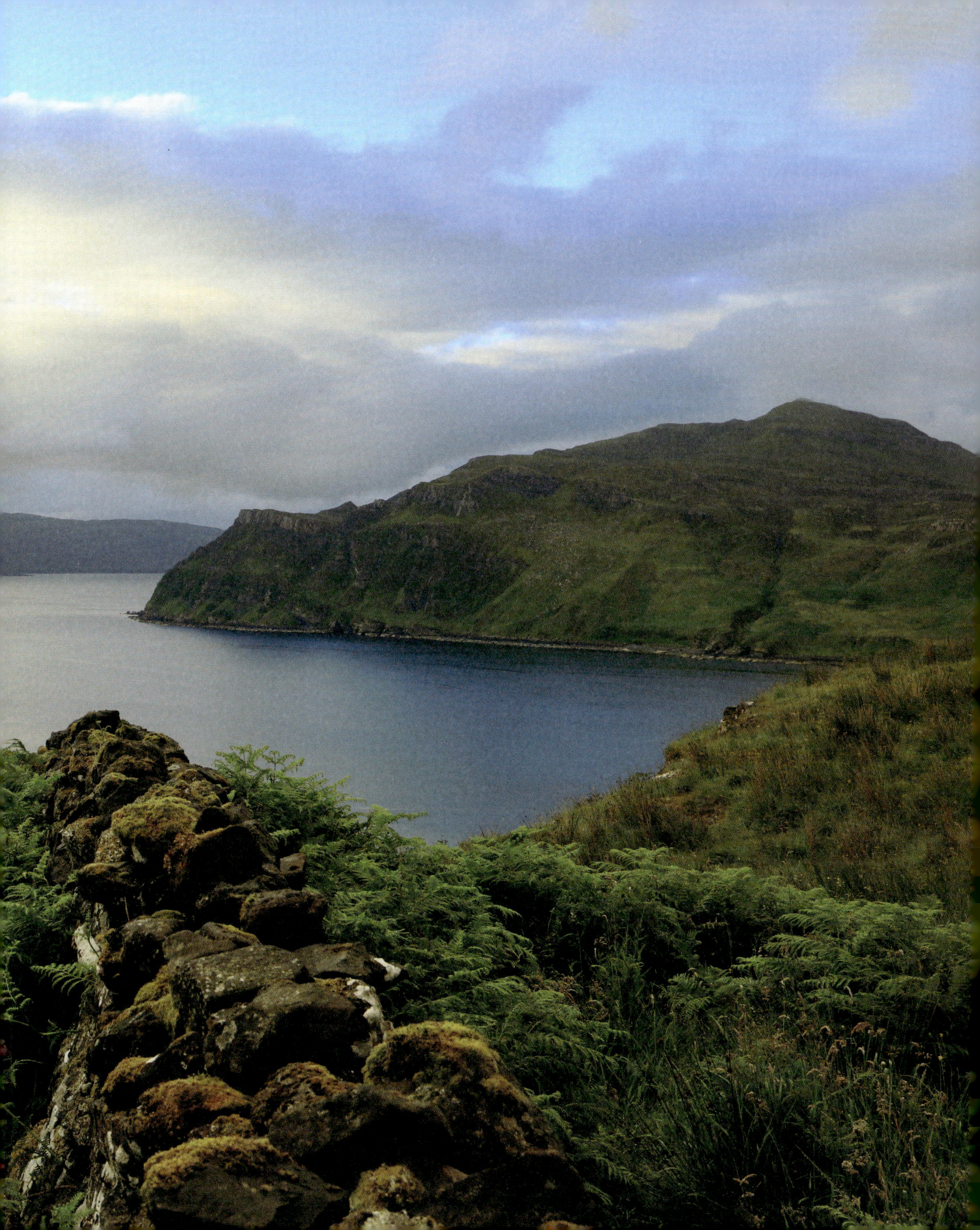

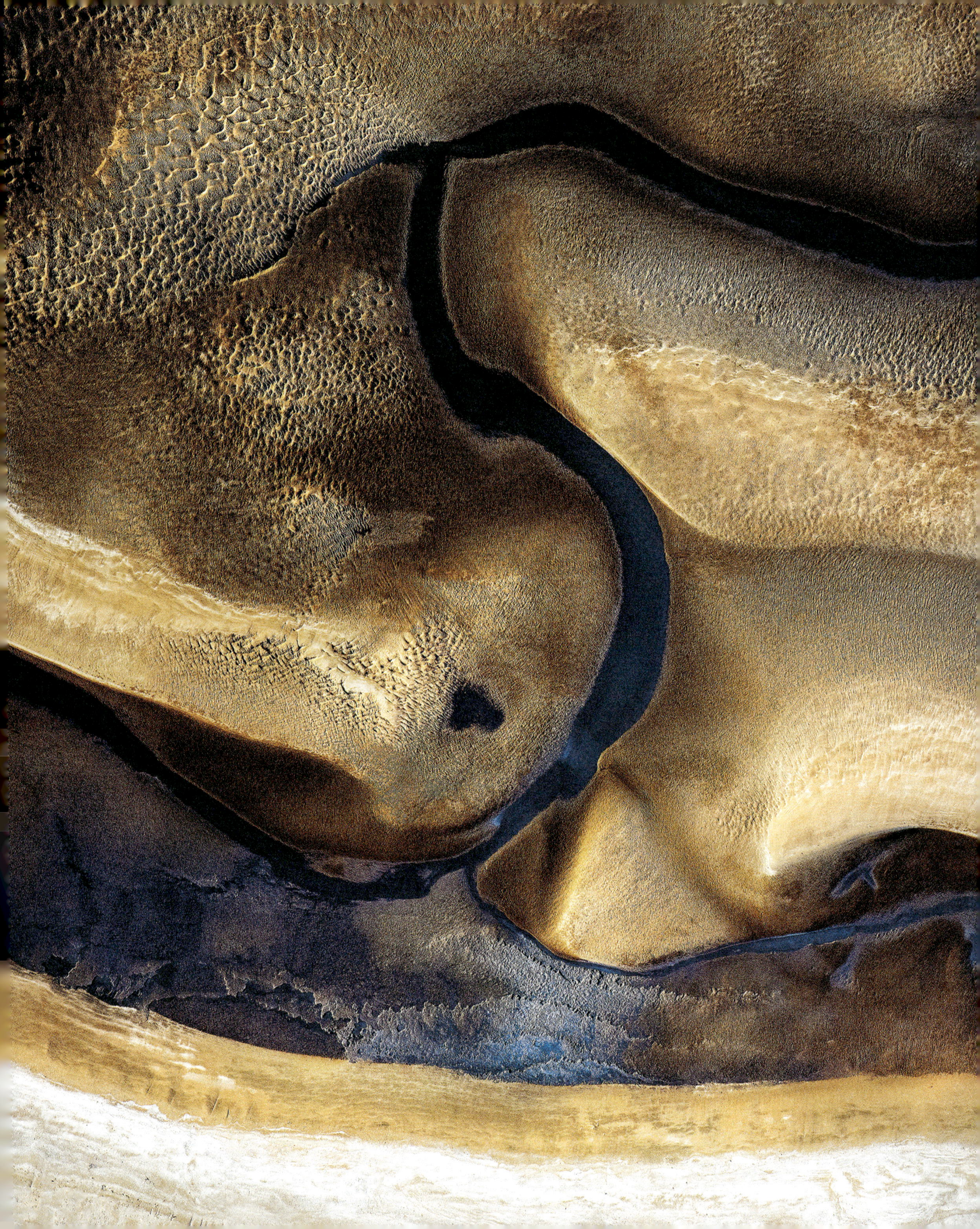

AUSTRALIA

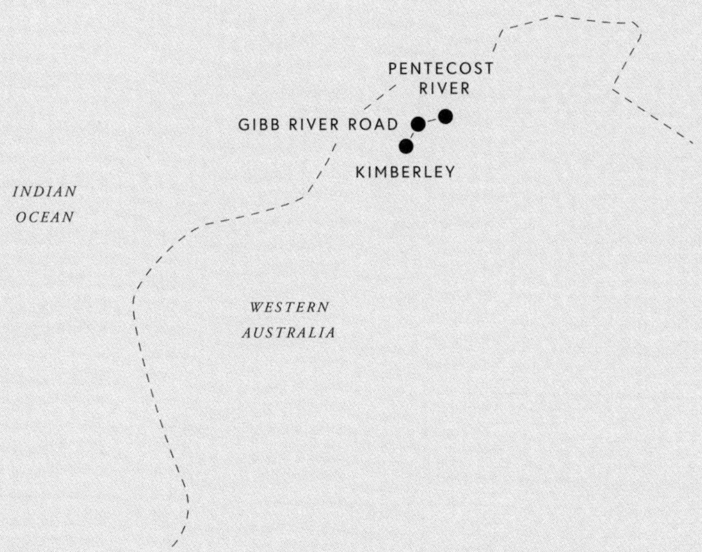

WORDS BY LIZ SCHAFFER

PHOTOGRAPHS BY TANIA MALKIN

Far Horizons

As a Sydneysider I grew up with water. In it, under it, admiring it. Walking to school I'd pass what has been rightly declared the most beautiful harbour in the world, while weekends would be spent diving beneath the waves of Bondi Beach. There was salt in the air and sand on the ground and, with my country boasting 35,876 kilometres of coastline, no shortage of scenic places to swim.

There are other memories too. Like counting the allotted seconds as I showered over a bucket, desperate not to waste a drop of water lest I face my drought-conscious mother's wrath. Australians, whether we're fully aware of it or not, have an interesting relationship with water. It is a fickle friend; unpredictable and ever-present, either as a wishful thought or smile-producing inducement to frolic. In Australia, waterways are the pathways that count.

Water is in our poetry and our lore – we speak of a man from Snowy River, swagmen drowned in billabongs and a homeland girt by sea. There are places where it appears to no longer exist, like the white salt plains of Lake Eyre that spring to life when the floods return, fish hatching from eggs buried for years in the caked earth as the divide between land and sky disappears. Up north, where the year is broken into the Wet and the Dry, water takes on a different meaning entirely. We need it for farming (after all, this was the country that grew up on the sheep's back), so we attempt to master it. But while we dam rivers and build lakes, there are constant reminders that we are at the mercy of this capricious element. Indeed, drought is never far from the minds of those who work the land.

We are an island nation and it is along the coast that most of the population clings. So I doubt I am alone when I confess that it took me decades to properly grasp water's significance. In fact, it wasn't until I ventured to the Kimberley, at the north west tip of Western Australia, that I witnessed the majesty of this country's waterways. This is the 'real Australia', the one they speak of in tales of the Outback. A place where the land is red, the sky is blue, and to survive you must be made of tougher material. Roads stretch into the distance, at times crossing crocodile-filled rivers like the ferocious Pentecost, and space is abundant. Yet even here – seemingly revelling in the contradiction – waterfalls fill hidden valleys, swimming holes tempt and the Gibb River Road (another lifeline through the wild and wonderful north) ends at the sea.

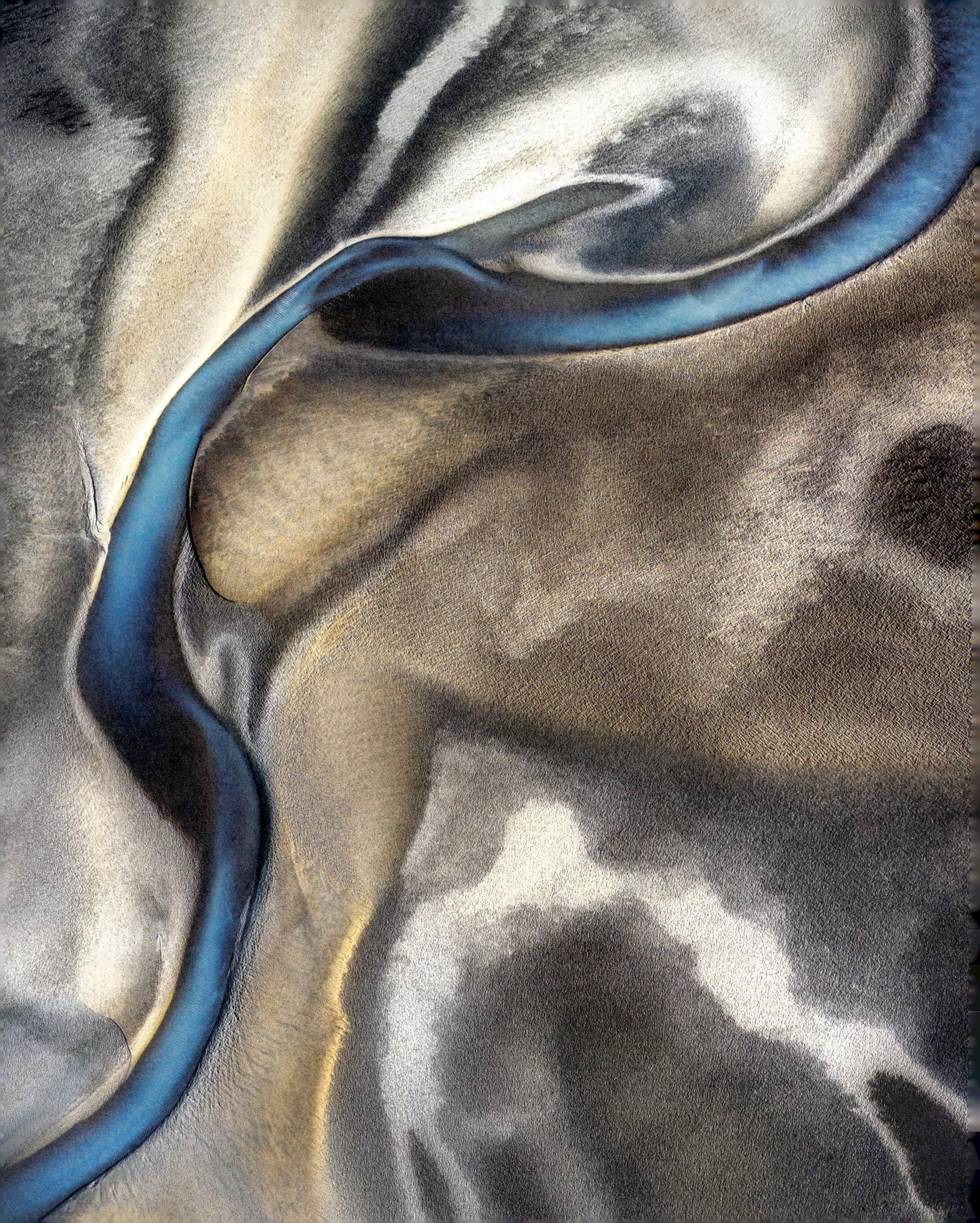

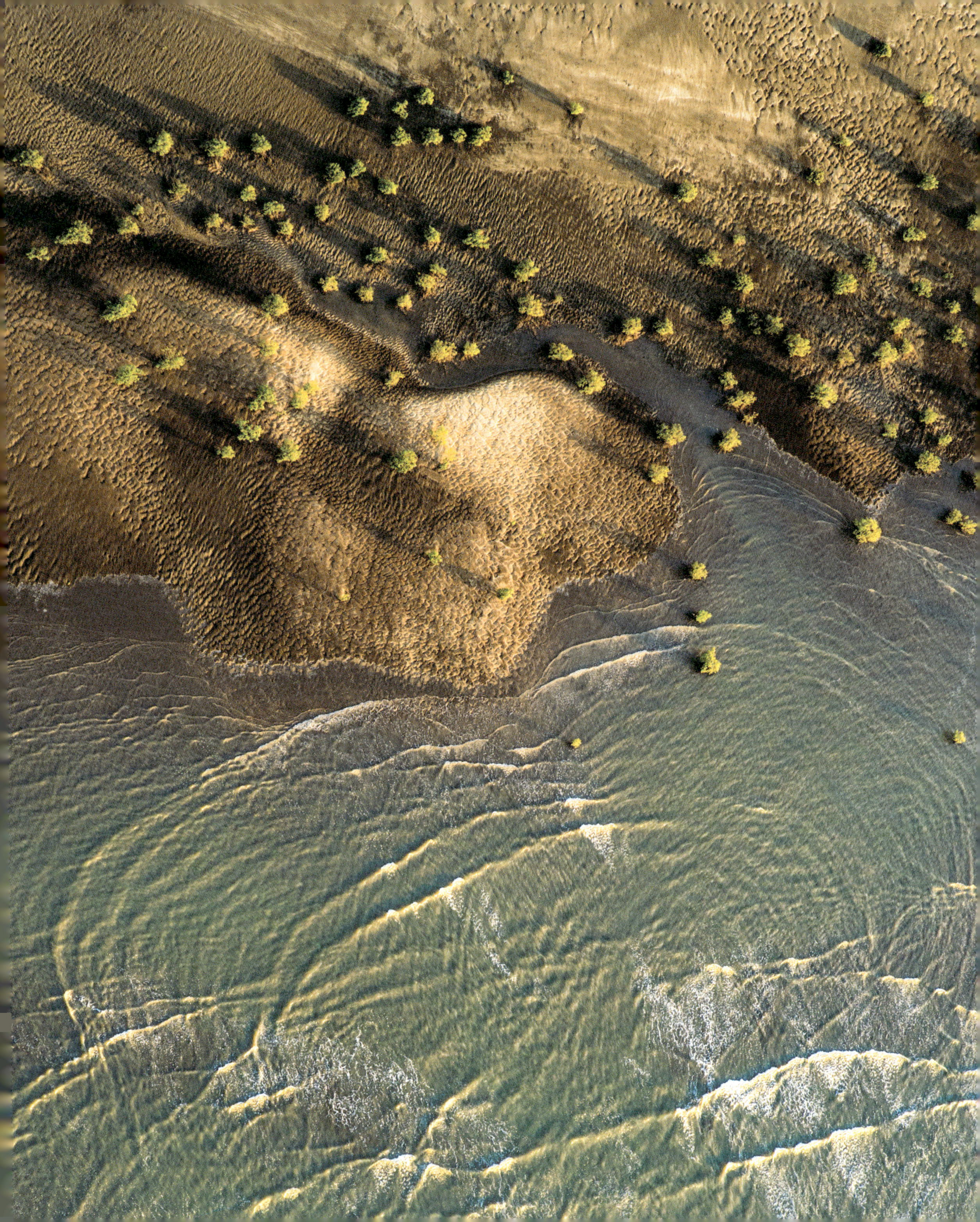

Australians, whether we're fully aware of it or not, have an interesting relationship with water. It is a fickle friend; unpredictable and ever-present, either as a wishful thought or smile-producing inducement to frolic.

To appreciate the marks of water you have to take to the air, as photographer Tania Malkin does. From here the earth ceases to be real, instead becoming a patchwork of patterns, the water carving its erratic path at whim. The hues are unexpected, with rivers coloured in shades of pink and green while the ocean glows. The earth itself is softened, as if it has been caressed over the years by tides long since evaporated, like a painting brought to life. On the ground you sense the might of these water-filled pathways, but from the sky you can't help but be humbled by their splendour.

Disparate and all-powerful, water here forms its own fractured path. Commanding and hypnotic, you want to follow it, capture it, understand (in whatever way you can) how it has allowed our country to take shape. While it may have taken me a while to truly grasp them, when I think of home it is these waterways I see. ⋆

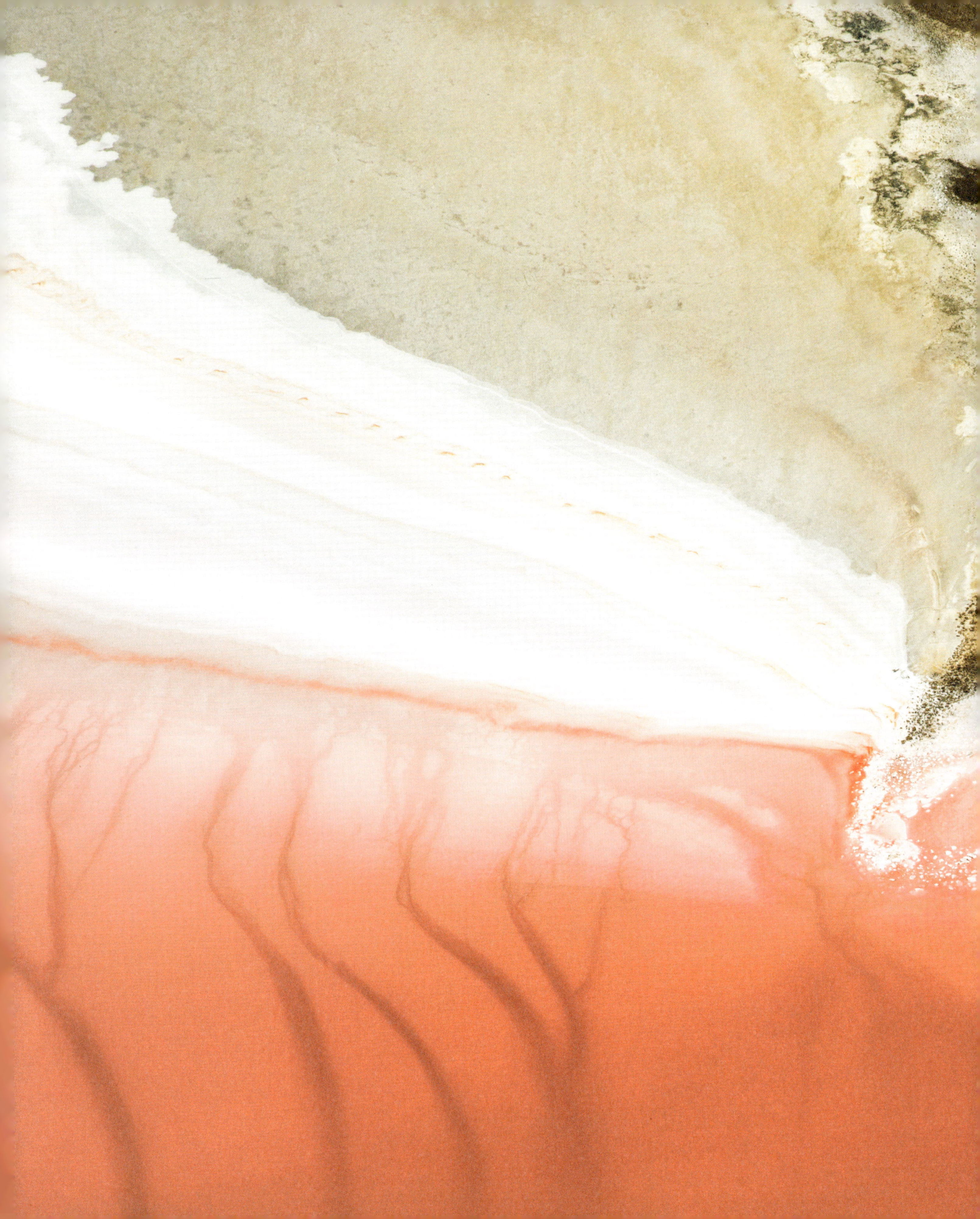

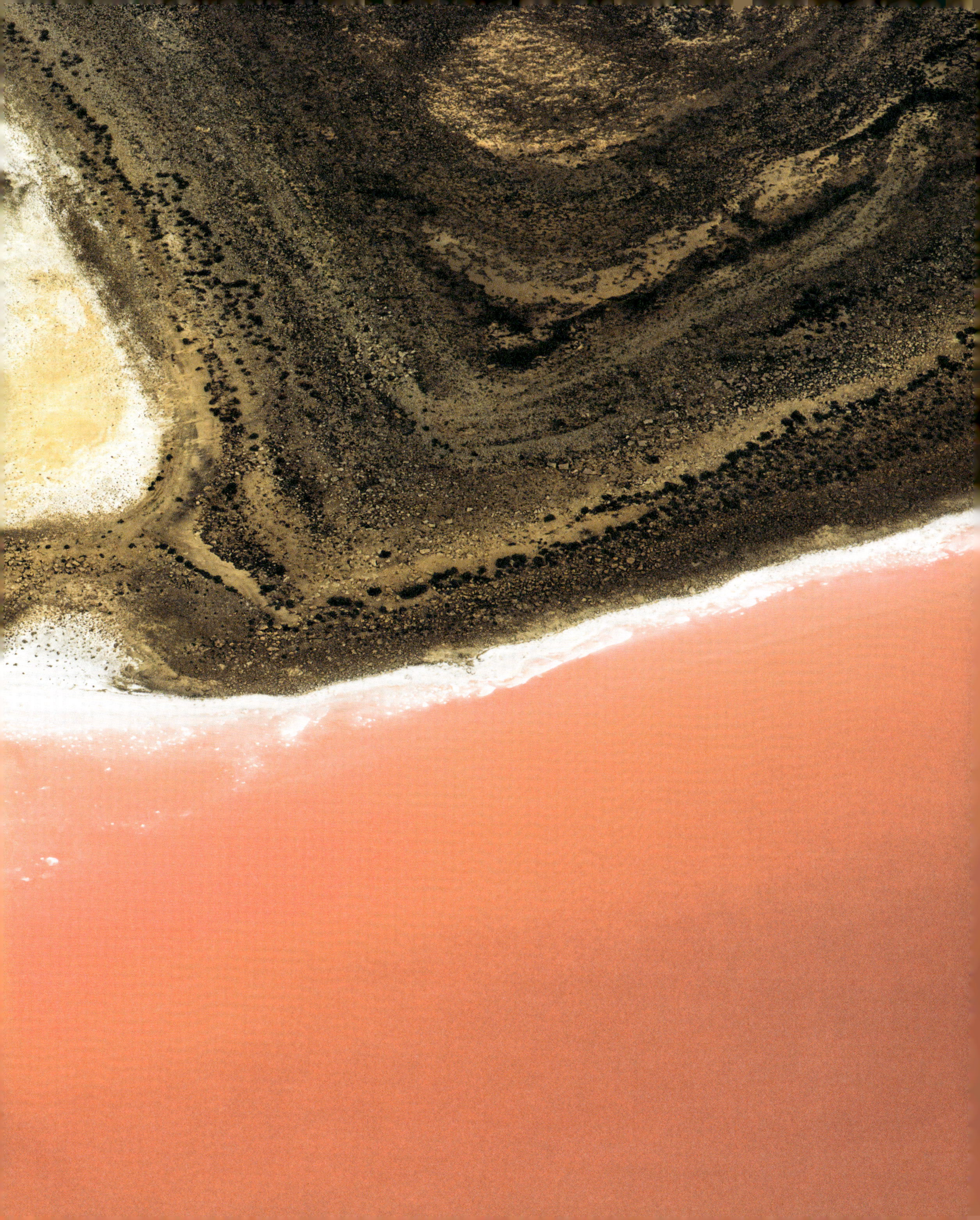

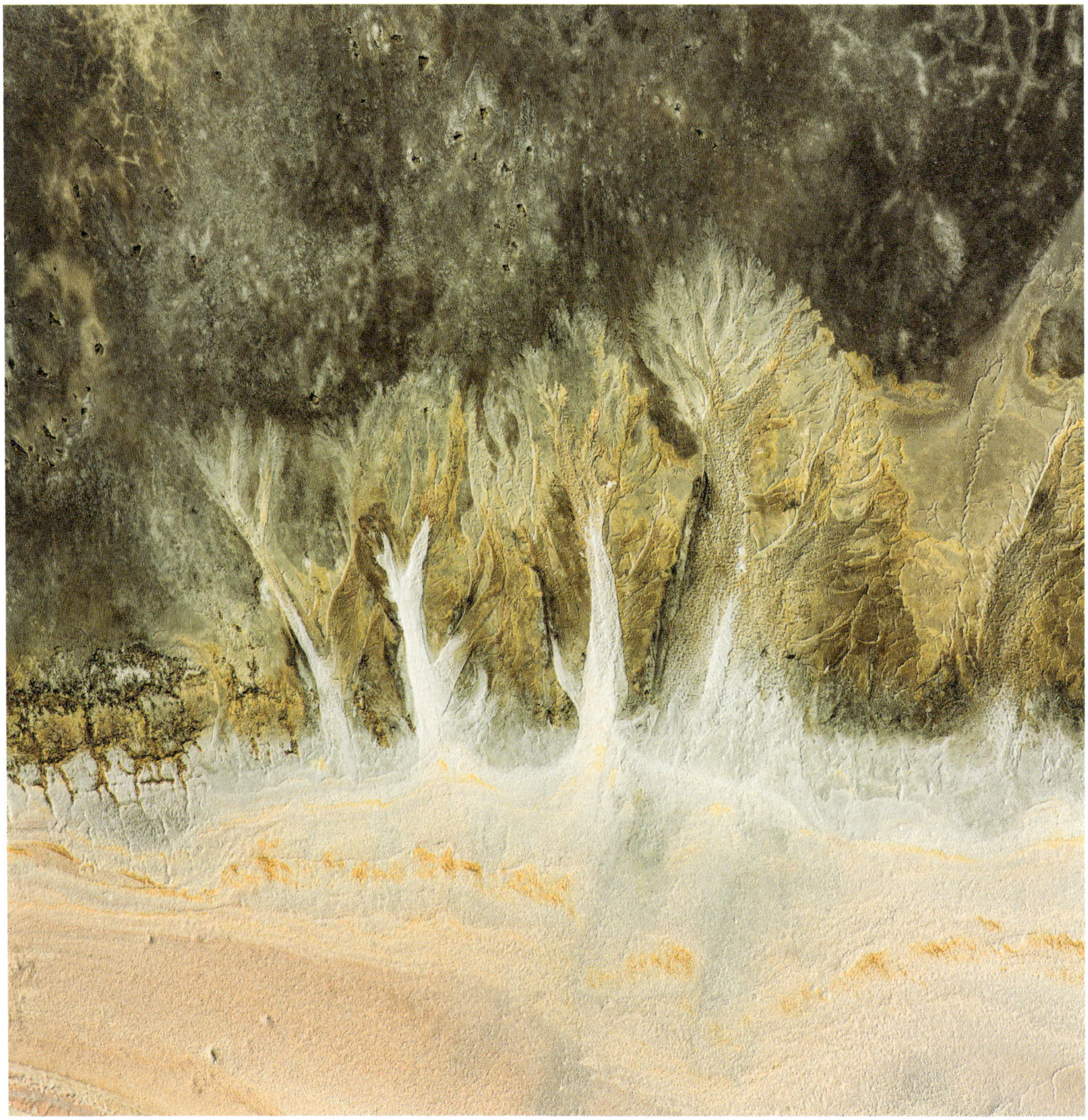

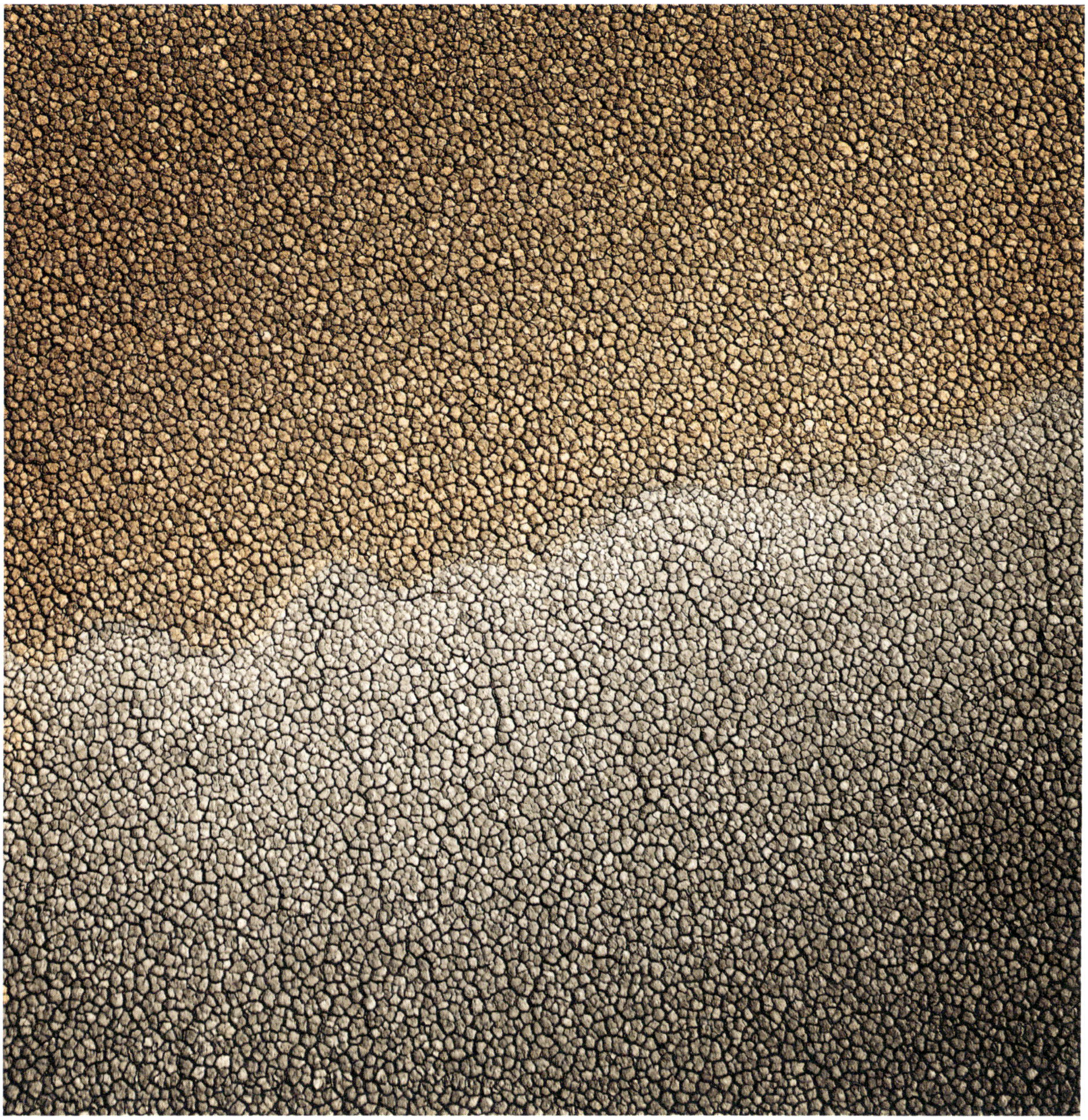

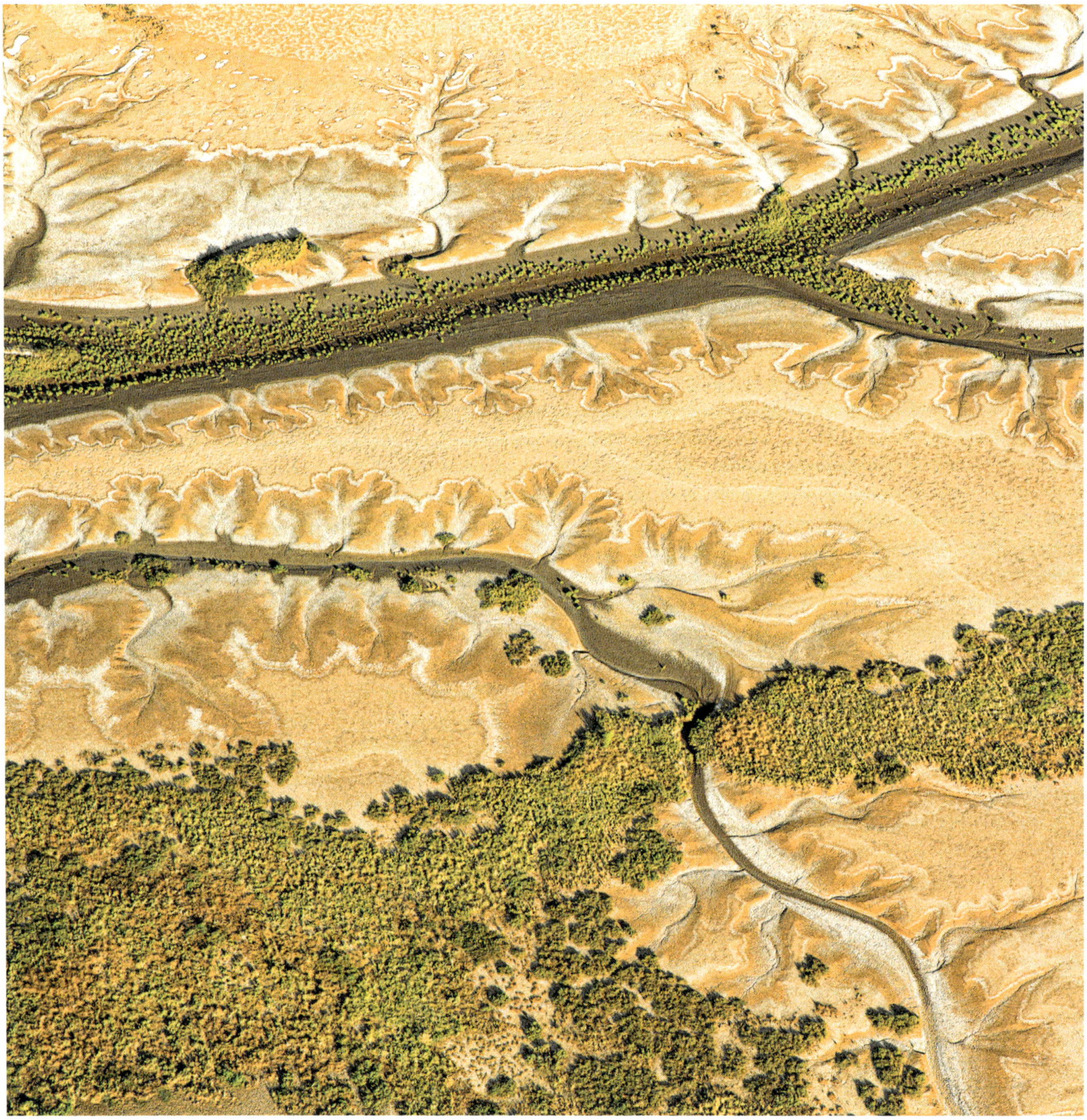

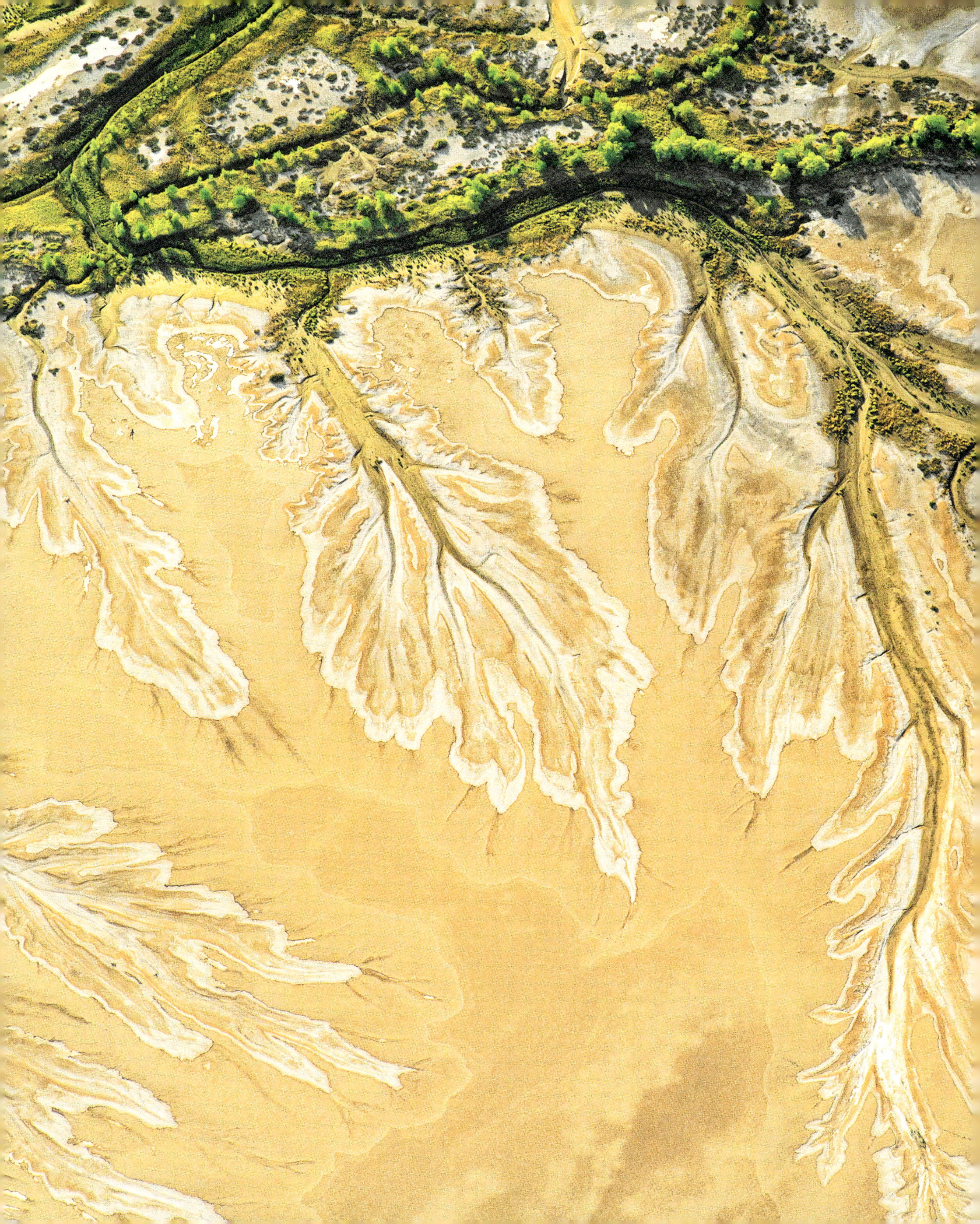

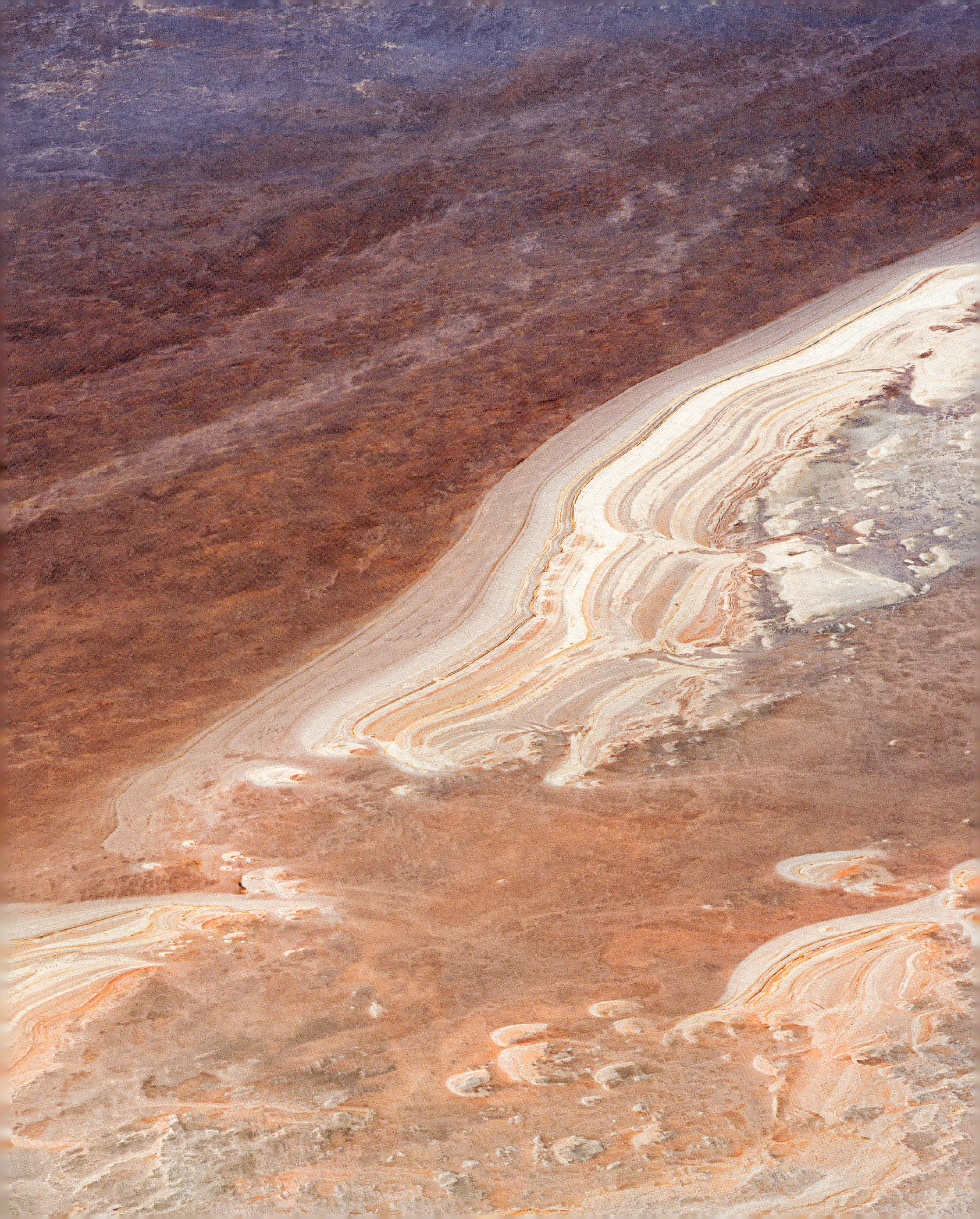

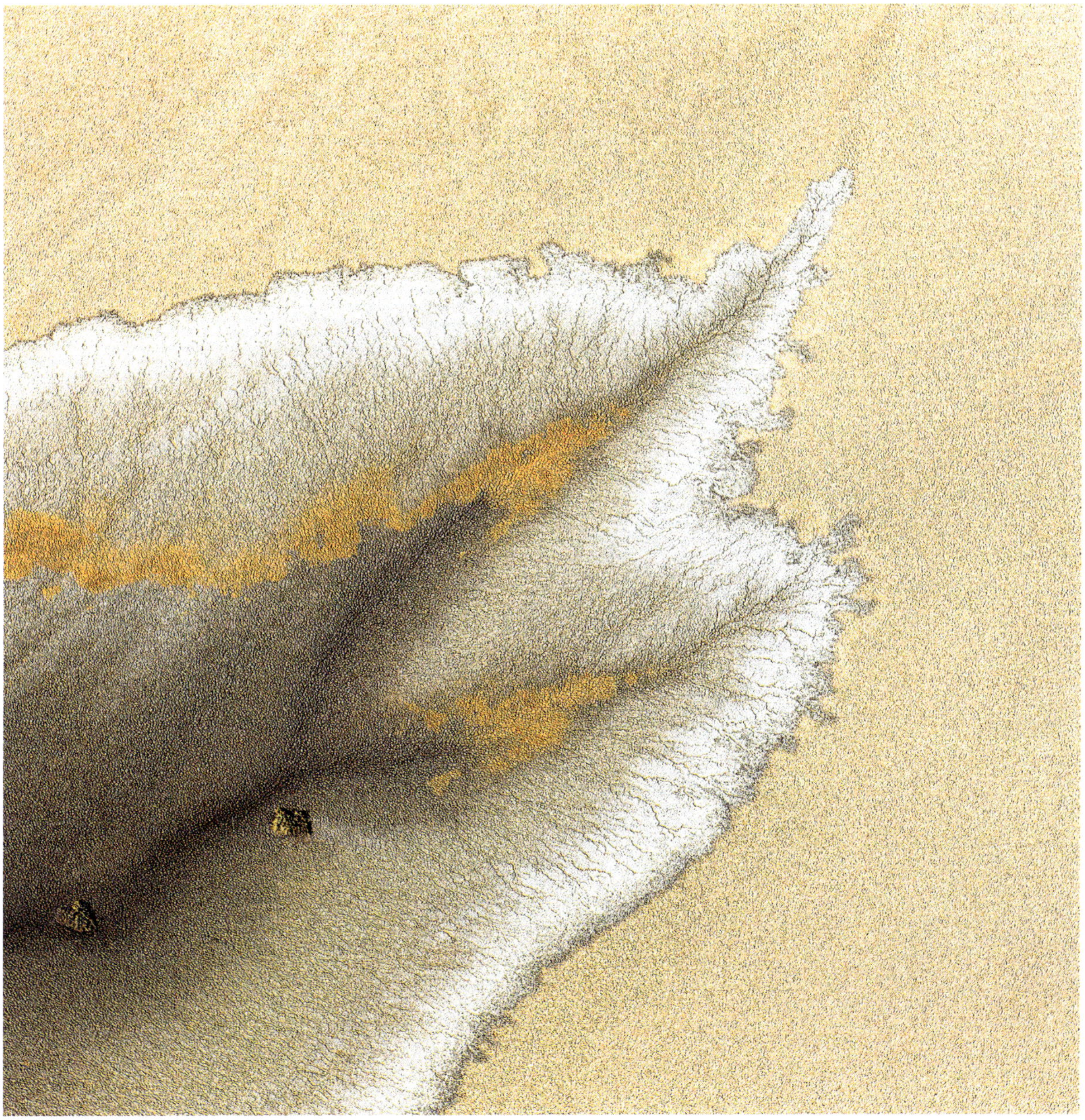

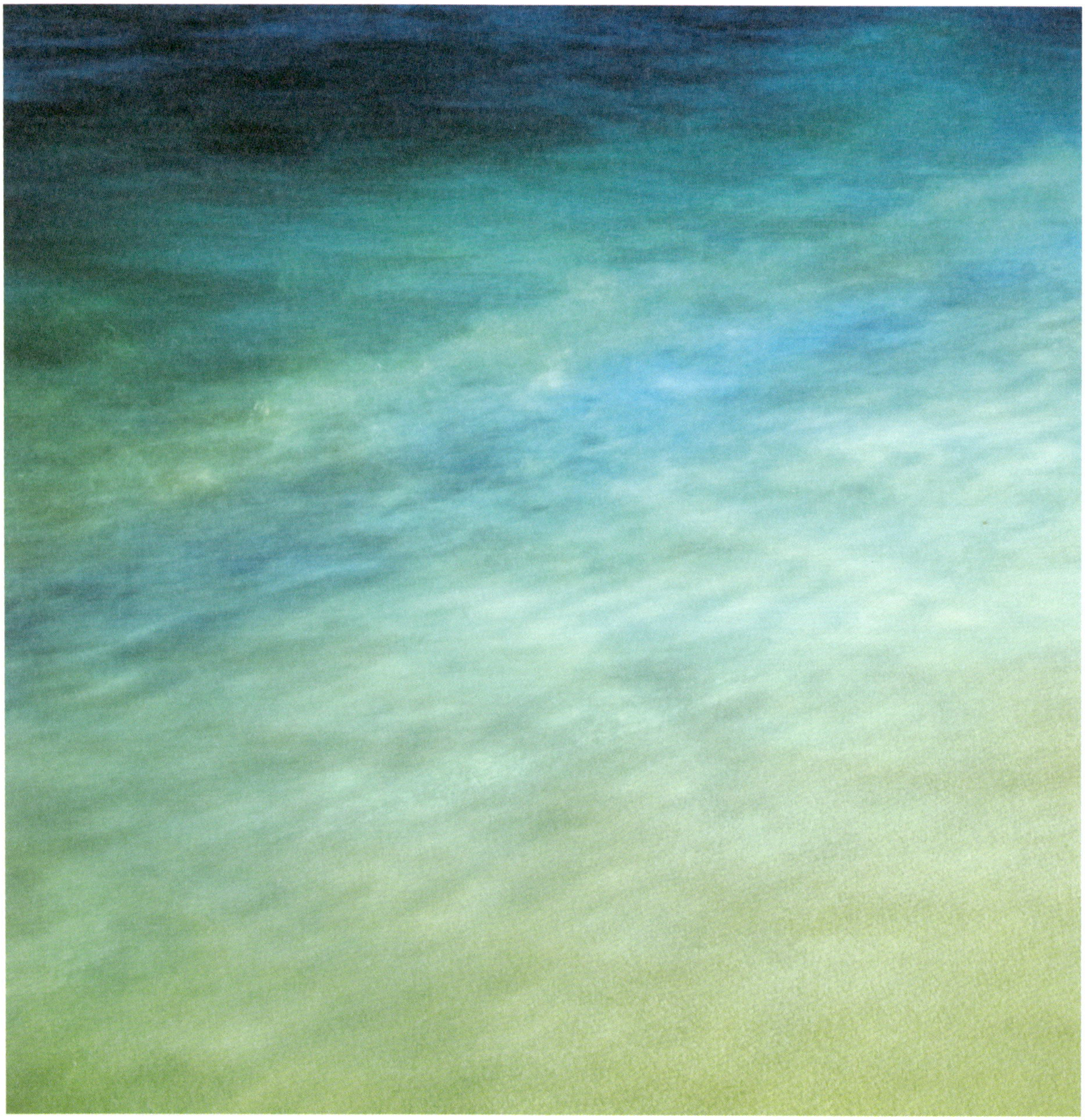

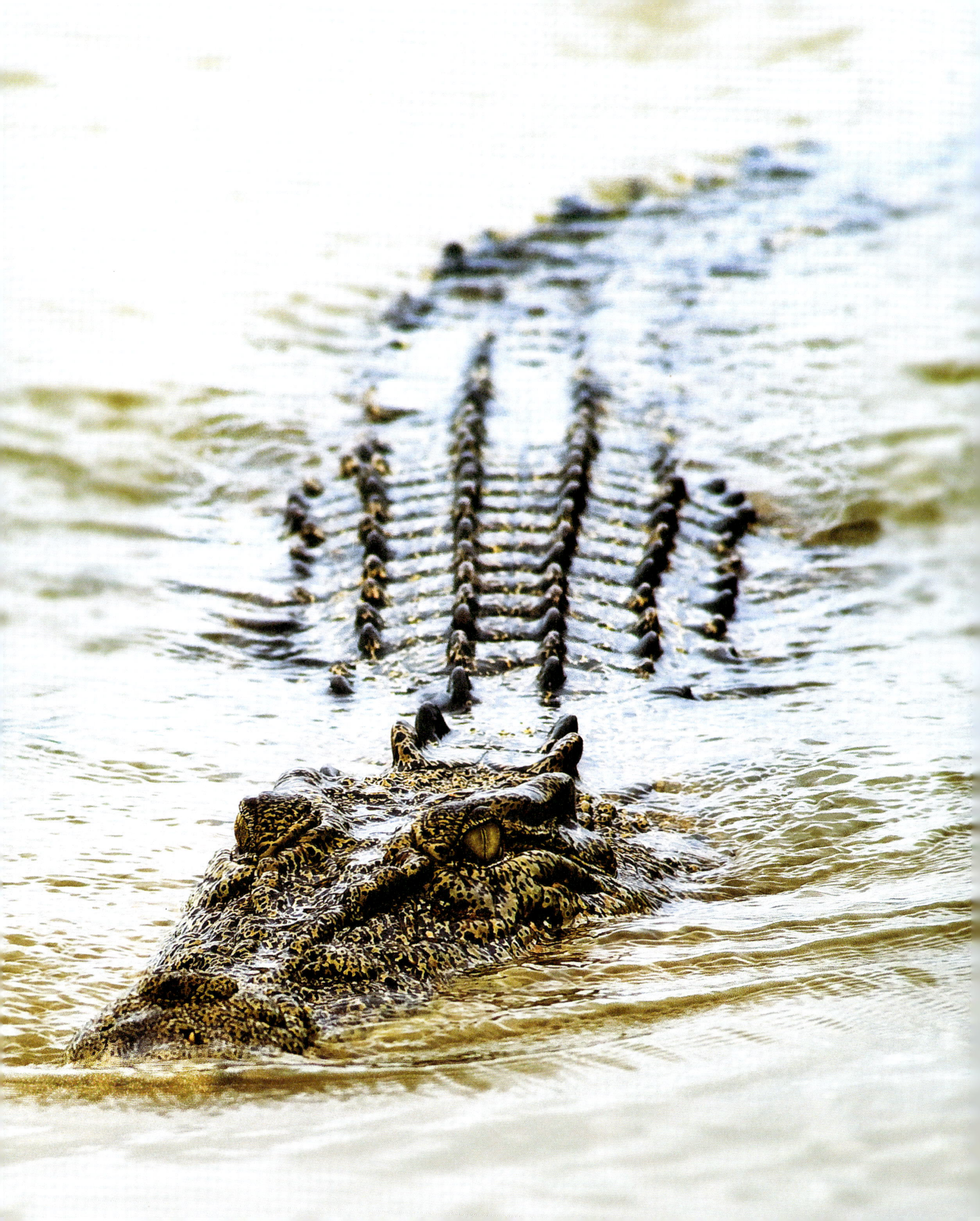

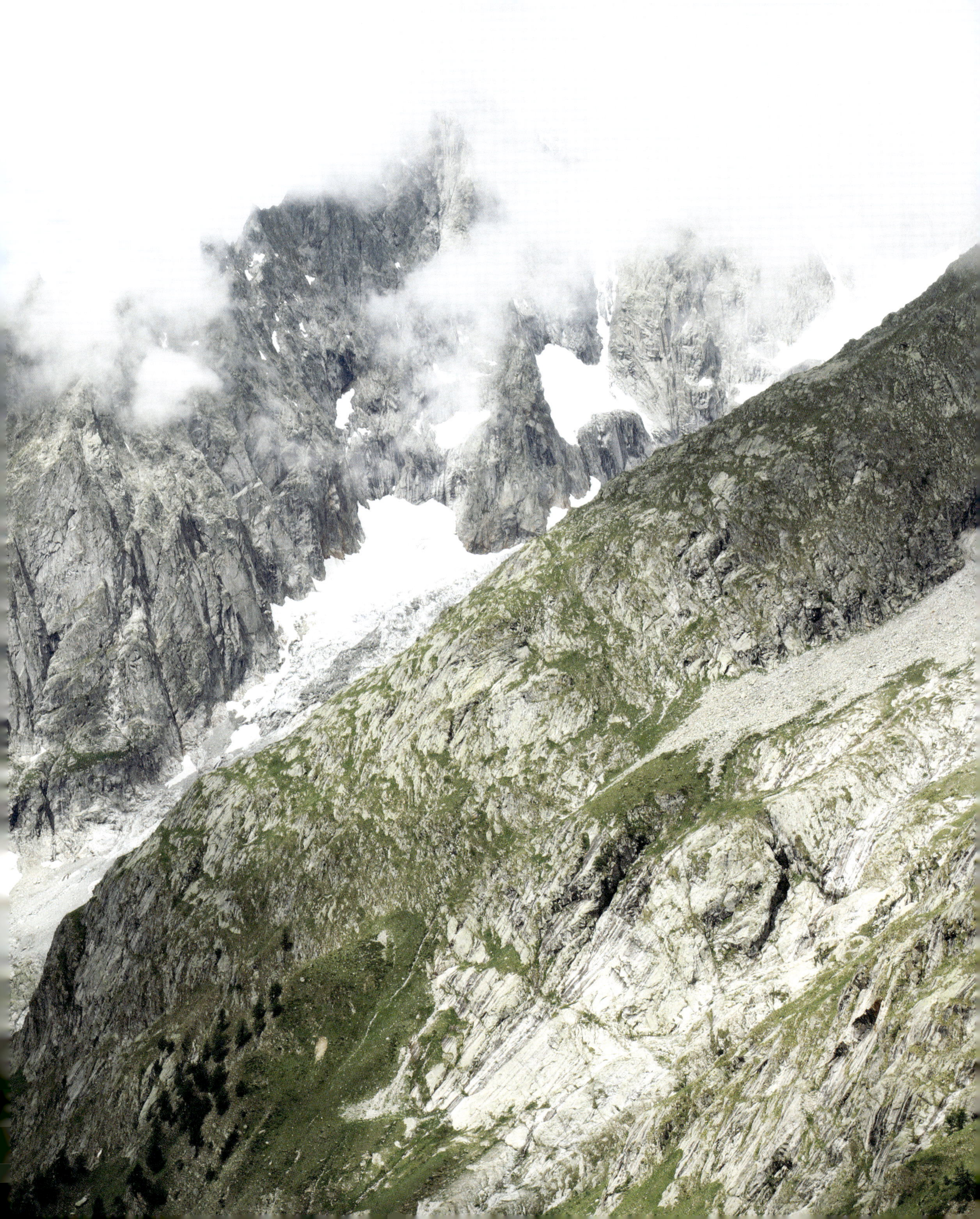

ITALY

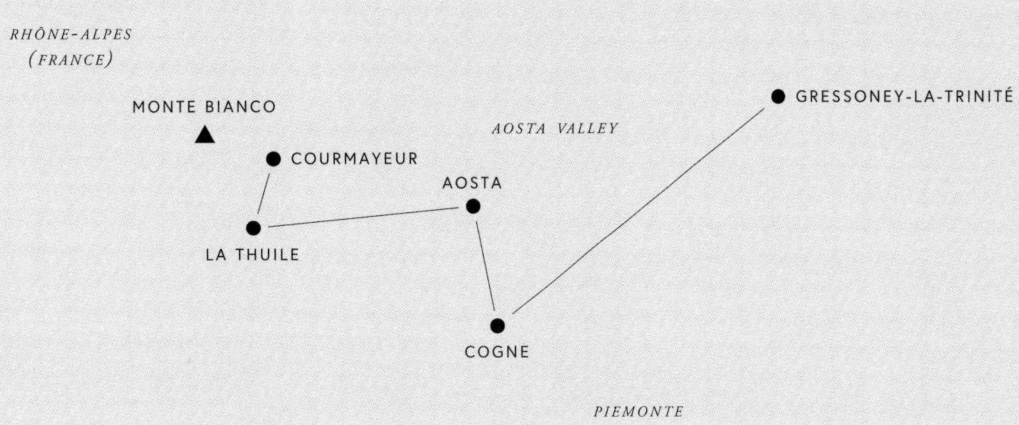

WORDS BY ANGELA TERRELL

PHOTOGRAPHS BY LIZ SCHAFFER

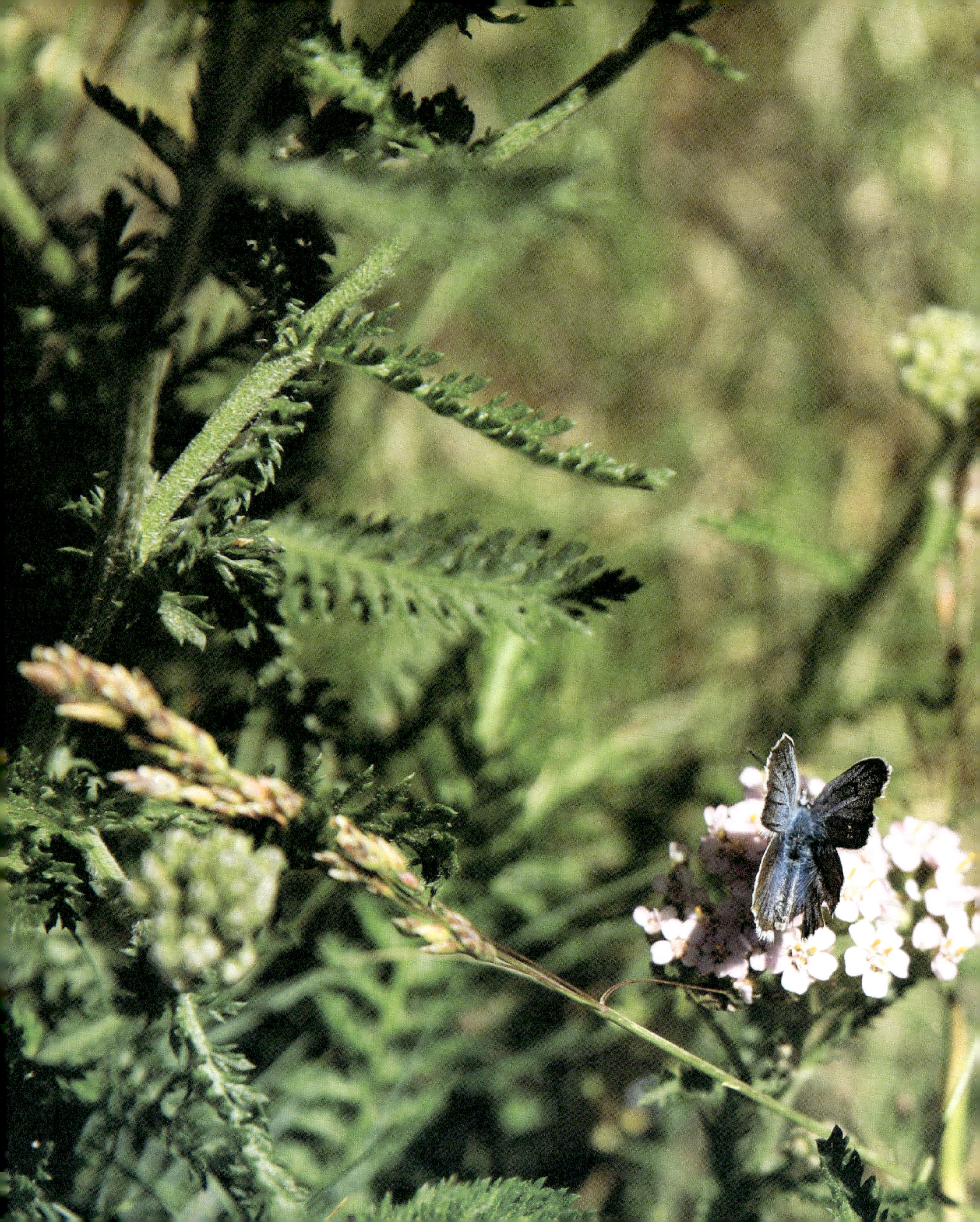

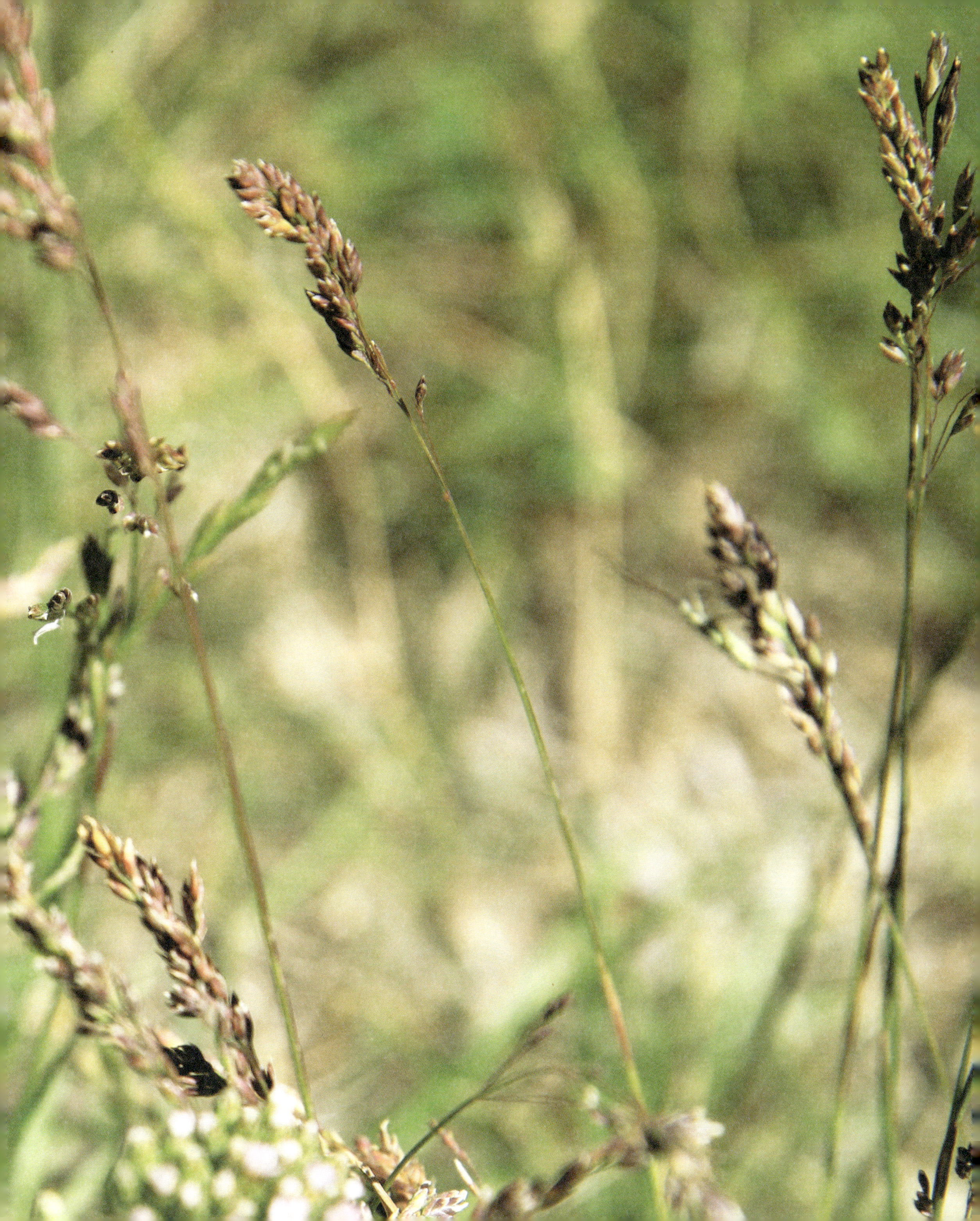

Terroir Tales

"A vineyard is like a son, nurtured by a family," muses Davide as we gaze over the quilted countryside, the hills and valley folds streaked with vines clinging to the sun-kissed earth and crested by terracotta-hued villages. "I love all that's behind a bottle of wine, the emotions, the ideas. It's personal. Things taste better when you know the story." While the scene before me was captivating, it was Davide's words that revealed the ardour behind Piemonte's beauty.

I wanted to explore this area by getting amongst it, so I'd turned to wine-besotted Davide Pasquero from Terroir Selection who took me cycling through historic villages (Neive being a particular standout) and along roads coiling through steep vineyards that made my heart pound as I began to understand why these vines are still largely tended by hand – just one of the factors that allows the Barolo from these hills to be viewed by many as the Ferrari of wine.

My mind wandered whilst pedalling. As the vineyards of the Lower Langhe rolled into the hazelnut groves of the Upper Langhe, the Alps remained a constant detail upon the horizon and I speculated on the treasures to be found if I extended my path through Piemonte and headed towards these distant, snow-capped peaks. This being Italy (where wanderlust and whim walk hand-in-hand), I succumbed to curiosity and, the next day, swapped my bike for a car and travelled across the Po Plain towards the siren's song: Val d'Aosta.

Even at its mouth the mountain grandeur was awe-inspiring. Aosta Valley may be Italy's smallest region but has its highest peaks – Monte Bianco standing as a sentinel at the valley's end. Driving along what was once the ancient route linking Rome to France, I passed the Roman bridge at Pont-Saint-Martin and chariot-wheel scarred road at Donnas, but it was the town of Aosta that held the most remarkable relics. Once rivalling Rome in magnificence, well-preserved ruins and the enveloping Alps helped me imagine just how formidable Aosta must have appeared to visiting emperors passing through its Augustus Gate.

Many epochs have left their mark here. Fairytale-like castles fill the valley and atop Coteau la Tour vineyards in Aymavilles I savoured Les Crêtes wine in a medieval tower, once a king's lodgings. Only 100 kilometres from Piemonte but a world away in terroir, the difficulty of cultivating vines on these granite slopes means Valdaostan plots are small but roots grow deep, wines such as Les Crêtes' Syrah and Fumin a luscious result of this mountain mineralogy. The Charrères

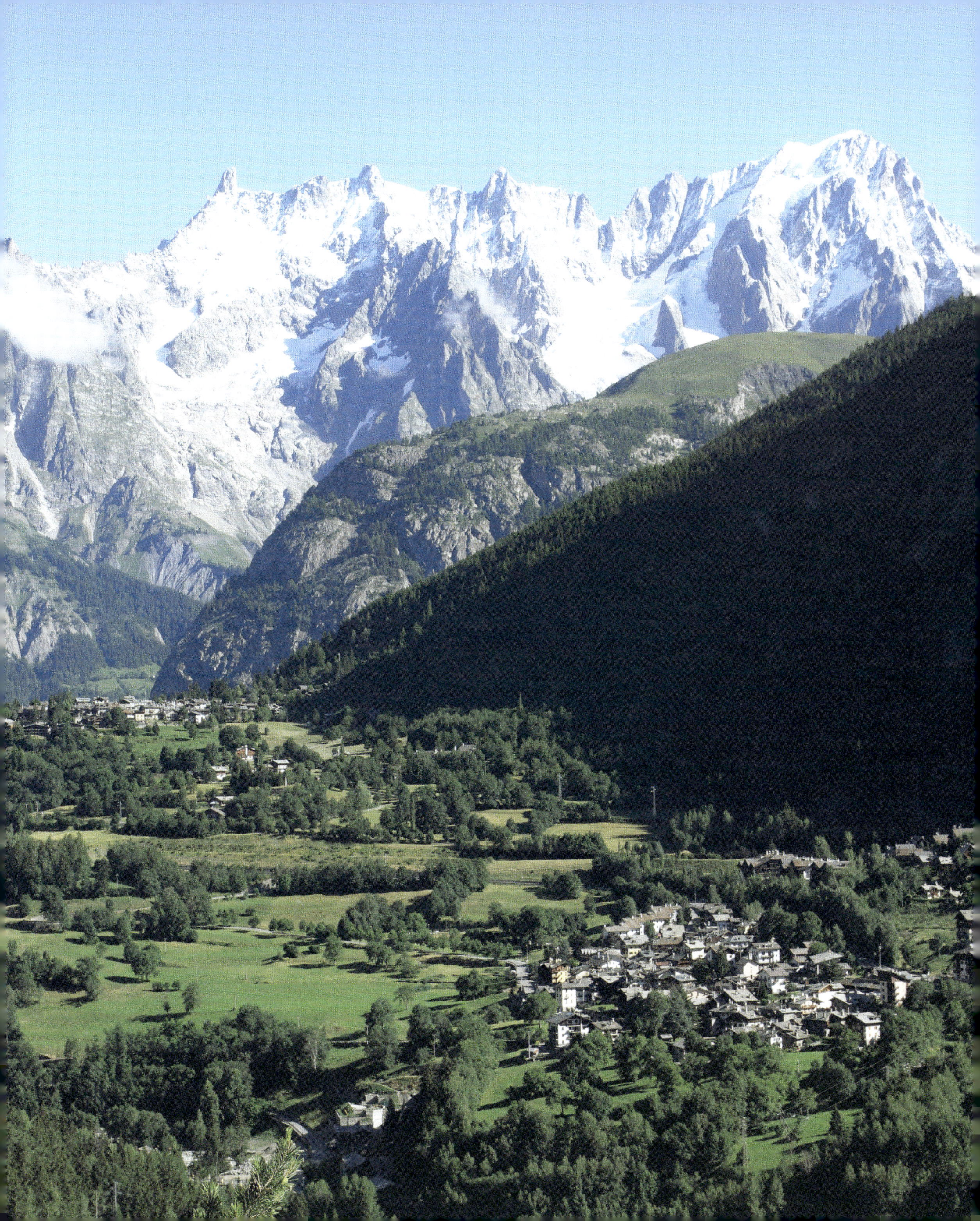

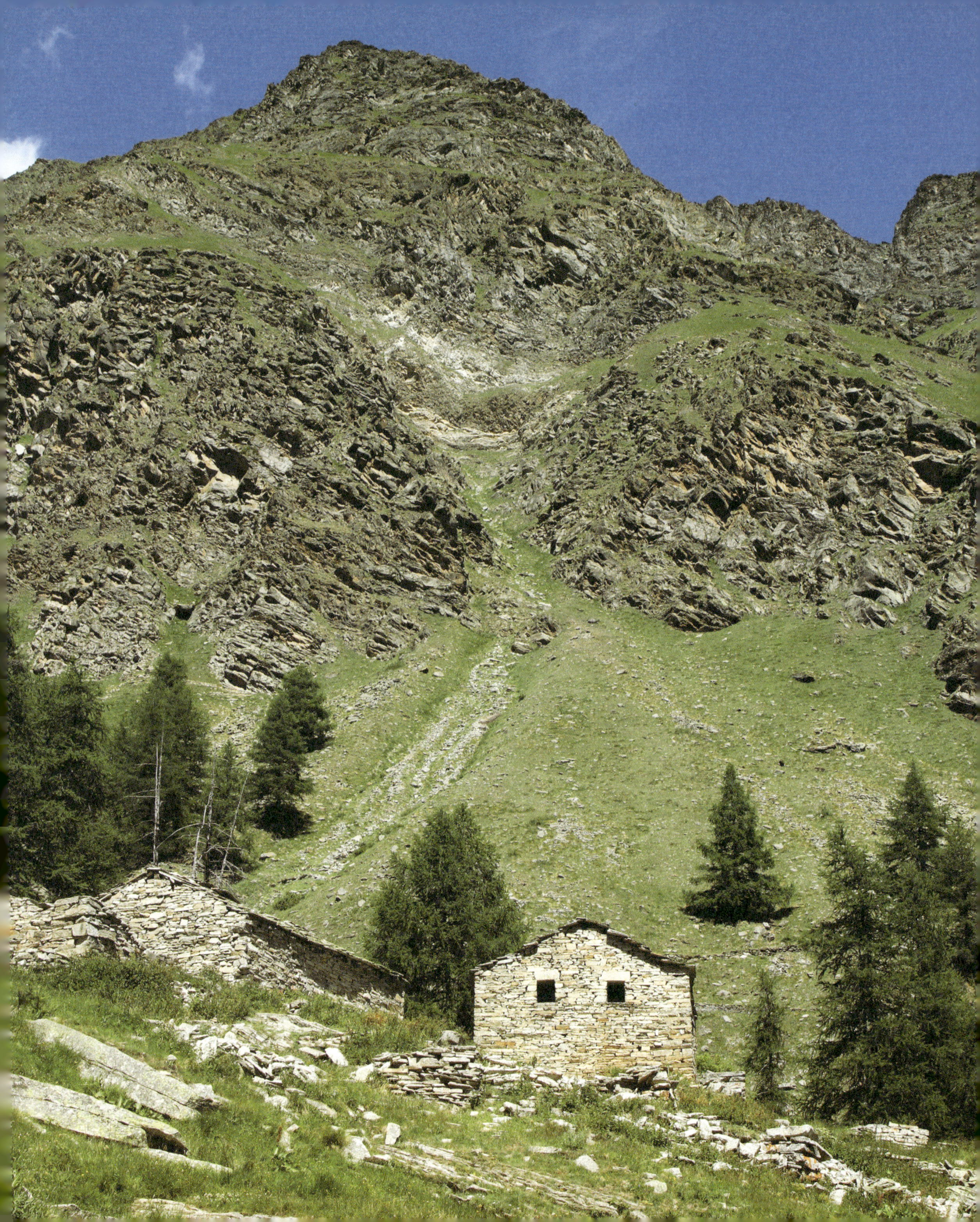

The Alps remained a constant detail upon the horizon and I speculated on the treasures to be found if I extended my path through Piemonte and headed towards these distant, snow-capped peaks.

family who own the winery have worked these hills for generations, and as I looked towards the serrated peaks sipping wine lovingly called 'son of the light', I appreciated that, as in Piemonte, there is fervour behind this land.

It was in the side-valleys that I experienced Aosta Valley's authenticity – scenes untouched by time and communities proud of the land they call home. Driving up the Lys Valley I passed villages suspended like balconies over the valley floor to reach Gressoney-La-Trinité, nestled below the Monte Rosa Massif, where the Walser culture remains alive despite the relentless creep of the modern world. These tenacious travellers settled in the area in the 11th century after walking over the Alps from Germany and it's comforting to see today's inhabitants safeguard this heritage, undertaking projects such as the restoration of centuries-old farmhouses into boutique hotels like the charming Wongade. With most of the interiors hand-carved or repurposed, Wongade not only provides a cosy place to rest your head but also showcases the local fare, which features so much more than polenta (although you will no doubt enjoy their hearty take on this mountain staple).

The gorge-like valley leading to Cogne was equally remarkable and it was easy to picture Hannibal and his elephants, who supposedly passed this way. Cogne is the gateway to Gran Paradiso National Park, the oldest national park in Italy and a nature lover's nirvana, and overlooks the wildflower-filled Meadows of Sant'Orso which are deemed an Italian wonder.

From Pré-Saint-Didier I followed the winding valley to Col du Petit Saint-Bernard on France's doorstep, pausing to admire the ruins of ancient storehouses and lodgings ravaged by time and altitude. Although the drive was relatively short, my mind was still filled with thoughts of the kings, explorers and pilgrims who had trodden this path before me when I returned to Nira Montana in La Thuile. This hotel beautifully captures the atmosphere of the forested mountains – hewn birch branches, timbered walls and art-like detailing offering a tranquil mix of contemporary design and rustic simplicity. So close to Switzerland and France, dinner at Stars Restaurant (following an Aperol and jaunt in the spa) reveals the influence these cultures have had on the regional cuisine, dishes like succulent trout adorned with ruby-red radish and sweet potato the colour of mountain sunshine a homage to the alpine *mélange*.

Every Italian region has its own flavour but it's the Aosta Valley's cultural mix that means many villages have their own unique ingredients. In Gressoney it is Toma di Gressoney, cheese made on the mountainside, and Chnéfflené pasta.

Cogne's specialty is Fontina cheese (beautiful when combined with chestnut gnocchi) and in Courmayeur it's Le Reve goats cheese produced by goats grazing happily on alpine pastures. At the homely Lou Ressignon restaurant in Cogne – named after a place you frequent for a midnight snack and chat – I even tried wafer-thin slices of cow's udder, surprisingly tasty when served with Lard d'Arnad and bread dripping in honey.

Food may be a window to Valdaostan identity but the setting is just as nourishing. Exercising here is delightful year-round – winter ski-fields becoming a myriad of summer hiking paths – so with the sun shining I donned my hiking boots, keen to explore the unspoilt landscape. From Gressoney I followed the Alpenzu Tour to mountain hamlets lost in time, passing an explosion of alpine colour along the way; the greens, yellows, purples and pinks of wildflowers perfect fodder for frolicking butterflies and grazing cows. Near Cogne I hiked a mule path from Valnontey, originally built for King Vittorio Emmanuel's hunting party but now an exhilarating route into the Gran Paradiso Massif. Clambering up the narrow trail I spotted ibex, chamois and marmots, but it was the magnificent vista and creamy hot chocolate at Rifugio Sella that were the real rewards for my valiant effort.

My journey had taken me into a realm of wonder. By and large, Aosta Valley remains a relative mystery to the rest of the world and I felt fortunate to have been able to unlock some of its charms for myself. Yet I was still tempted to travel further, Monte Bianco's magnificence enticing me to rise above the valley floor and see what lay beyond.

Life is full of twists and turns and in Italy following your heart is always advised, so, not surprisingly, I found myself the next morning on Skyway Monte Bianco heading towards the 'Roof of Europe'. Soaring over rocks faded with age and gnarled by the mountains' force, I contemplated the panorama ahead and the many pathways still to follow. ⋆

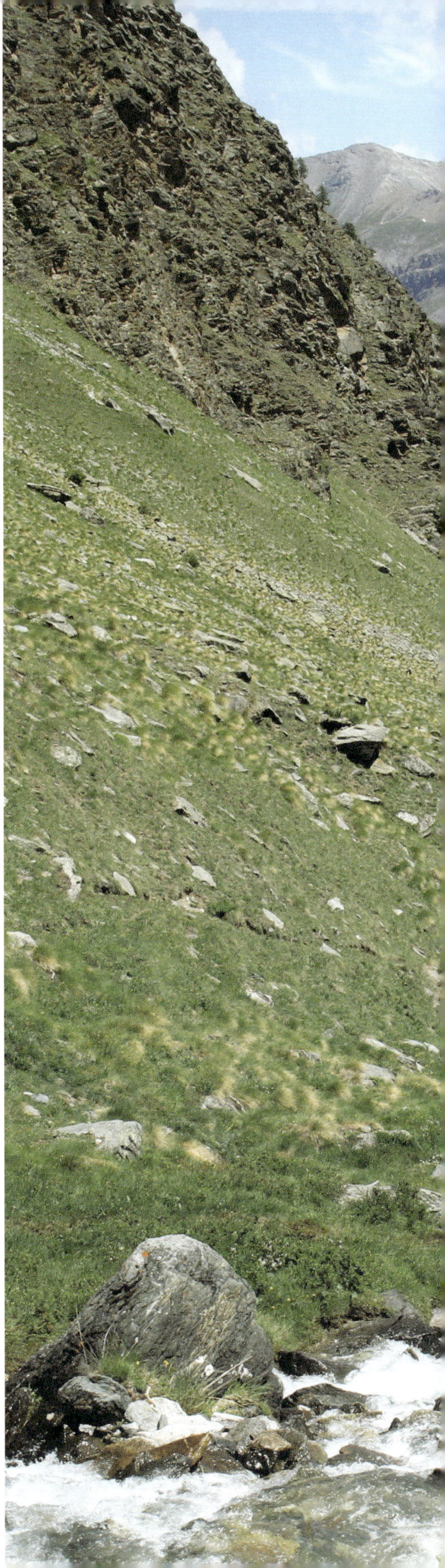

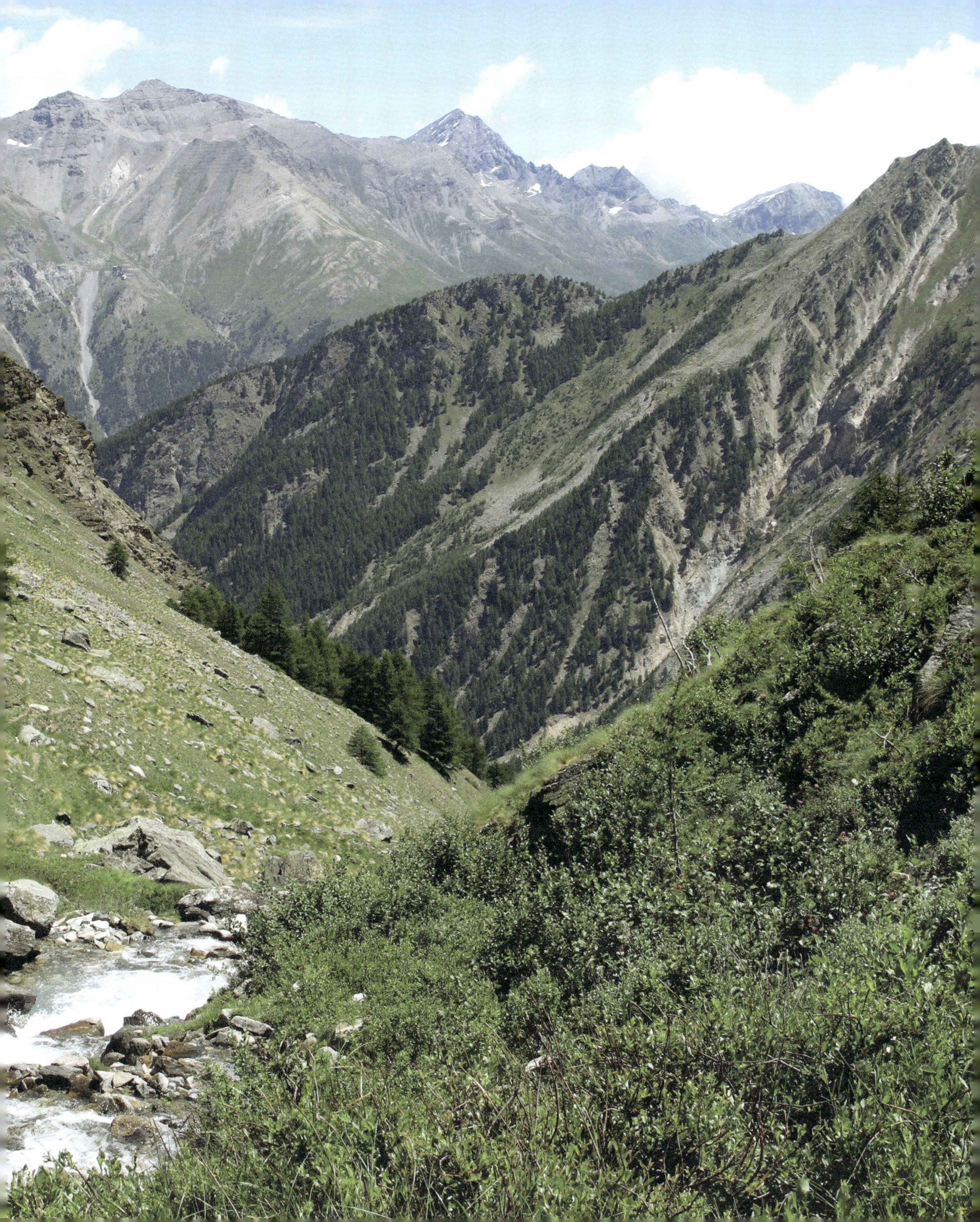

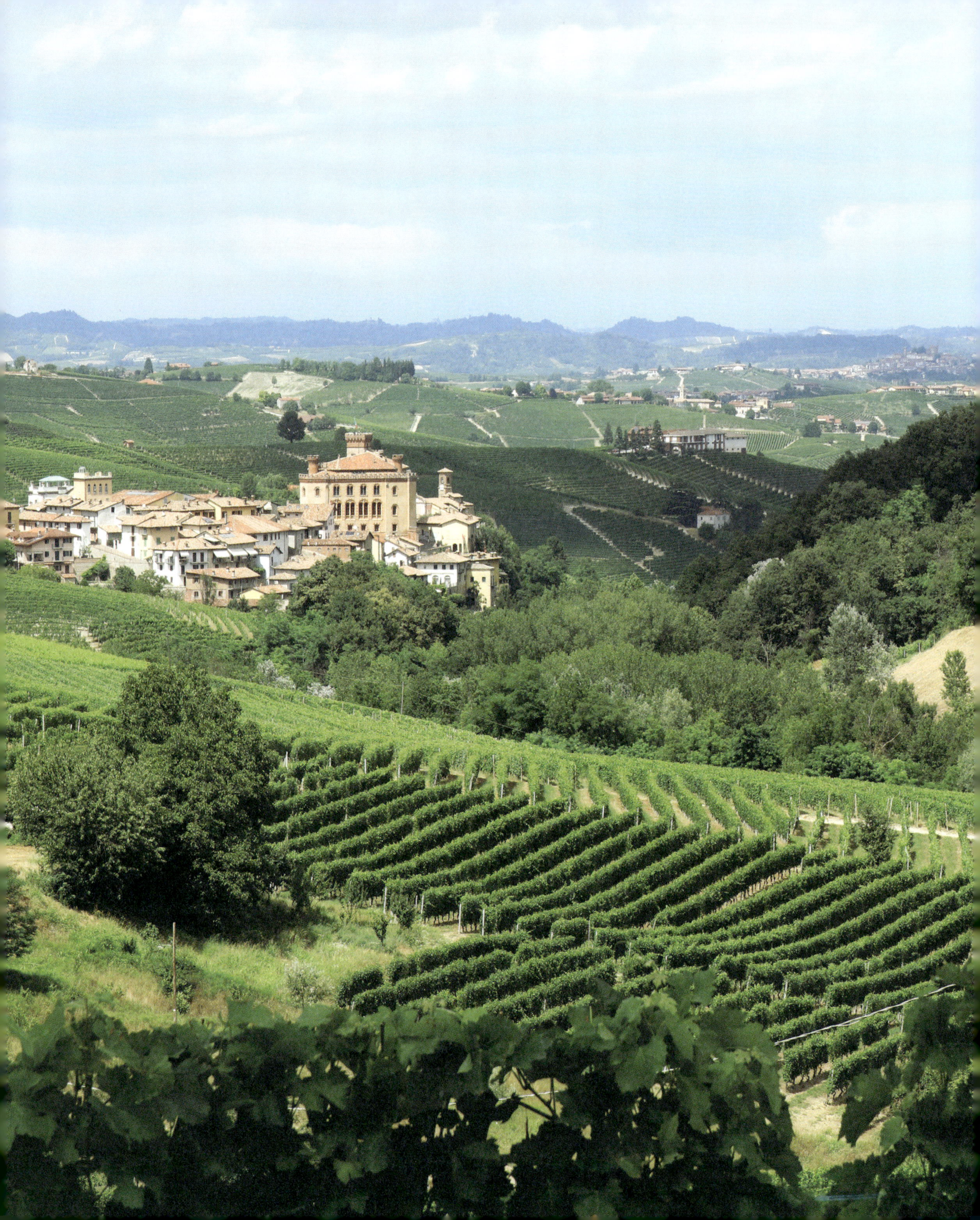

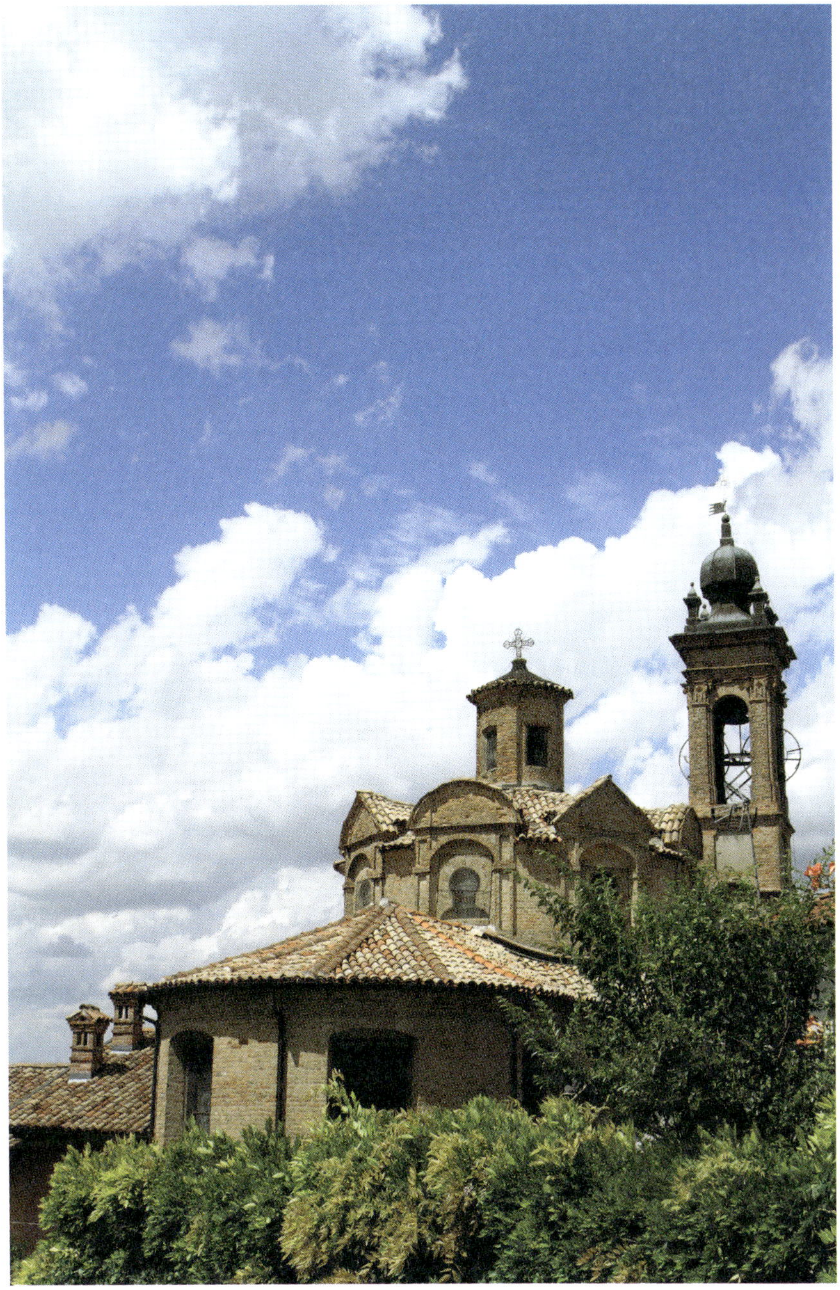

In Piemonte's Neive time stands still
and Barolo is the tipple of choice.

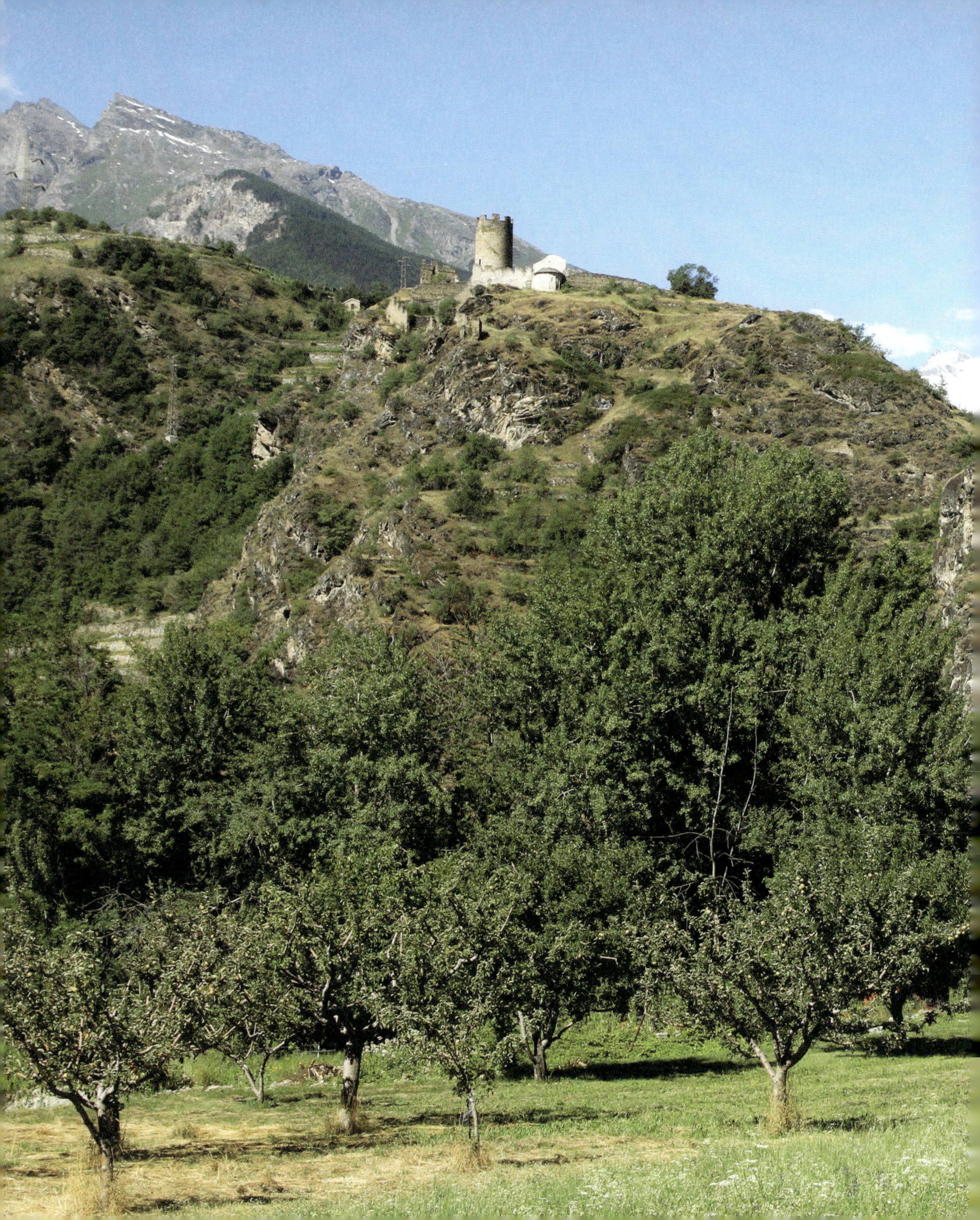

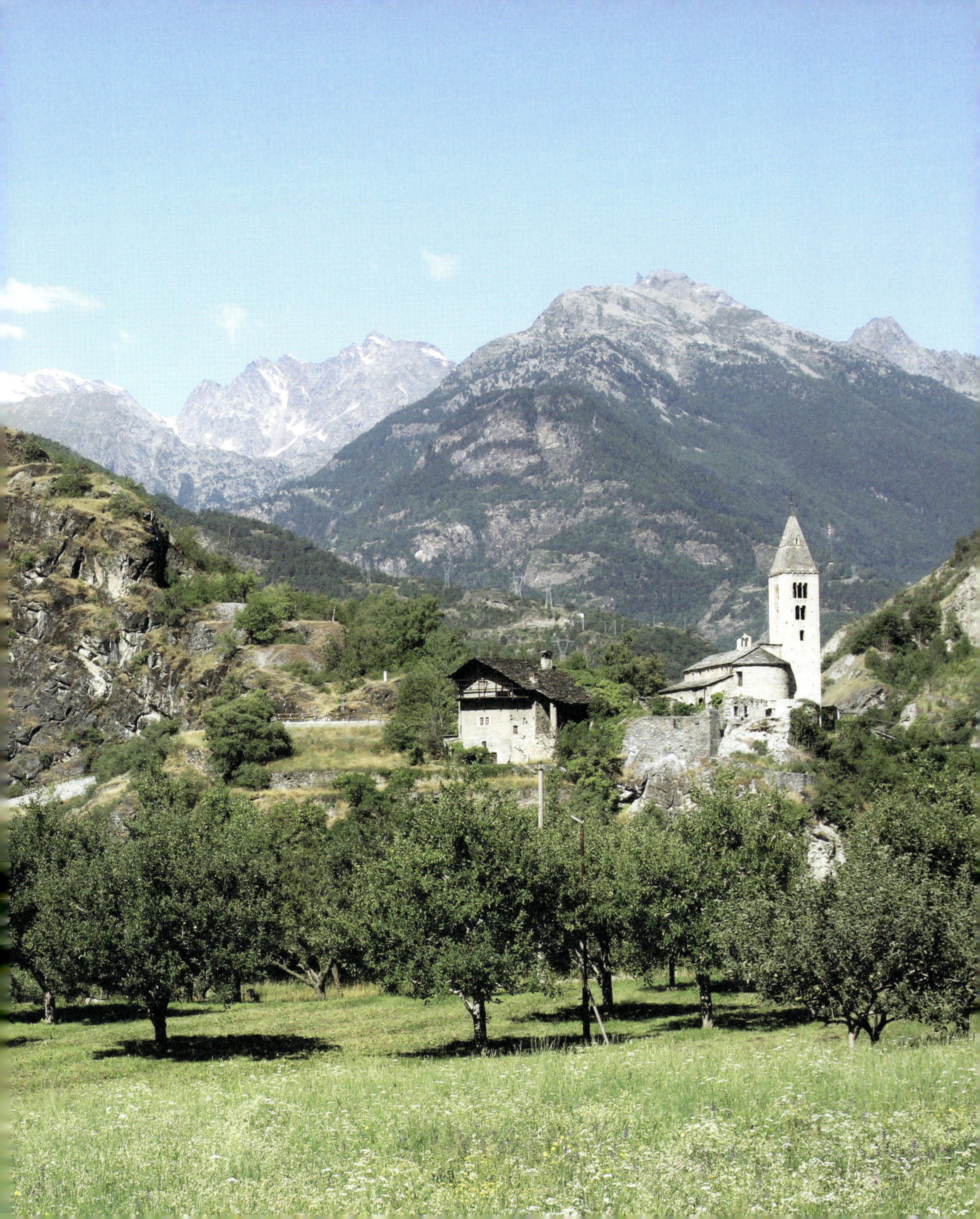

SWEDEN

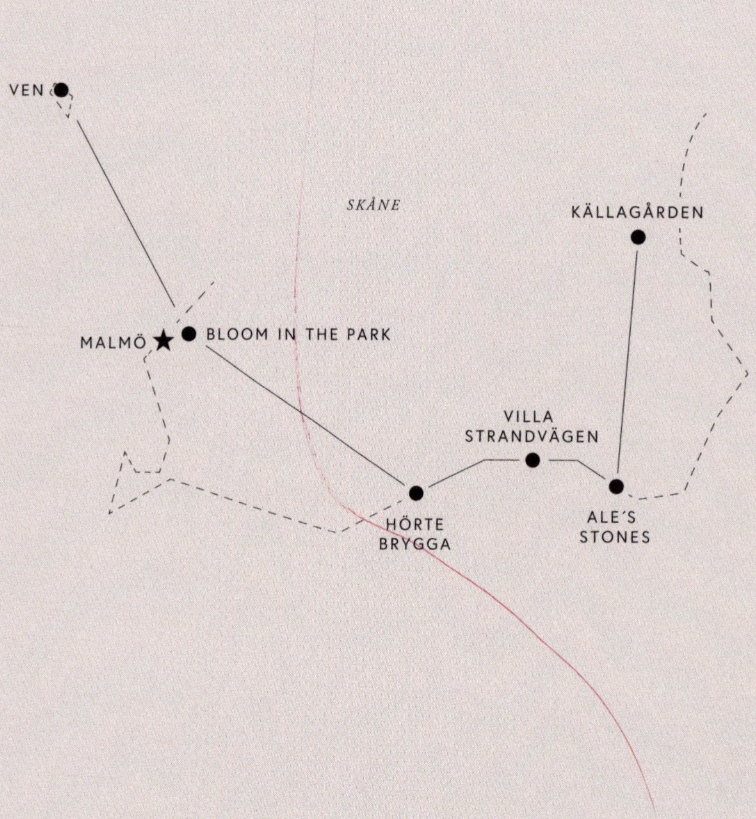

WORDS BY JEN HARRISON BUNNING

PHOTOGRAPHS BY TOM BUNNING

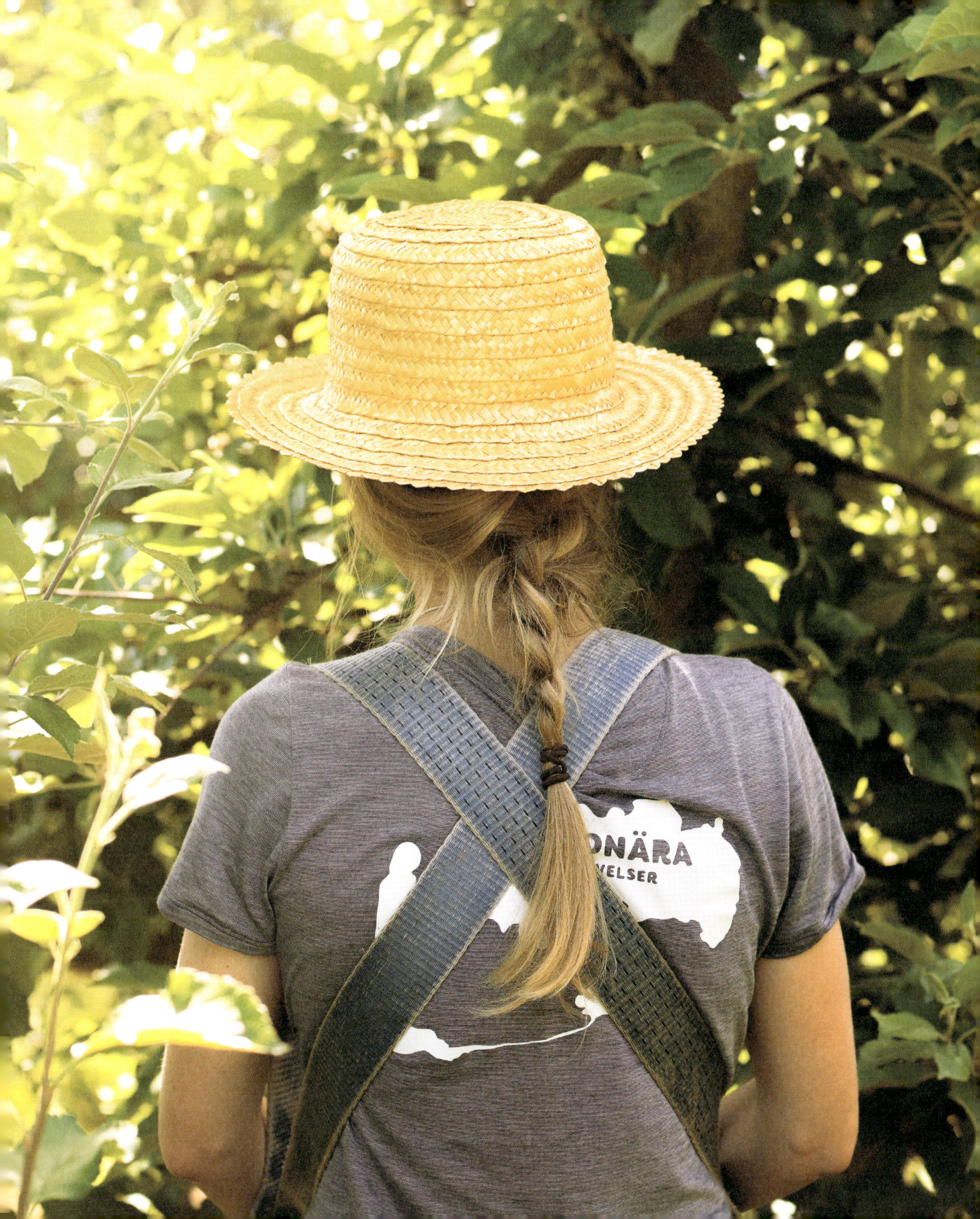
ONÄRA
VELSER

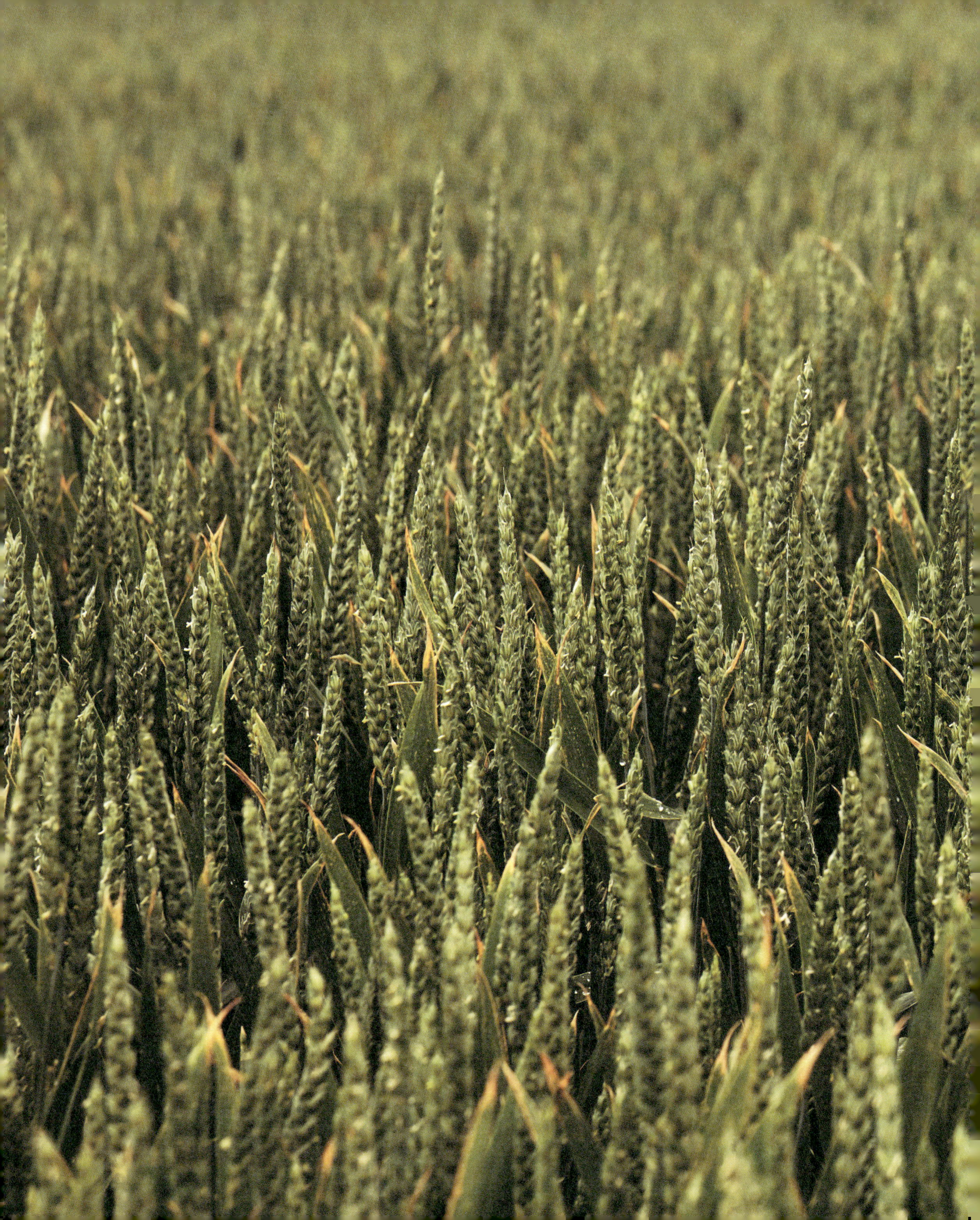

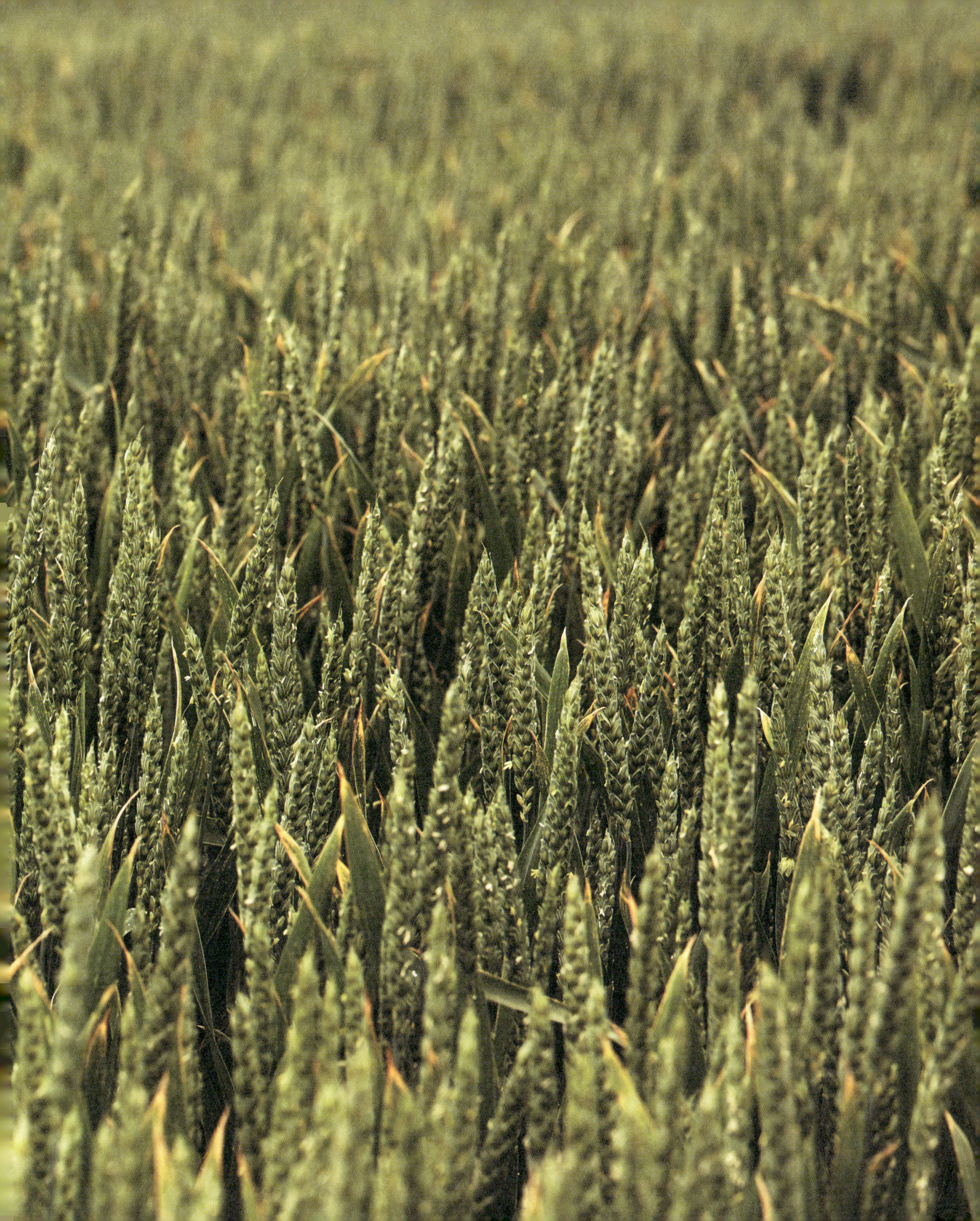

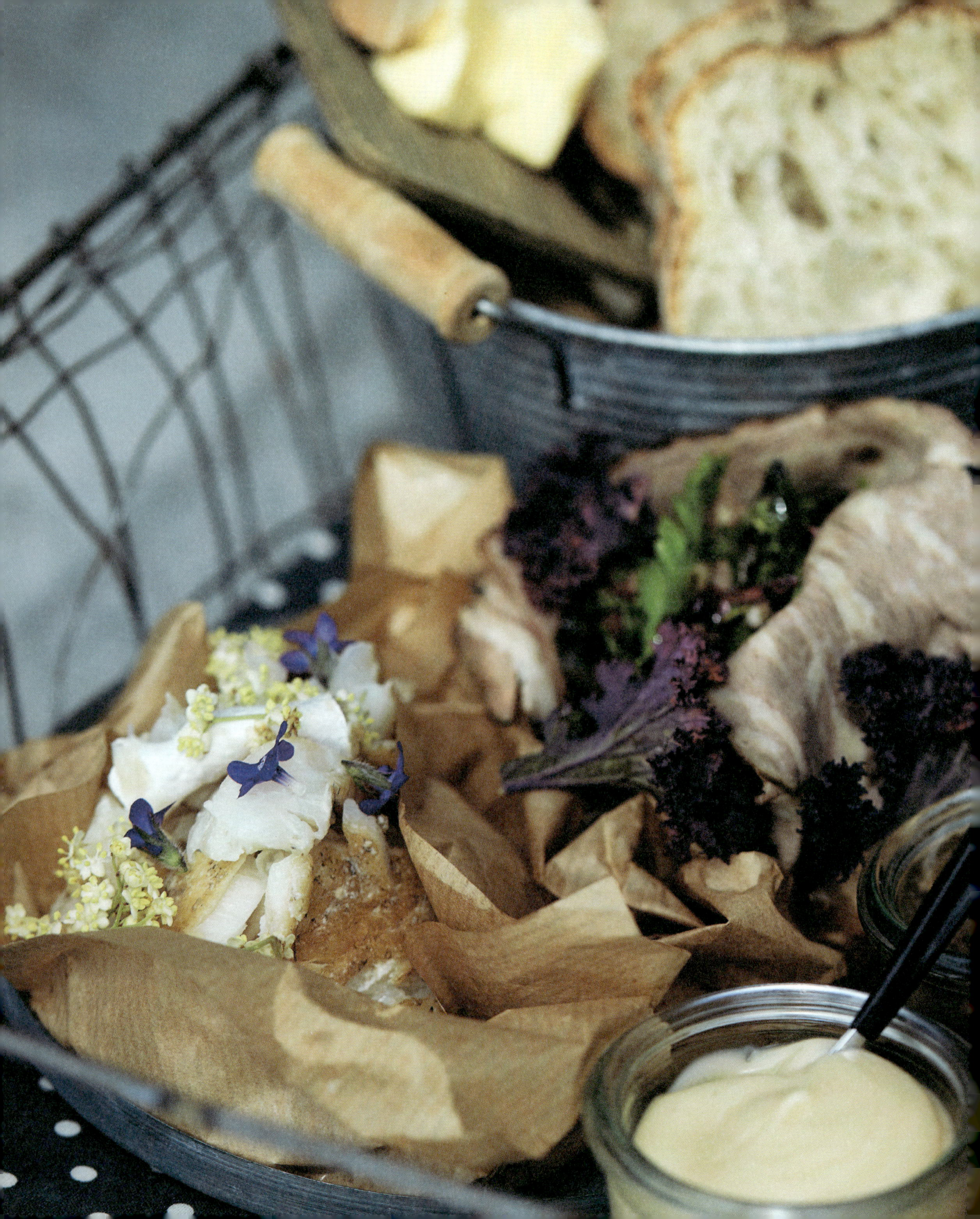

Through the Larder

With its undulating fields, vast plains, forests of roaming beasts and chorus line of orchards and vineyards, Skåne more than deserves its moniker of Sweden's larder. This is the most fertile land in all of Scandinavia: a kingdom where the earth is queen and the farmers her knights. Add a liberal sprinkling of passionate producers, brewers, sommeliers and chefs – some returning home having honed their craft in Stockholm's stellar culinary scene, others succumbing to the siren song of the south – and you'll find that Skåne is a veritable Narnia for foodies.

We left London at dawn, bumbling bleary-eyed from plane, to train, to automobile, arriving just in time for lunch at the waterside oasis of Hörte Brygga where husband-and-wife team Martin Sjöstrand and Emma Andersson have carved out a little piece of paradise from a converted twine house in an old eel boat harbour.

There's no menu to consult, no prices to be examined and no dish of the day. You simply take yourself into the kitchen, pick up a picnic basket and await your turn to have it filled with small dishes by the chefs themselves. There are delicate shoots, cold cuts of home-cured meat and smoked fish, freshly-baked sourdough, pickled vegetables and zingy dips. Perhaps you'll choose a locally-brewed cider to wash it down with, before taking your basket to one of the long sharing tables, or off outside to find a quiet spot to yourself. It sounds low-key, and it is, but this is not your average waterside cafe. This is stripped-back fine dining inspired by the land, sea and sky's seasonal offerings, prepared and served by Michelin-starred alumni in the most unassuming style, the chefs working amidst their guests, stopping every so often to change the record on the turntable.

As befits a corner of the world surrounded by water on three sides, much here is linked to the sea and its rhythm, a sense that became ever more apparent as we climbed the winding path through poppy fields some 37 metres up to Ale's Stones high above the village of Kåseberga.

Some believe these 59 standing stones form an astrological clock, others that they're part of a burial monument laid out in the form of a ship's tumulus. But whatever the truth behind its creation, we can be sure that standing amidst these ancient megaliths and gazing over the rolling water, with huge gulps of Baltic air in our lungs and the weight of human history on our minds, we felt our shoulders shrug off just a little more of the hurly-burly of our city home.

Designed in 1899 by Danish-born architect Peter Boisen, Villa Strandvägen sits in a quiet corner of southern Sweden's most southerly tip, amidst lush gardens and woodland. With its seven cosy bedrooms, splashes of New England-inspired florals and collection of black and white photographs lining the walls, this unassuming wood-panelled country home delivers Swedish coastal luxury with a generous dash of romanticism. You could come here for the interiors, to relax in the luxurious Salt Creek Spa at the adjoining Ystad Saltsjöbad hotel, for a drink on the herb-scented terrace. Or you could just come to eat, with a capital E.

This is the stage of Daniel Müllern, who has earned a Swedish Chef of the Year title, a coveted listing in *The White Guide* (the Nordic version of *Michelin*) and a string of television appearances. A star of the Swedish cooking scene, he returned home to Österlen to apply some of his gastronomic magic to the Ystad Saltsjöbad hotel's restaurants and banquet hall. When the opportunity arose to transform the inn next door into a boutique offshoot of the main hotel, with an intimate dining space for 40 guests, Daniel jumped at the chance.

Forget dining at the chef's table, at the Villa you feast in the chef's kitchen, the vast vintage French oven taking centre stage as, with the sun finally dipping behind the trees, course after course appears at your table, often in the hands of the chefs themselves. We feasted upon rice paper-thin parmesan crisps speckled with tarragon oil, a tartare of salmon with fresh cucumber and horseradish crème, asparagus with poached eggs and home-grown lovage, and tender chicken with earthy morrels and tangy chives. This is rustic Swedish cooking at its best: food inspired by the seasons, elevated from a humble provenance by the finest of local ingredients and delicate plating. After a palate-cleansing rhubarb duo of sorbet and consommé to bring us back to our senses, we rolled upstairs to bed under the eaves, drifting off into the sweet satiating sleep of the well-fed.

The morning revealed itself to be full of the joys of early summer, with pale blue skies filled with gently chuffing clouds. If there was ever a perfect day to wander an ancient apple orchard, this was it.

Tucked away betwixt the sea and the rolling heaths of Brösarp, Källagården is home to a 17th century farmhouse, some 60 acres of apple, pear and plum orchards, a smattering of wild cherry trees, and a small flock of sheep.

We met farmer Helena Rimsfors for a breakfast of apple juice and mutton salami: all home-grown, of course, as is Helena. Born and raised on her grandparents' farm, after a spell away from Skåne exploring the north and studying tourism she returned to run the property with her father. A decidedly modern farmer, she is conscious of her duty to handle the land and its offerings with a light touch, but also of her responsibility to keep her grandparents' legacy alive.

Clambering aboard Helena's trailer we set off on a tour by tractor, stopping along the way to wander into dense, leafy corridors of trees bearing romantic-sounding *Ingrid-Maries, Wintergolds, Fridas* and *Summerreds*. We trundled on uphill, admiring weighty *Romas, Gravensteiners* and *Glosters* in varying stages of fruiting before the tractor halted in a sun-dappled clearing where a small apple press was awaiting its production line. We chopped and turned and pressed our pail of *Fridas* into sweet, cloudy juice, before sitting awhile on the grass to enjoy the fruits of our labour in great, thirst-quenching gulps.

The island of Ven rises out of the Øresund Strait between Landskrona and Denmark and, like so much of these parts,

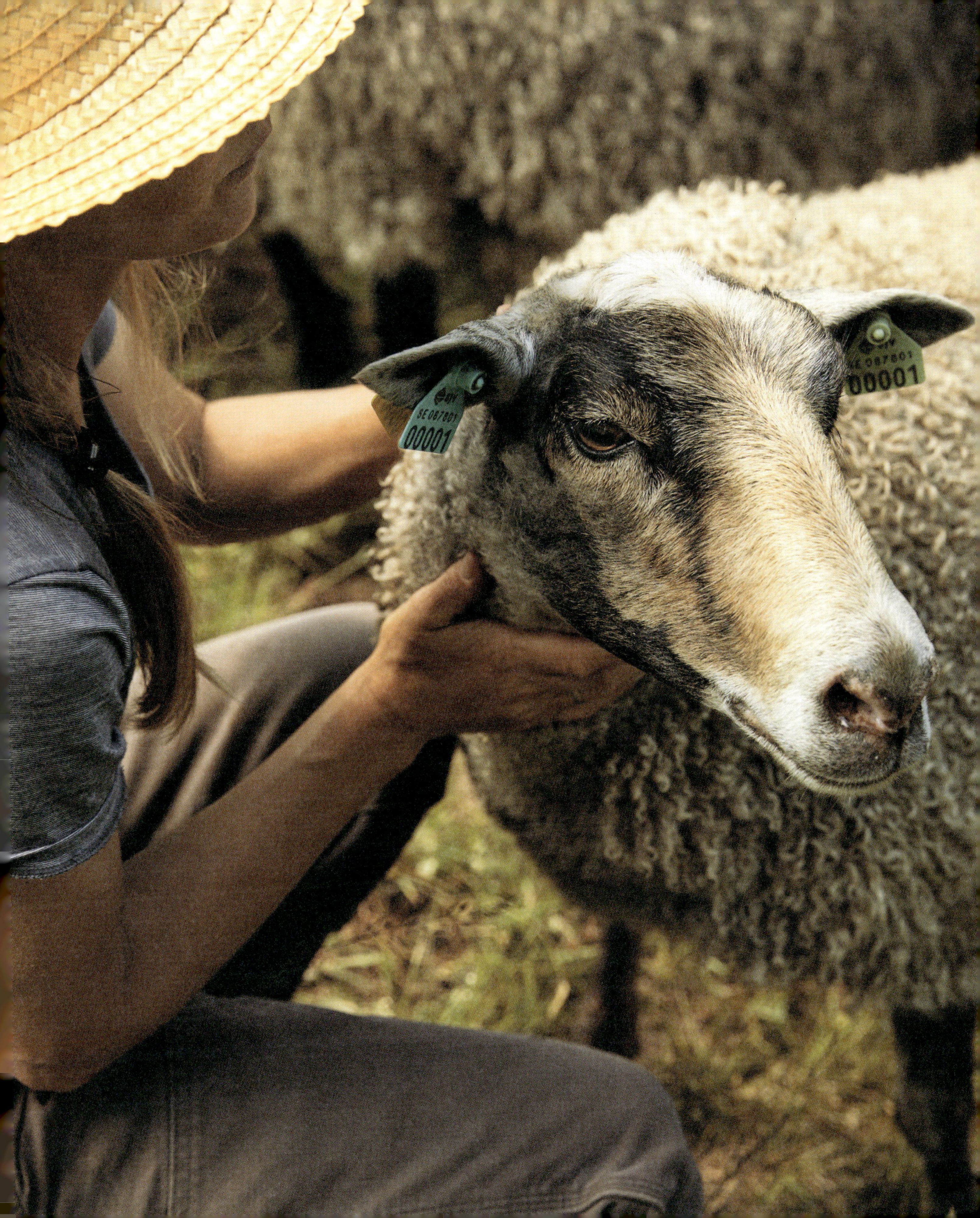
SE 087801
00001
SE 087801
00001

was passed to and fro between Danes and Swedes, before finally being ceded to Sweden – along with Skåne, Blekinge and Halland – in the 1658 Treaty of Roskilde.

The history books may chart Ven's territorial claims through Dano-Swedish warfare but the tale of its beginnings is rooted in Scandinavian folklore. So one legend goes, the female giant Hvenhild decided that the topography of southern Sweden would be improved by hills, so walked over to Zealand in Denmark to collect a few clods of earth in her apron to scatter on its flat landscape. On the way back her apron strings burst and one of her clods dropped into this water, becoming the island of 'Hven', now known as Ven. Whatever its origins, its most appealing present-day charms for these gastronomic tourists came in the form of a bicycle ride to a distillery and the promise of lunch.

The family-run Spirit of Hven distillery produces organic pot-distilled vodka, gin, rum, eau de vie and schnapps, much of it made from grain grown on the island itself, but it is their single malt island whisky that they're best-known for. After a dram to check the quality of their *Tycho's Star* single malt (smooth, rich and dangerously moreish), we weaved our way uphill to take in the panoramic view from the graveyard at the medieval church of Saint Ibbs, before cycling through increasingly fat raindrops to the haven of Restaurant Ella. At this unassuming eatery in one of Kyrkviken Harbour's stone boathouses, chef Henrik Ljungqvist treated us to local cod fresh from the morning's catch, spiked with pale pink caviar pearls and served with island-grown asparagus. A deliciously summery feast rendered even tastier by the feel of woolly jumpers about our necks and the sound of a growing gale lashing the windows.

Our arrival into Malmö was heralded by clear skies and sunshine. This, the third largest city in Sweden, feels rather like elegant Stockholm's tousle-haired and carefree younger sibling. It's a cauldron of old town grandeur, modern architecture, lush parks, winding streets and even a beach complete with 19th century open-air swimming baths.

We met Sweden's first female Michelin-starred chef Titti Qvarnström over by the beehives at acclaimed restaurant Bloom in the Park. Titti had just returned from running the magical-sounding Pure Food Camp Sweden: four days of foraging, harvesting, butchering and open-fire cooking in the Mittskåne woods with fellow chefs, writers, and foodies. Food Camp is just one of the projects this generous young chef has on the go. Indeed, Titti has made it her personal mission to inspire others to get back to nature, care about where their food comes from and support fellow foodies – an ethos that's behind her recent book, *Malmö Cooking*. There was no one better to introduce us to Malmö's thriving food scene.

First stop, Malmö Saluhall – a bustling market hall that's home to grocers, butchers, florists, fishmongers and ice cream parlours in a formerly dilapidated 19th century freight depot – and then on to the Rosengård district. Here we found Mat- & Chokladstudion, owned by Joel Lindqvist who pioneered the current Nordic trend for using bursts of colour, unusual shapes and unstructured organic plating in pastry work. It may look as sweet as pie, but this is no ordinary pudding; his ice cream, pralines, cakes and other sweet (but not necessarily sweet) treats inspired by nature and spiked with ingredients from Joel's larder. His shelves bear pickled hazelnuts, fermented sour cherries, strawberry vinegar, dried lingonberries, woodruff, elderflower and more, much of it gathered under that glorious Swedish foragers' right, the law of *Allemansrätten*.

There was just time to meet vegetarian-turned-butcher Ola in her charming additive-free, all-organic deli Ola & Ko before heading to Titti's garden to gather herbs, flowers and fruits for our evening at Bloom.

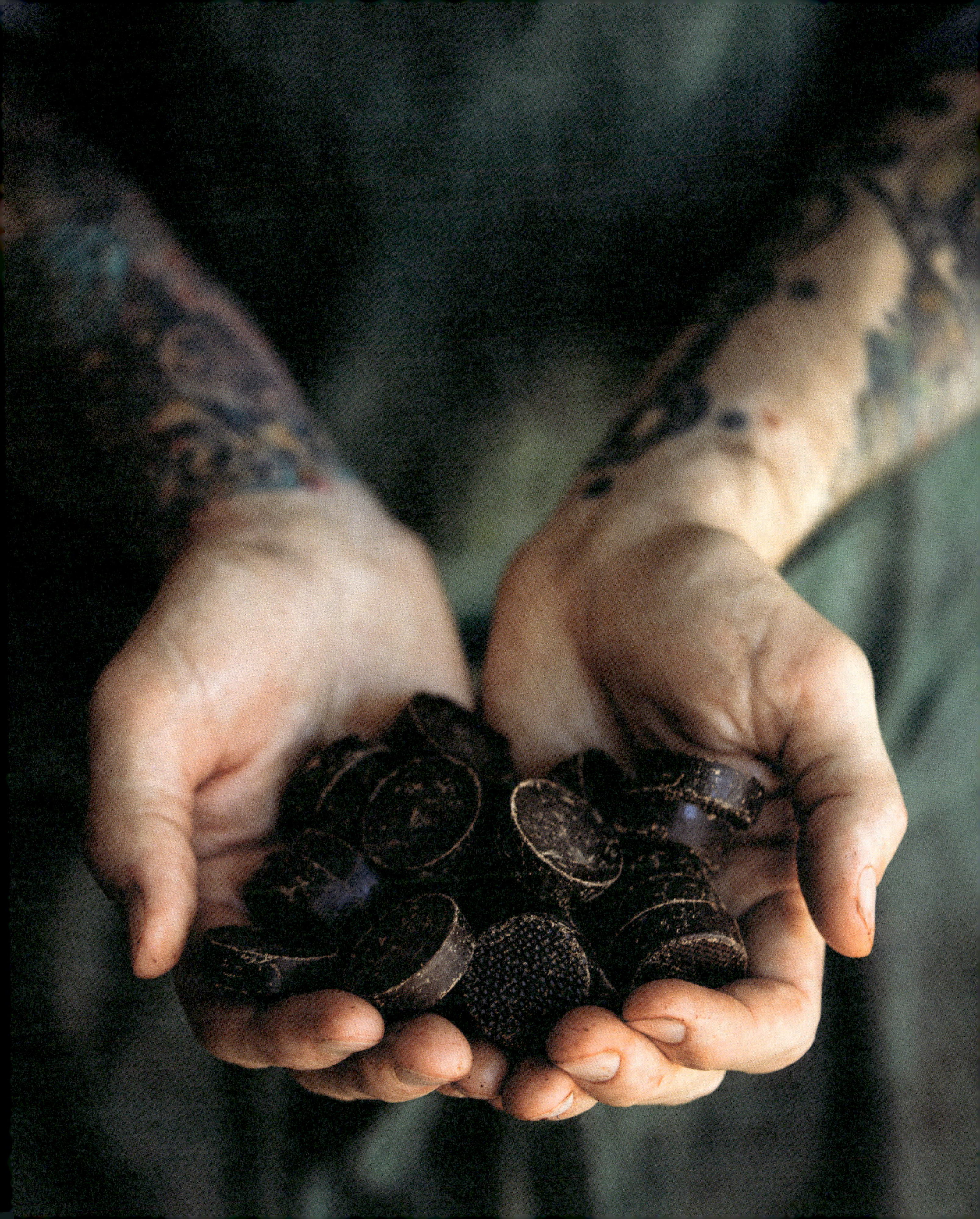

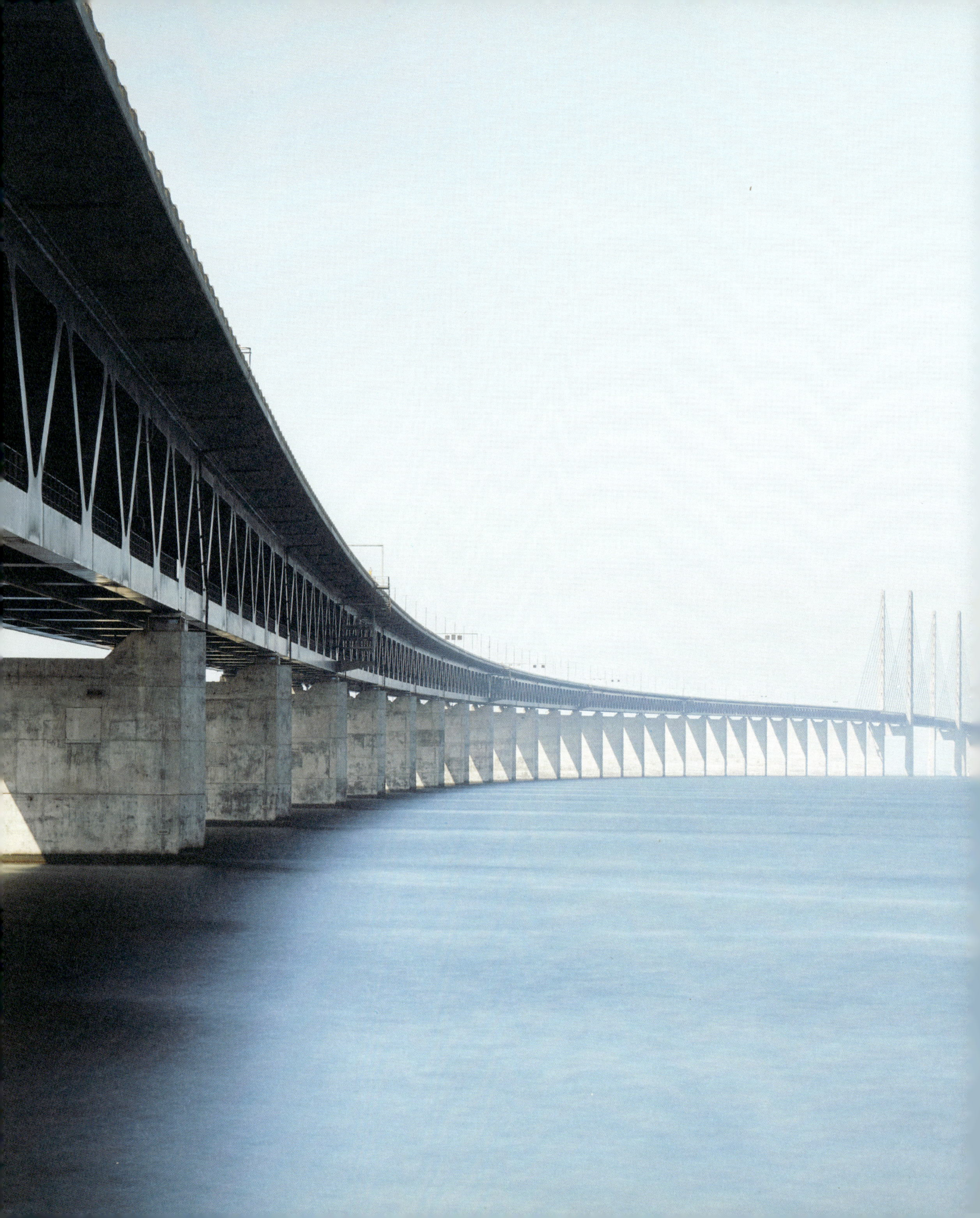

Dining at Bloom is like being a supper party guest in the home of a thoughtful and genial host. Tables are staggered but we all eat together, each group encouraged to dine at a pace that suits the weather and mood. On a balmy evening, why not pause between courses and watch the carp gliding under the water of the lake?

And what of the food? This is not just cookery, this is sorcery; crisped roots with jewelled orbs from the sea, *cigarillos* of sweet shoots dipped in herbed sauces, succulent fowl with earthy juice and soft seasonal fruits scattered with crunchy soil. Mysterious delight after delight, course after course.

With bags packed and takeoff looming, we indulged in a final *fika* on Ribersborg Beach before walking along the coast in the shadow of the vast Øresund Bridge, reflecting on all we had experienced. Our journey along Skåne's earthy pathways was more than just a rifle through larder shelves. It was the next page of our love affair with Sweden's producers, harvesters, makers and creators. An affair seeded in nature, watered by like-minded souls, and harvested by a bout of culinary wanderlust. ⋆

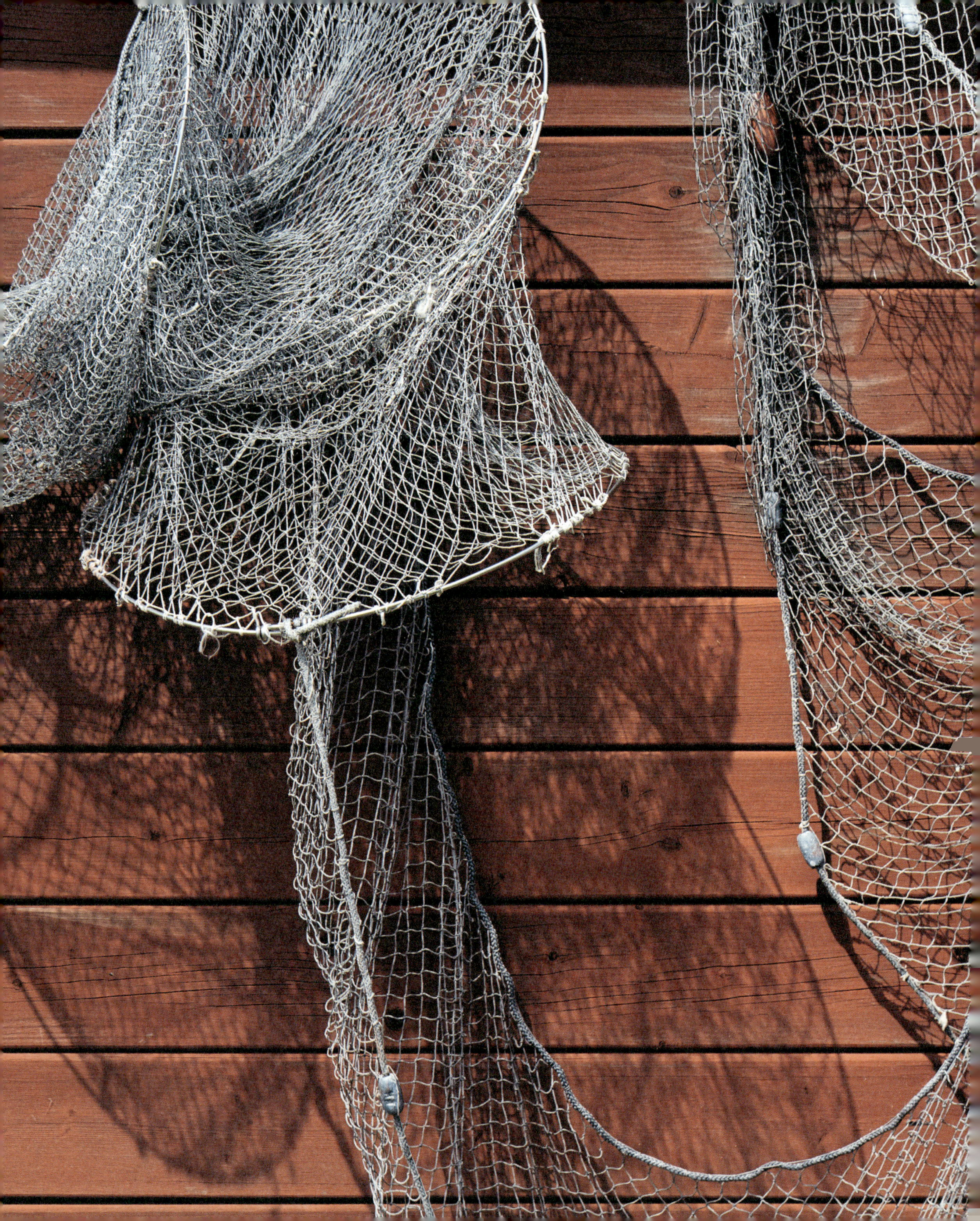

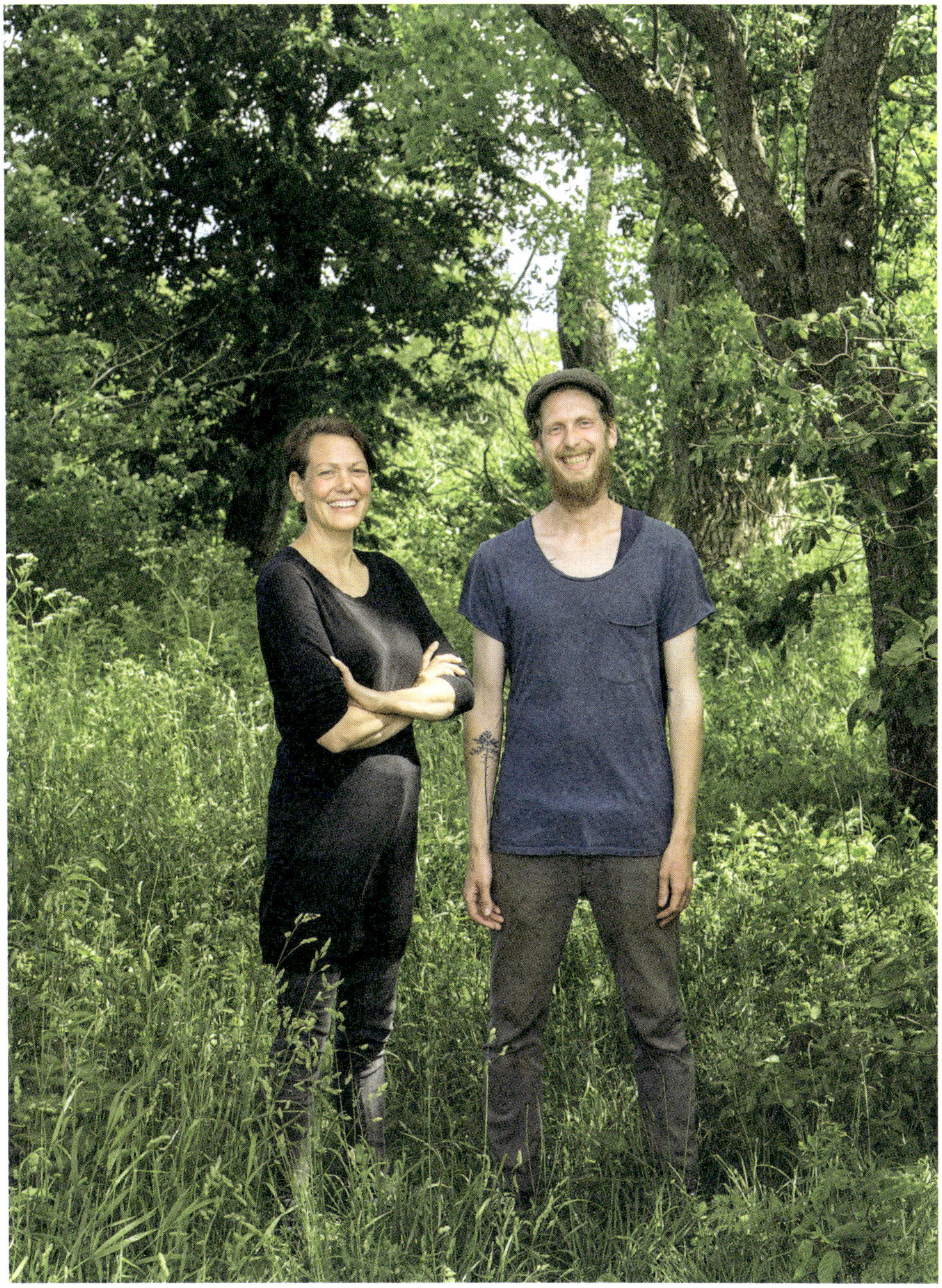

Martin Sjöstrand and Emma Andersson of Hörte Brygga.

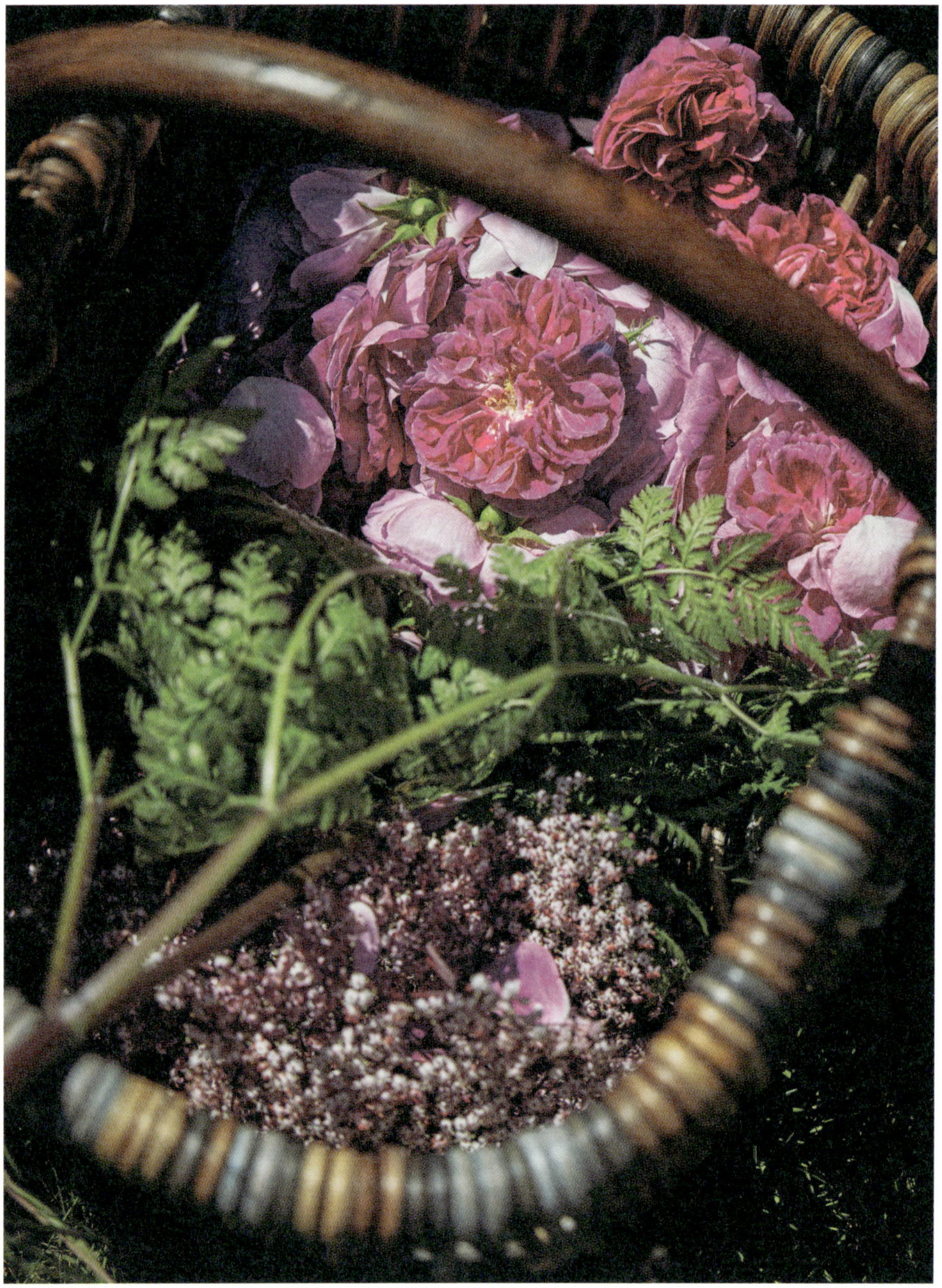

Chef Titti Qvarnström collects flowers for Bloom in the Park.

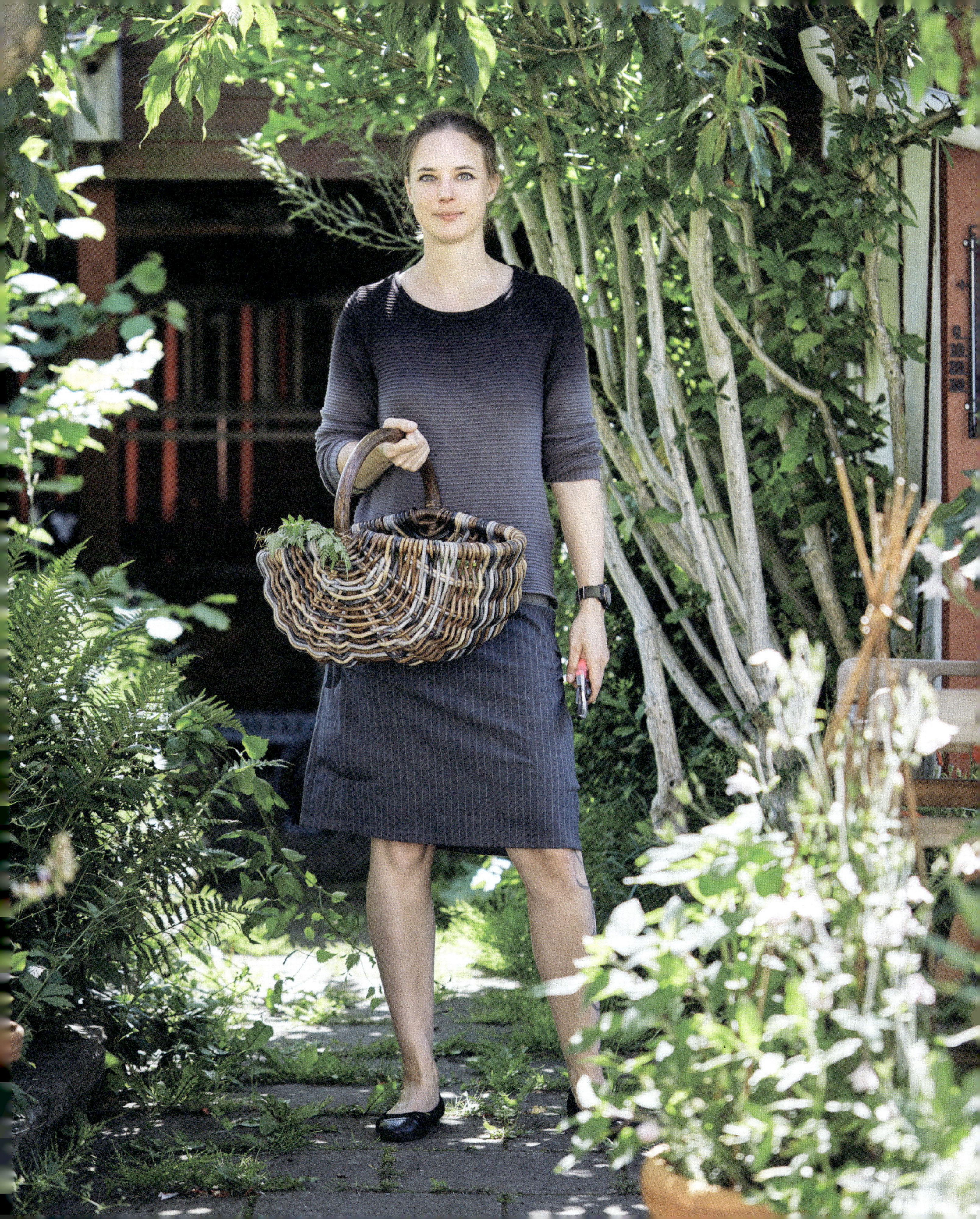

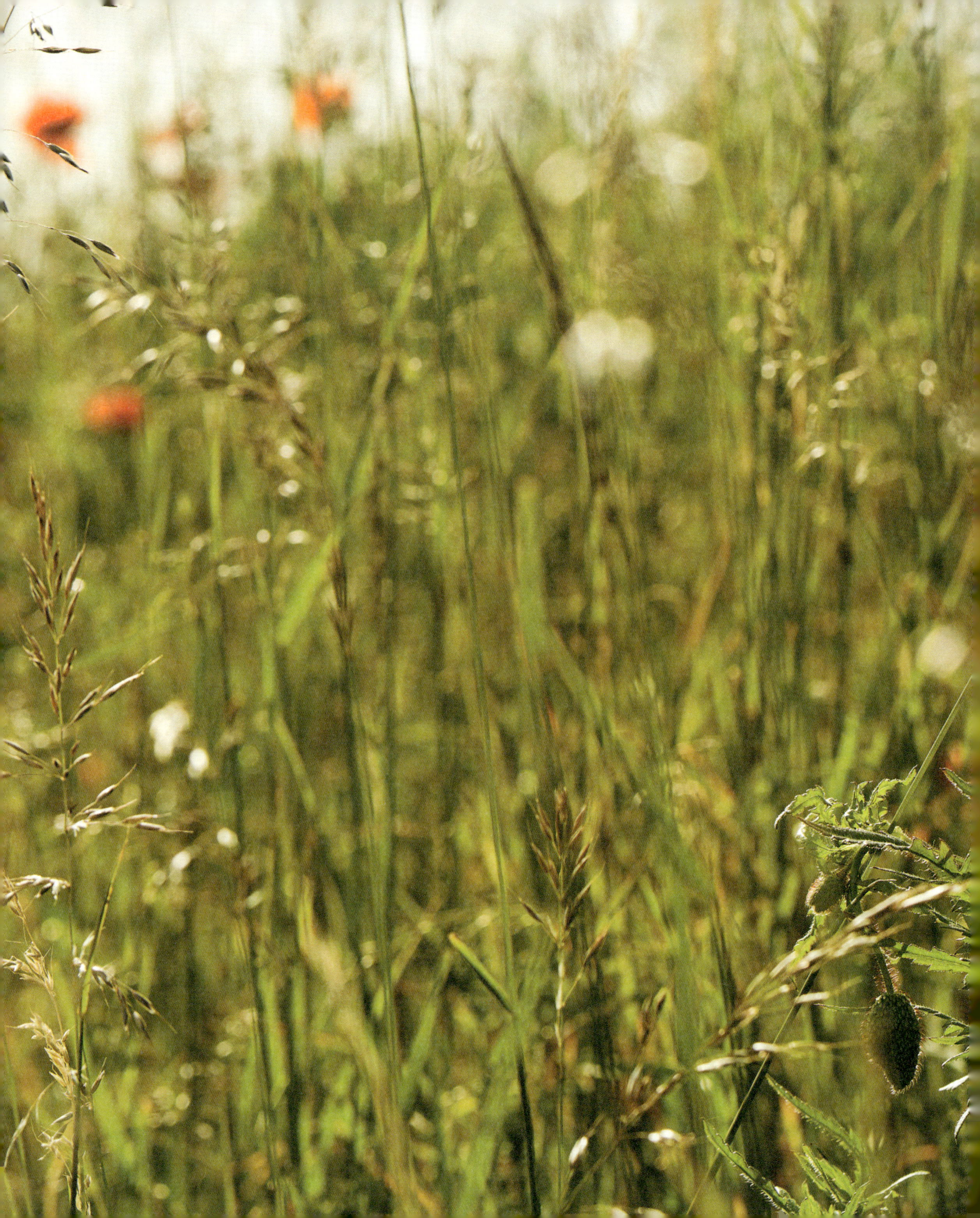

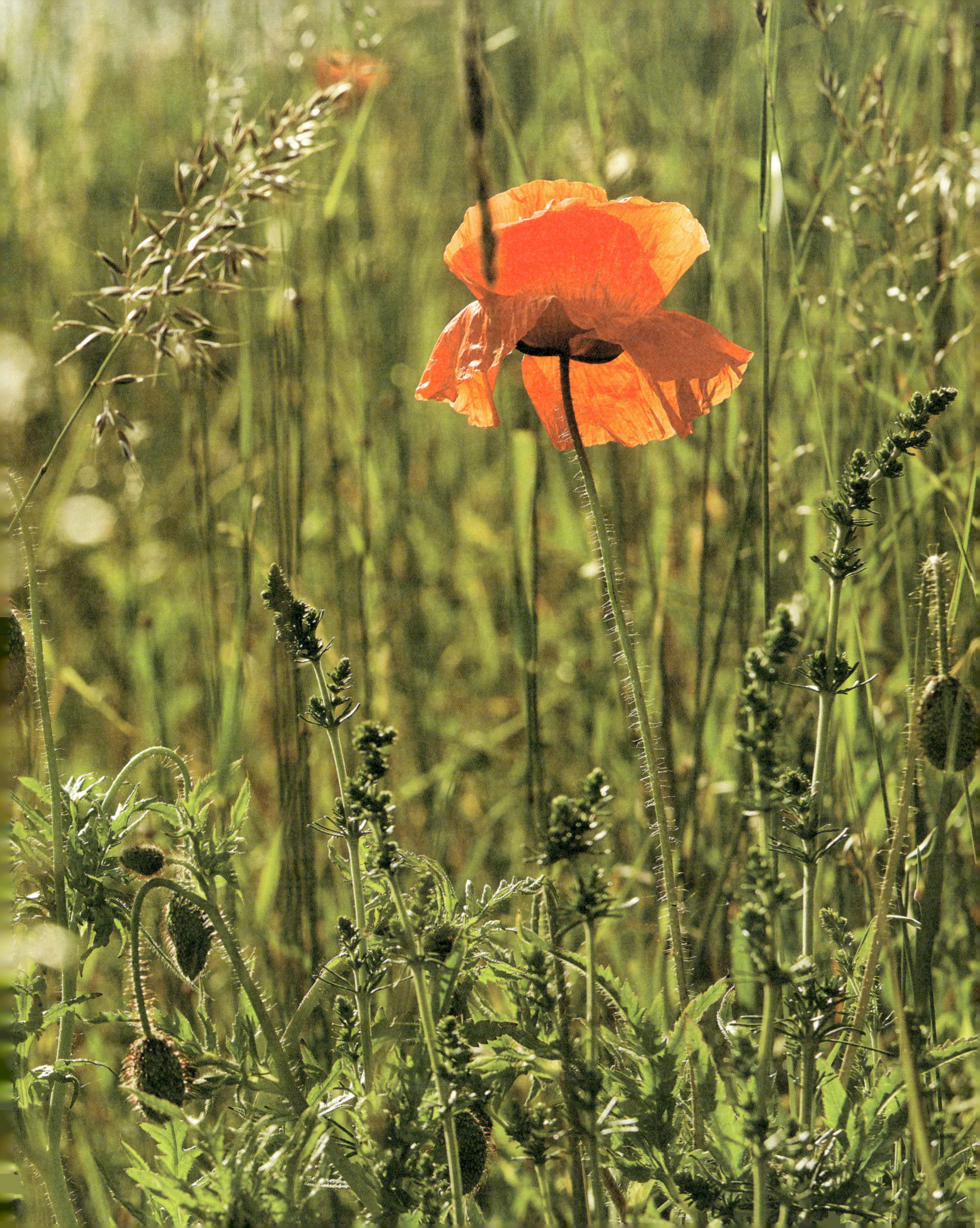

CANADA

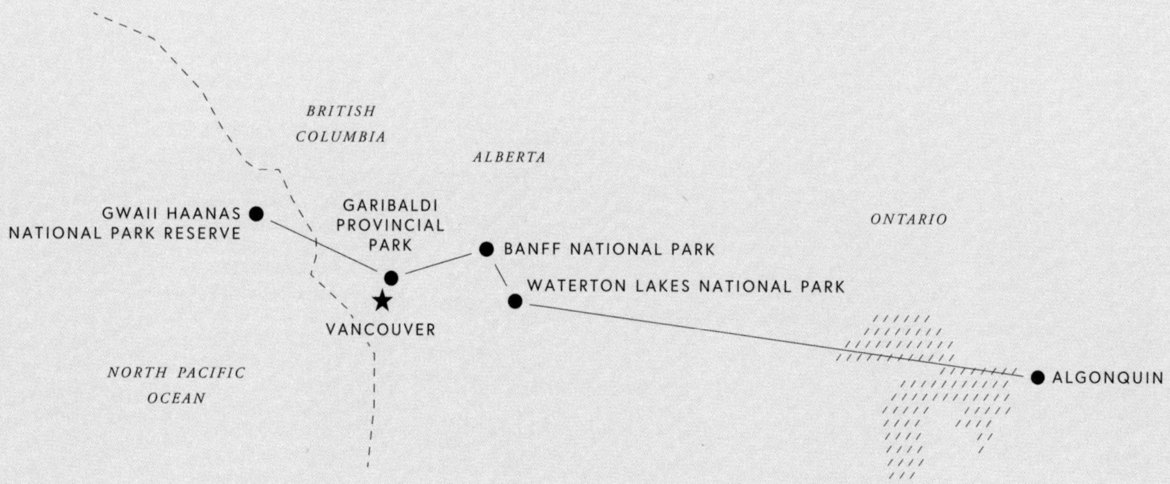

WORDS BY SHAUN PETT

PHOTOGRAPHS BY BETH SQUIRE

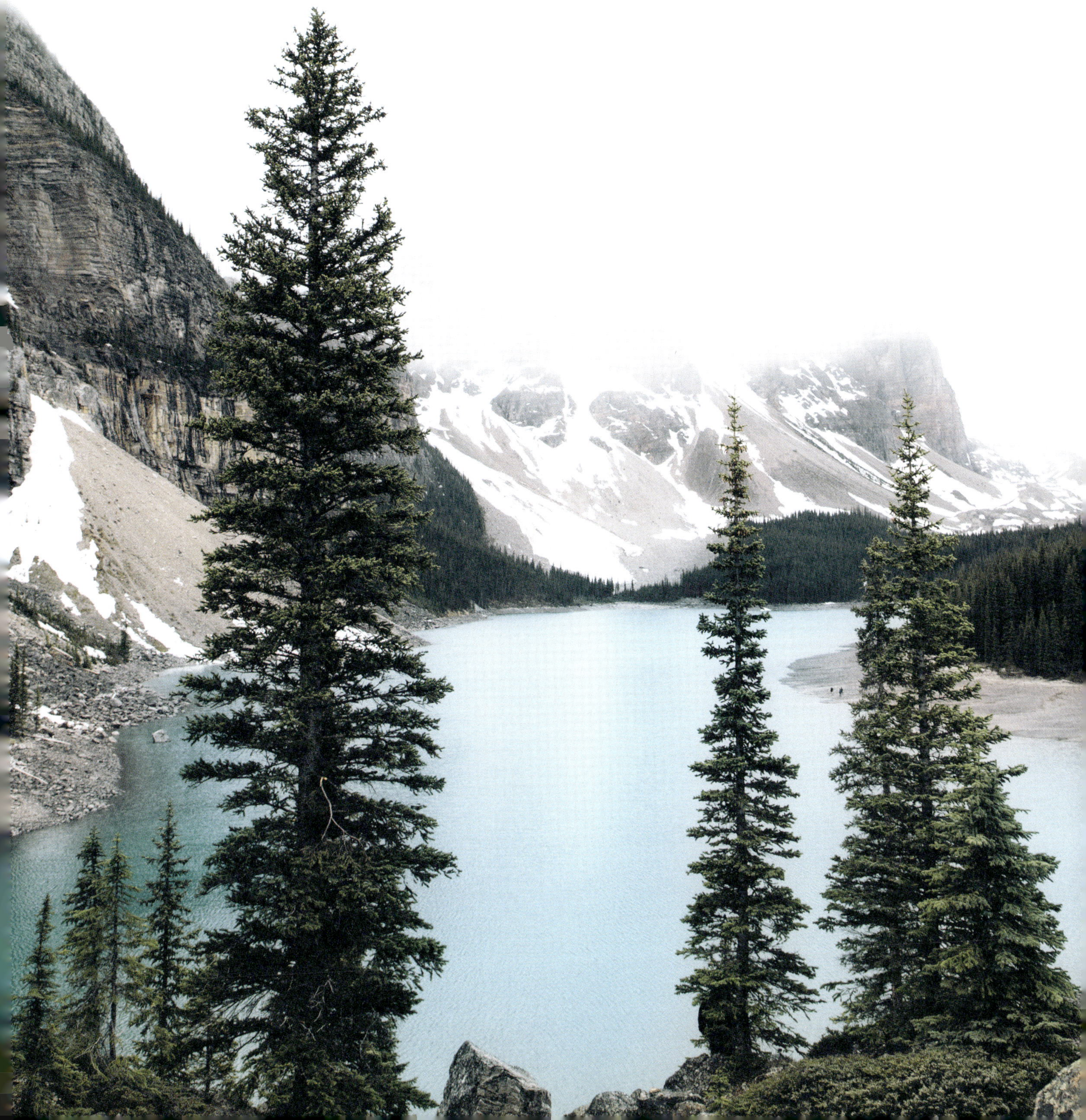

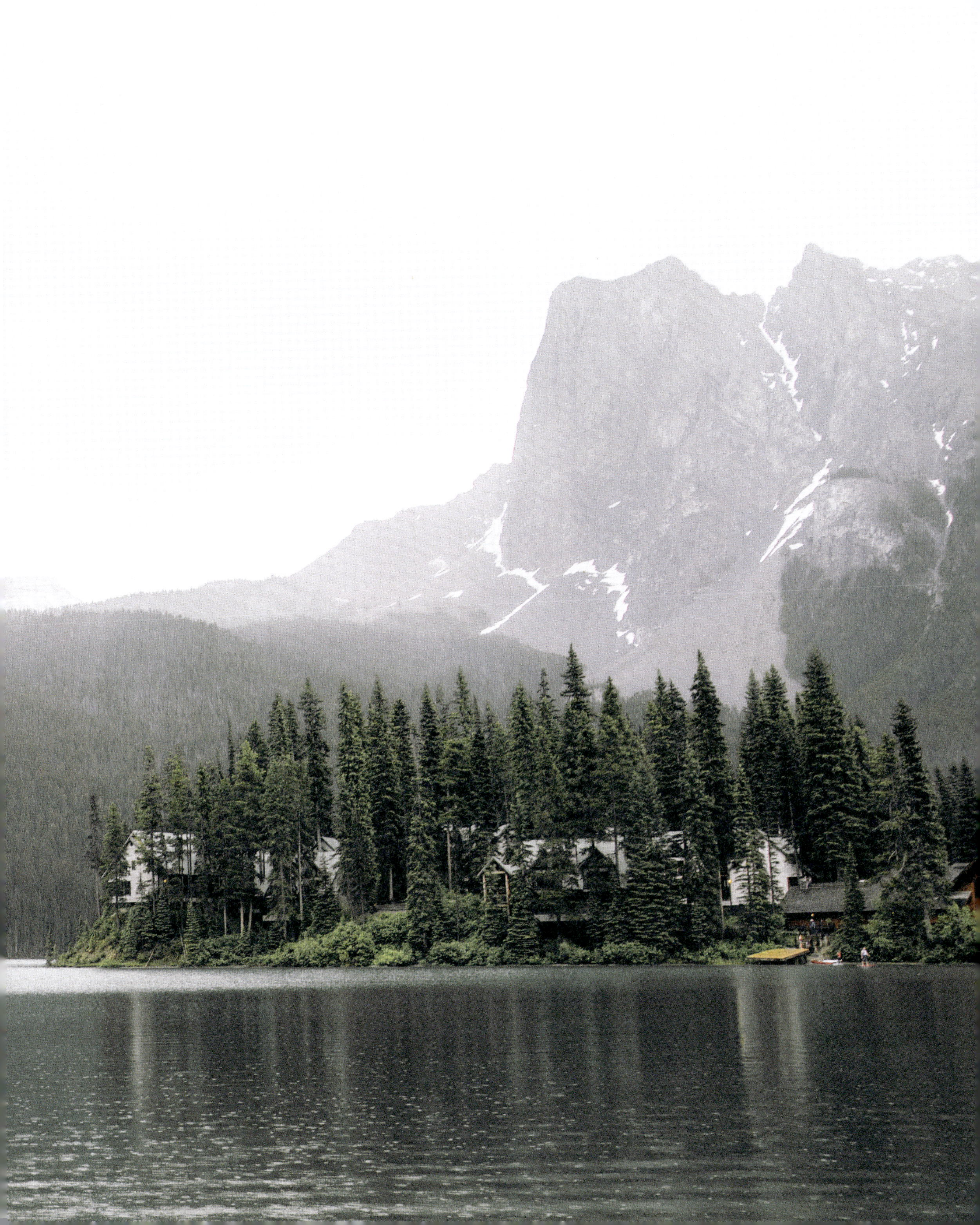

The Great Escape

How far do you have to go to get lost?

When I was young my suburban home in Ontario backed onto a forest. It wasn't a large forest, but it was a kingdom for a kid, the greatest toy possible. No matter the season I'd descend the path, cross the stream, climb the hill and be gone, spending hours roaming through the gulches and gullies, building forts of leaves and snow, playing in the ponds and streams, or just sitting in the silent noise of the woods until one of my parents called out for dinner and I would return from my private realm.

This childhood seems quintessentially Canadian – although defining Canadian identity has always been difficult; with no linguistic or national base, it's a country of varying shades and multiplicities. And yet a connection to – or simply the presence of – nature has often set Canada apart: the wild, remote and awe-inspiring images of the North, and the dense pine and verdant coastal rainforests found in the paintings of the Group of Seven or Emily Carr. For the first colonisers, this unknown wild was a danger. 'Survival', as Margaret Atwood has argued, characterised the early Canadian mentality. And though modern progress tells us the wild has been conquered, we are again thinking about nature from our urban dwellings, craving what we have been missing.

Vancouver is like my childhood home; surrounded by the sea, forests and mountains, one can step out the door and soon escape the metropolitan cacophony. Follow the 28 kilometre seawall that traces the city and you'll end up in Stanley Park, Vancouver's greatest treasure – in fact, the first act of the newly formed city council in 1886 was to protect this land. Compared to the other great urban parks of the world, Stanley Park still feels like wilderness, free of sculpting or manicuring and boasting a forest of half a million trees. It is an oasis for so many; an escape, if ever so brief, from the pressure of modern life, where one can be inspired by the natural setting. Indeed, between Second and Third Beach you can often find artist Kent Avery balancing stones as he has for nearly two decades; beautiful, ephemeral sculptures that seem to defy gravity until the tide rises and washes them away.

Vancouver ends suddenly on the steep slopes of the North Shore Mountains, unable to climb higher. Not much further beyond these homes there's skiing and backcountry camping and hiking, all with kaleidoscopic views of glassy Vancouver, now tiny amongst the peaks and alpine lakes, and west to the blue Georgia Straight and Gulf Islands. On Salt Spring Island you'll find back-to-the-land hippies and modern

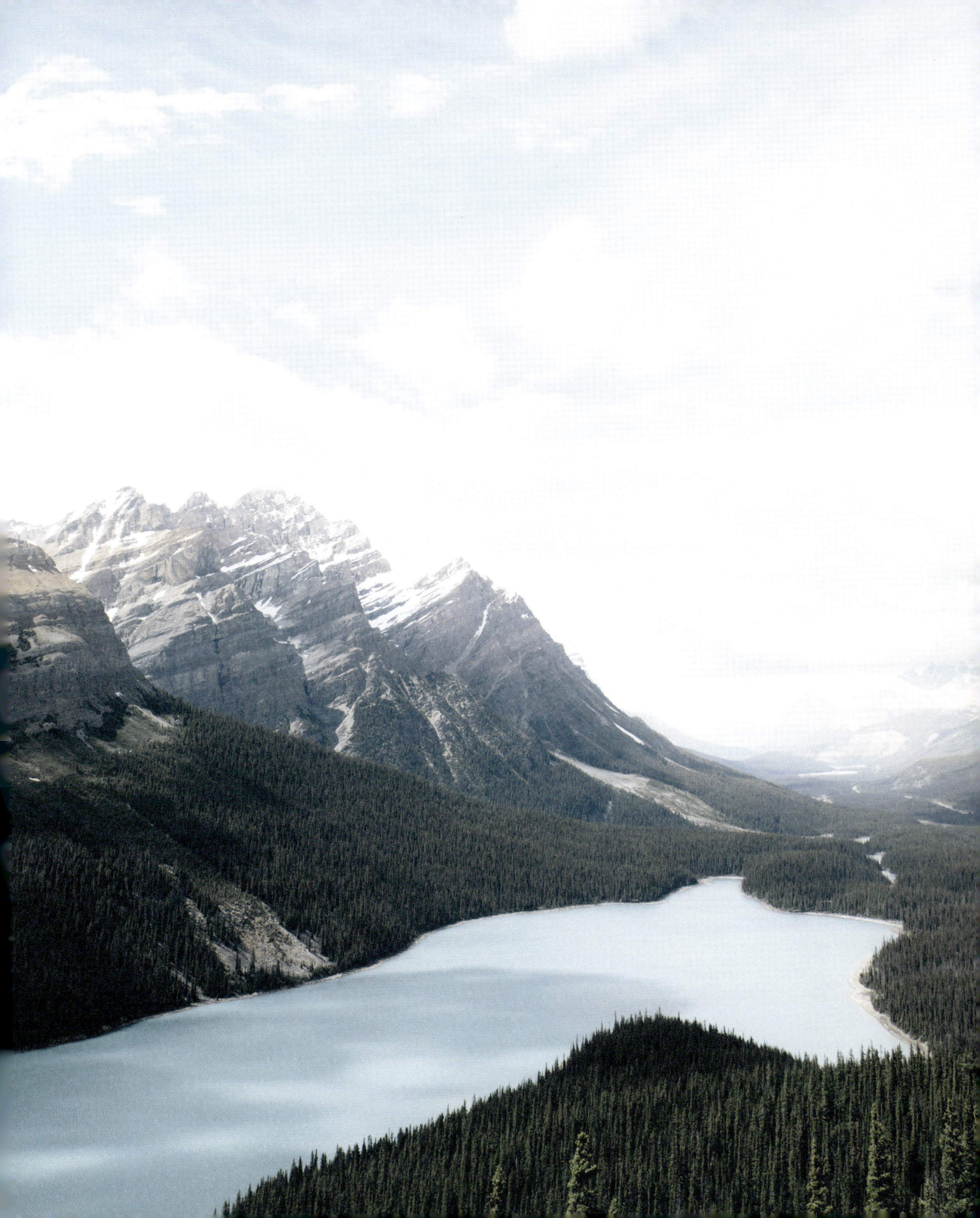

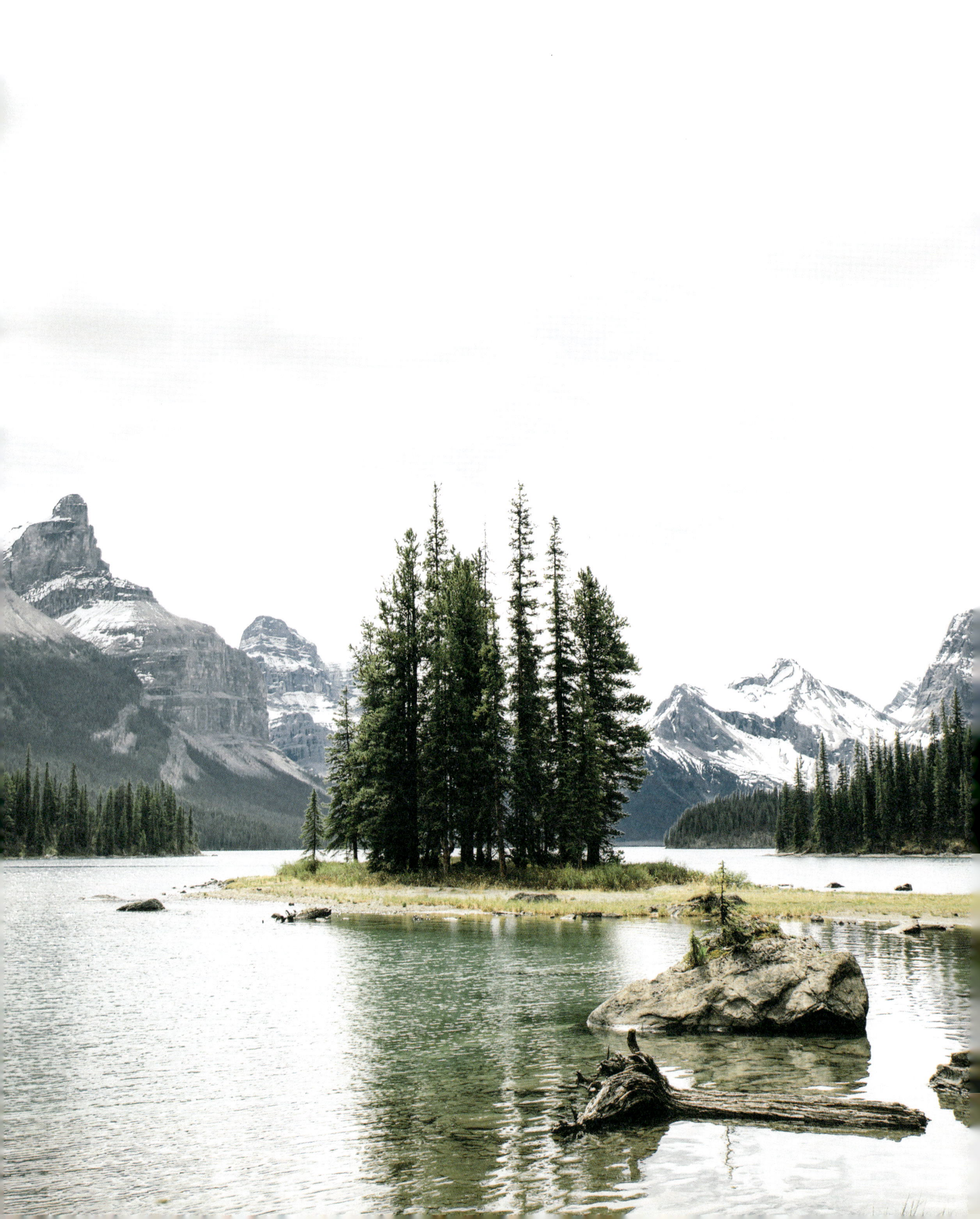

artisans at the farmers' markets, while on neighbouring Galiano Island the restaurant Pilgrimme, housed in a secluded wood cabin, is representative of the new generation of chefs exploring the Canadian terroir of sea and land.

Connecting Vancouver to Whistler, the Sea to Sky Highway feels like takeoff as you trace Howe Sound, pass the outdoor playground of Squamish, and then speed up through rainforest into the Coast Mountains. Whistler itself is an alpine Disneyland run by Australians. It's not tranquil, but it does make a base for discovering the surrounding Garibaldi Provincial Park. My partner and I pitched our tent just outside town along the churn of a glacial-fed river. The next morning we took on the Wedgemount Lake Trail, which ascends unceasingly for almost 1,200 metres, with a final scramble over boulders and scree, to reach the blue alpine lake cradled in the mountain bowl. A glacier nestles in the hills at the far end and we gingerly walked over it, this frozen time capsule trickling beneath our feet. It was the first time I'd been so close to a glacier and to me it was a shock, like an alien life form. So strange was it to my urban sensibility that I couldn't quite reconcile my existence with its own – and how my actions so far away are threatening its future here. Before descending we refilled our water bottles from a mountain stream (crisp, delicious water is one of the joys of Canada's wild) and made it down with jelly legs.

Calgary, a.k.a. Cowtown, has always been the spiritual home of Canada's West, of rodeos, cowboy hats and petroleum. However, it is also the gateway to the Rocky Mountains. You can see the serrated, iced-white peaks from the city. Given its proximity and iconic status, Banff National Park (Canada's first and the third-oldest in the world) attracts millions of visitors and traffic jams – but there are modes of escape and private pockets of wilderness to be found. To get away from the crush you can visit one of the several backcountry lodges which, depending on the time of year, require you to hike or cross-country ski in. The lazy can take a helicopter.

South of Calgary, Waterton Lakes National Park straddles the US border, creating the first International Peace Park with Montana's Glacier National Park. Often overlooked, Waterton has the same spectacular scenery with a fraction of Banff's visitors. And the chances of seeing wildlife, especially bears, both black and grizzly, are high.

When I was young my family took canoe trips to Algonquin, which, on a map of Ontario, appears like a great green heart. Each year, in the dark of winter, my parents phoned the reservation line, usually got a busy signal, and tried again until they were able to reserve our campsites. Heading north, you soon enter the Canadian Shield with its rolling rock crust and boreal forest. Despite its size and popularity, Algonquin's 2,400 lakes can still feel empty. Time slows as you learn the new routine: you hang your food from trees (hoping to deter the bears), camp on islands and fall asleep to the varied and mournful song of the loon.

Sometimes you have to go farther to escape. With two-thirds of Canada's population living near the US border, the vast North holds an extreme density of solitude. Aulavik National Park in the Arctic has an annual visitor rate of a dozen or less. In western Newfoundland, Gros Morne National Park is one of the only places in the world where you can visit a lunar-like landscape, created by the earth's mantle having broken through the crust. Meanwhile, kayaking along the north coast in the Bay of Exploits puts you in Iceberg Alley – if you time it right.

The archipelago of Haida Gwaii sits off the north coast of British Columbia. For a visitor, there's a slow dawning of magic while touring the ancestral home of the indigenous

Sometimes you have to go farther to escape. Given that two-thirds of Canada's population live near the US border, the vast North holds an extreme density of solitude.

Haida, who have sustained themselves from the land and sea for more than 13,000 years. A sea-kayaking trip in the remote Gwaii Haanas National Park Reserve feels like a paddle around the edge of the world. At times Japan, just over the water's horizon, seems closer than the rest of Canada. Here, the largest remaining collection of carved mortuary poles still stand on the island of SGang Gwaay, a monument to times and people past. Epidemics decimated the population during the 19th century and the villagers who survived left their longhouse homes to the elements. Piece by piece the poles are being allowed to decay and disappear: the Haida believing that everything comes from the earth and returns to the earth.

Canada – and the land before it – was built on pathways into the wild, those tentative steps and strokes leading further and further into the future. Still we're walking and paddling, still we're figuring out this land and this identity. The country may be vast but there's surely a path to wherever you might want to go. ★

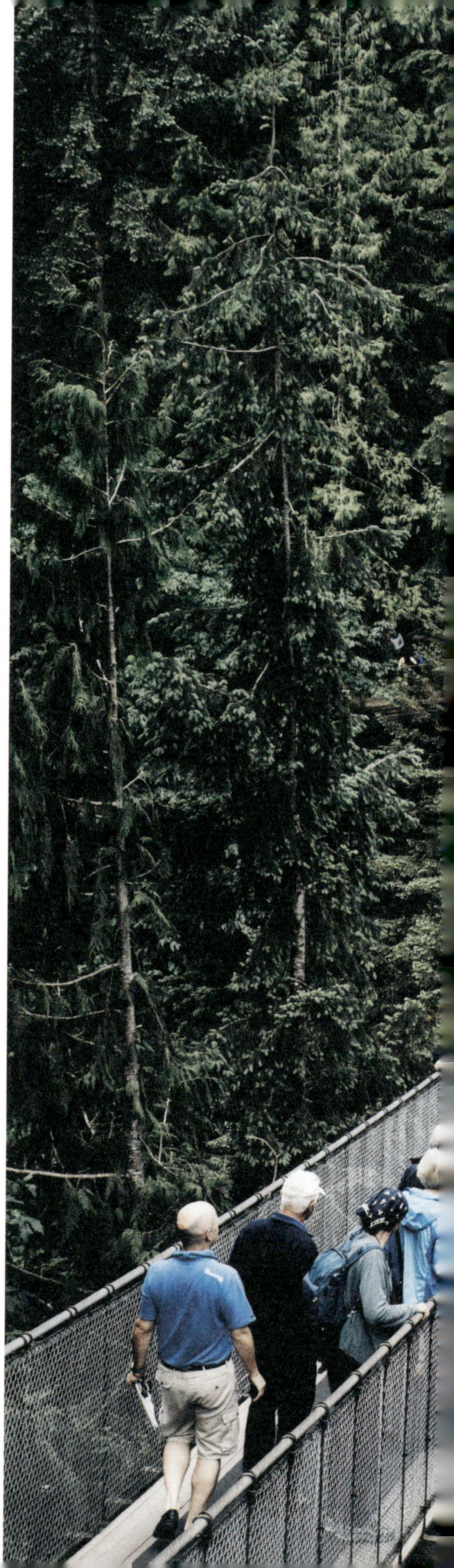

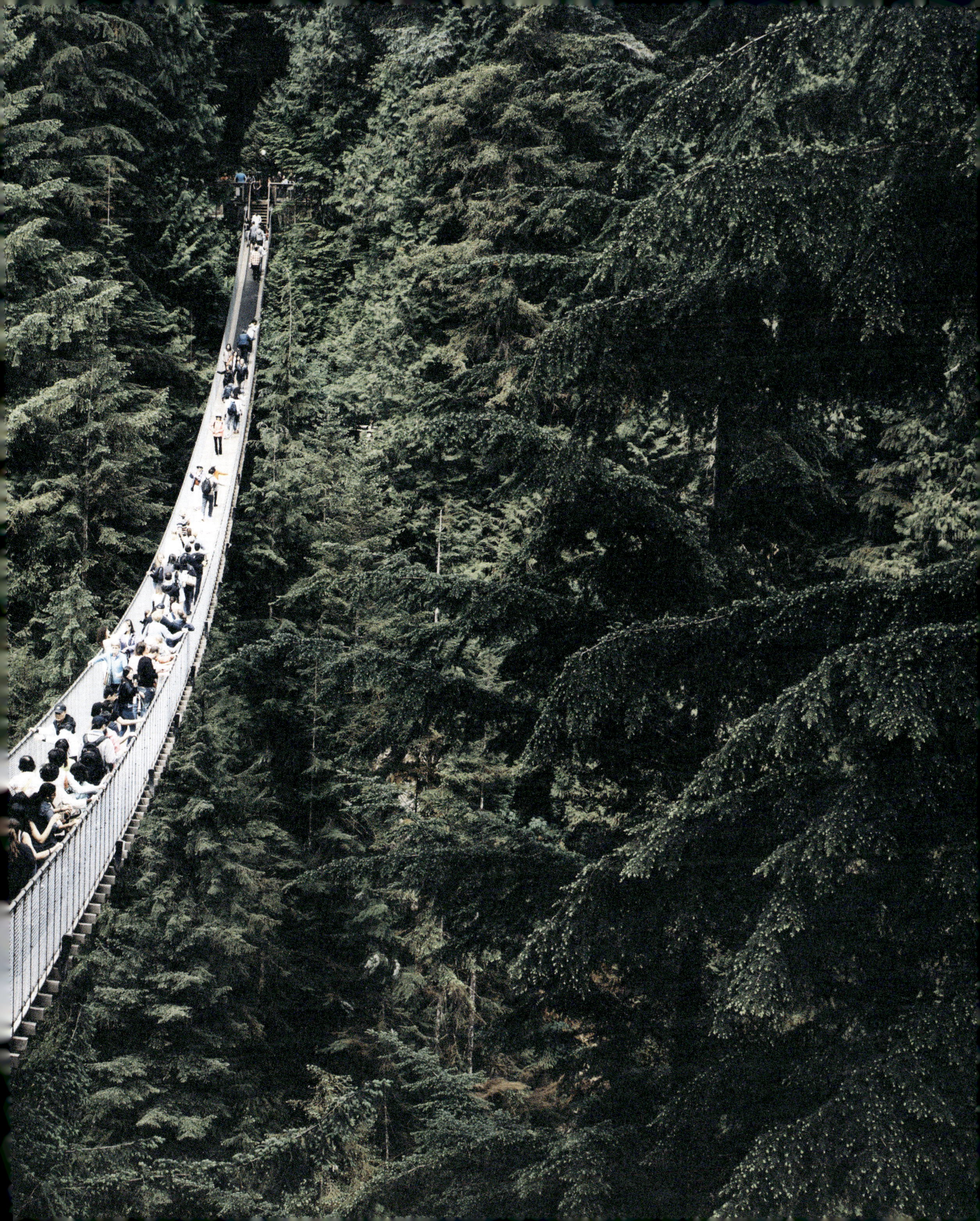

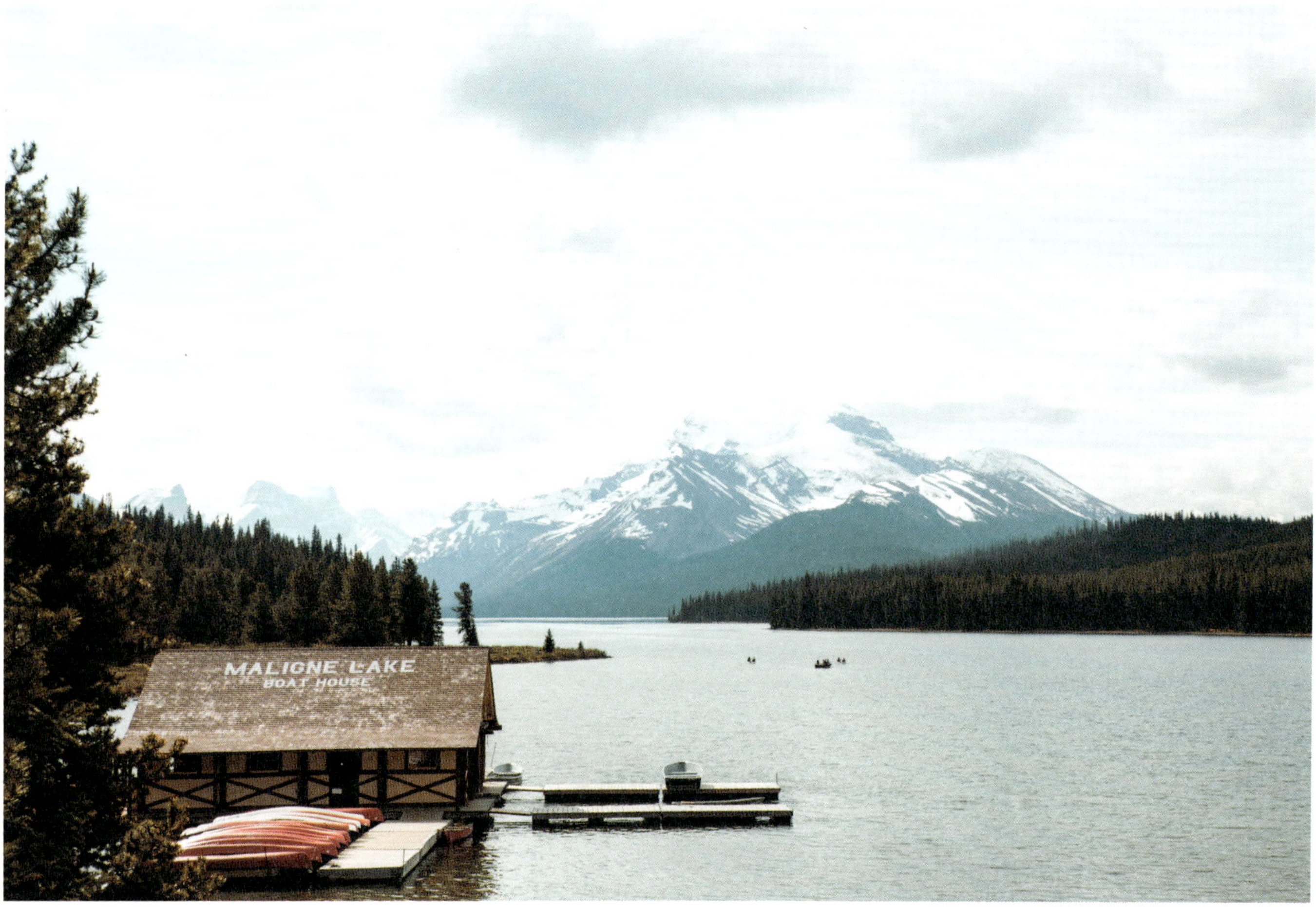
MALIGNE LAKE
BOAT HOUSE

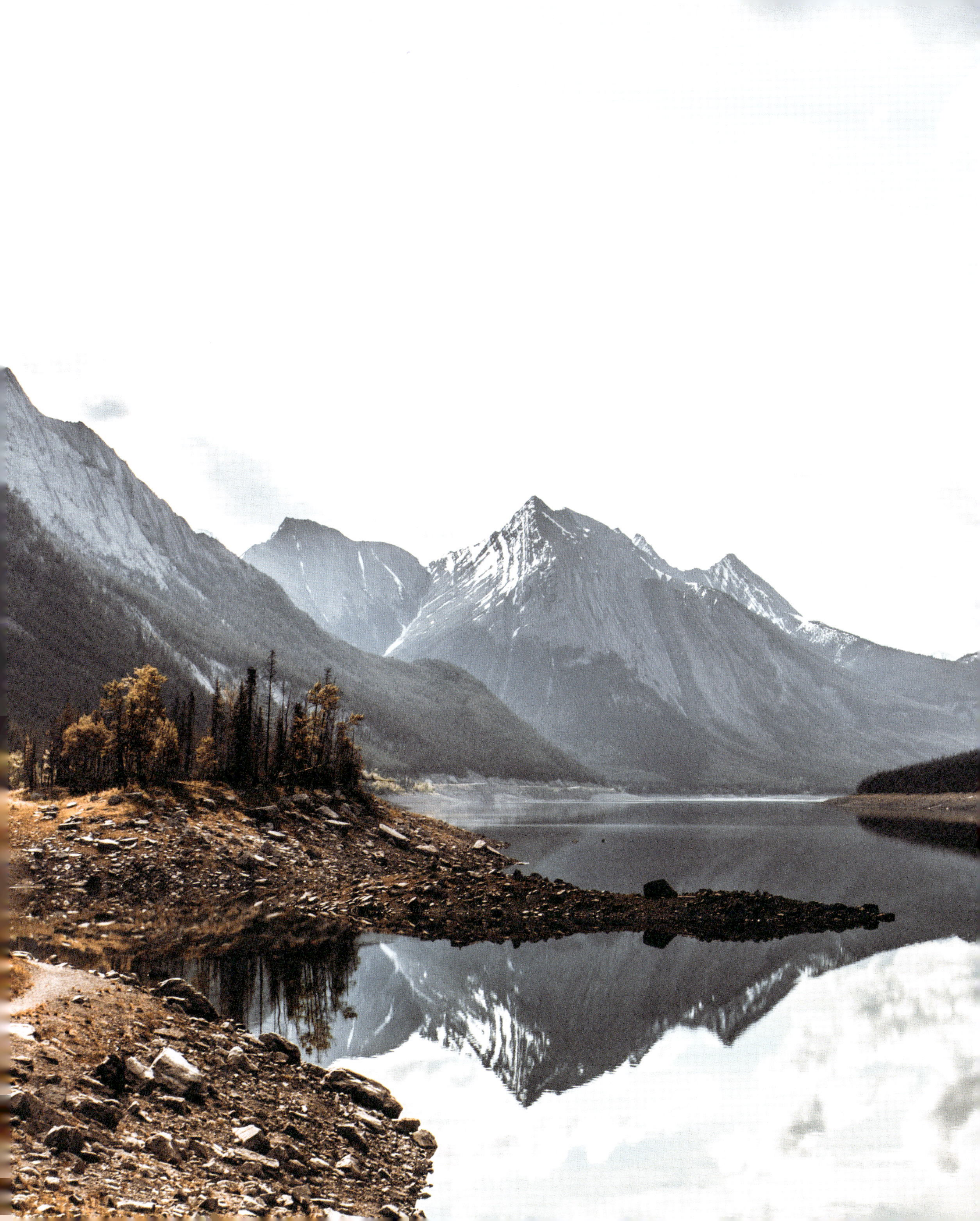

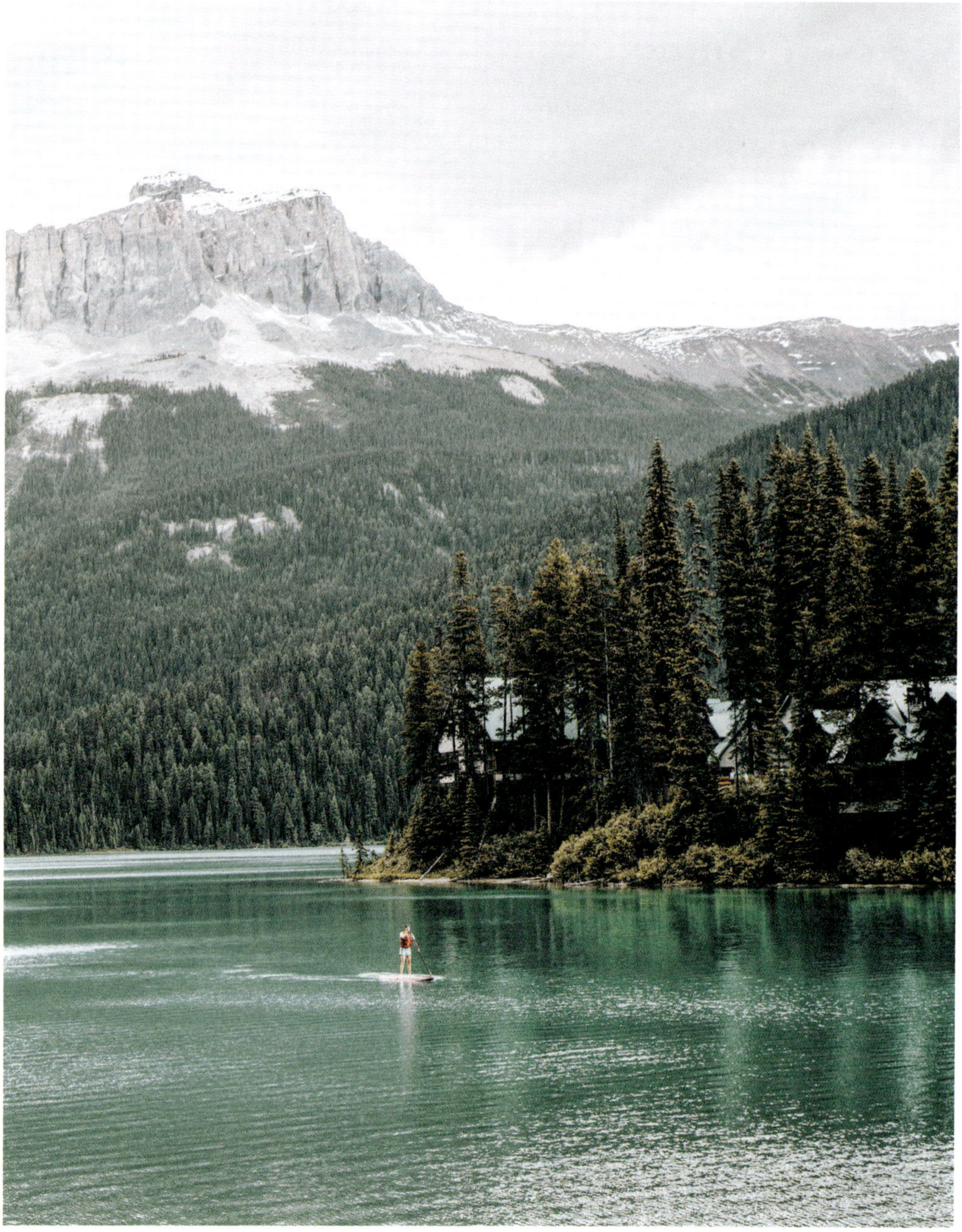

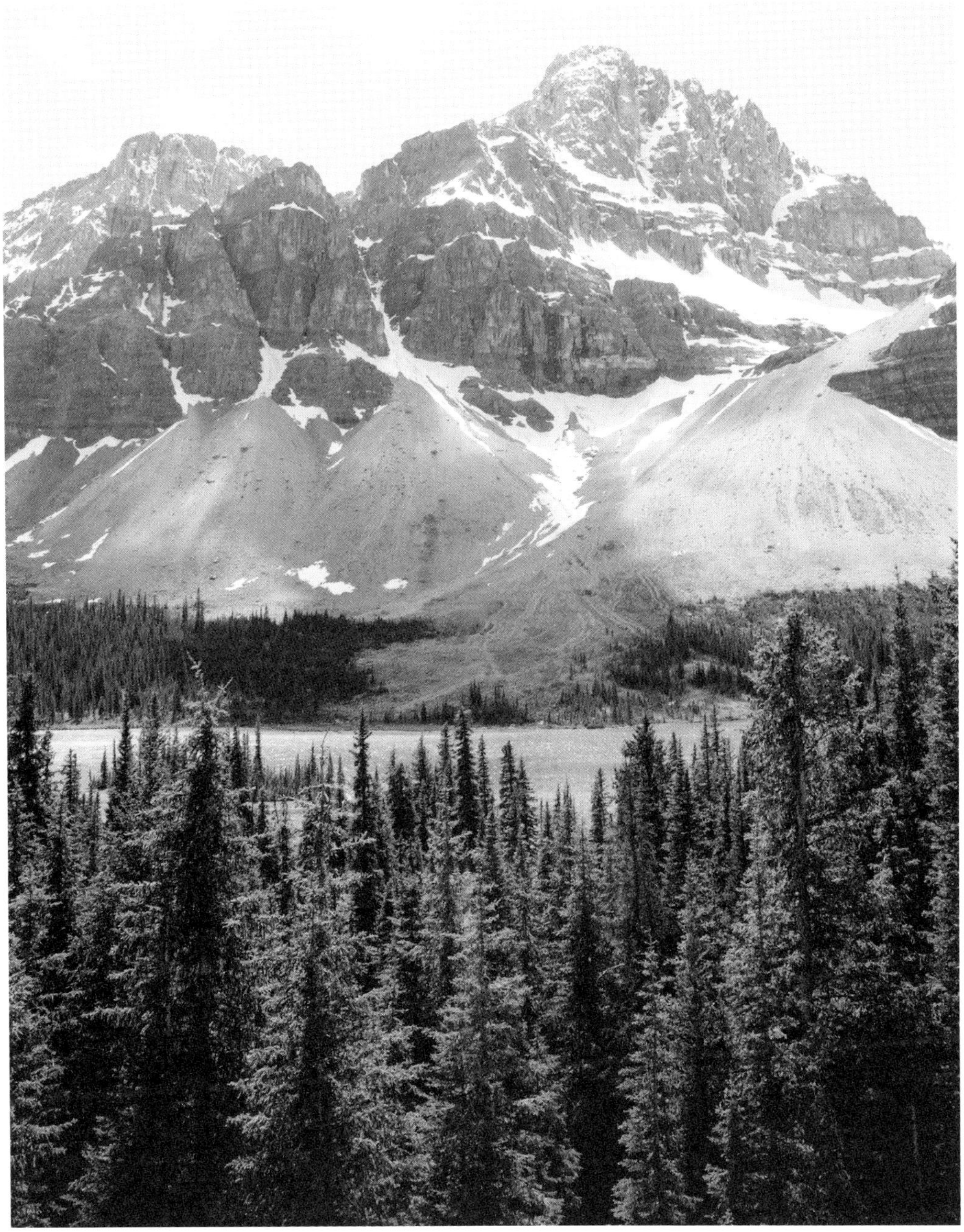

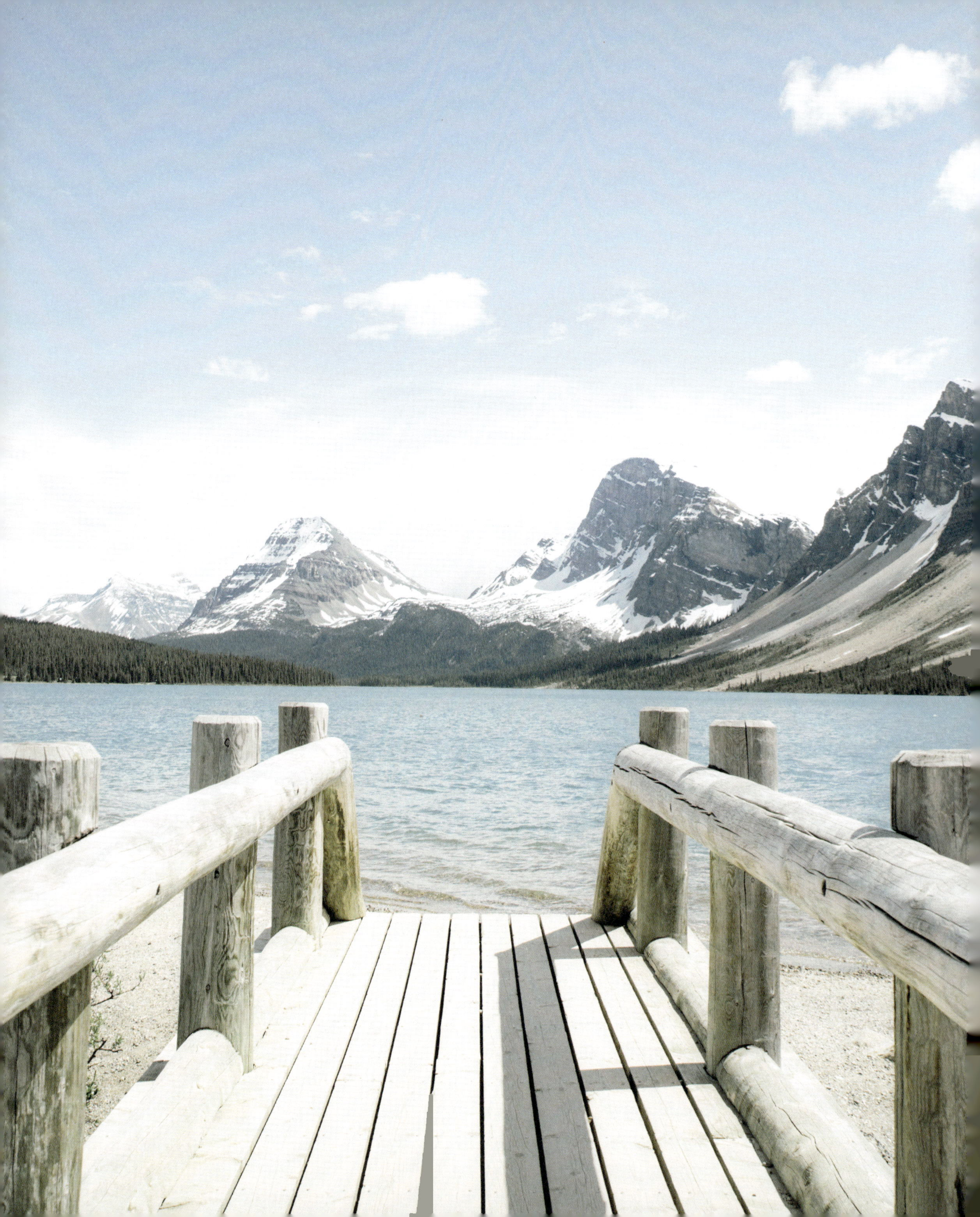

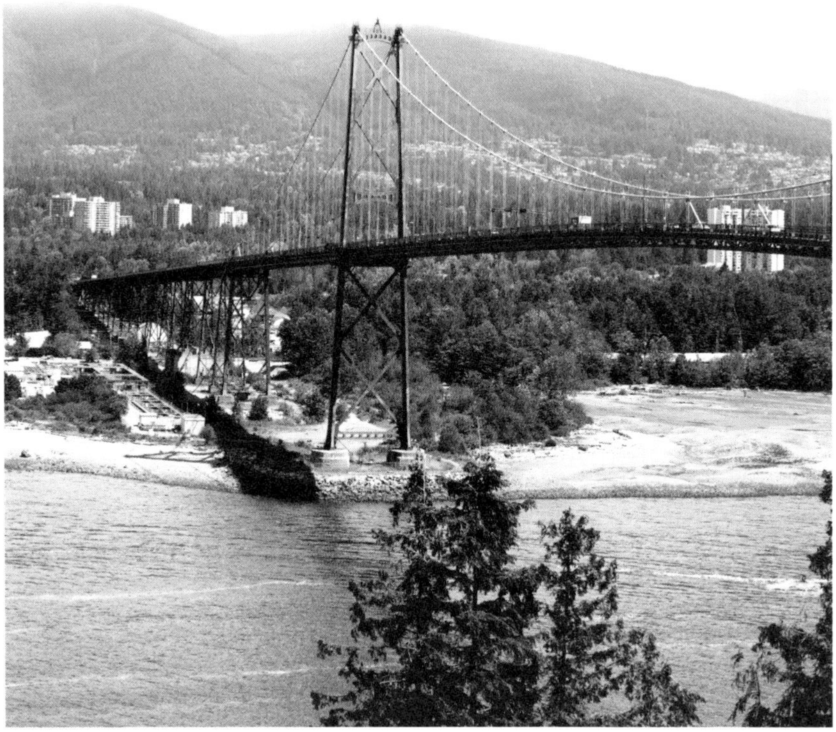

JAPAN

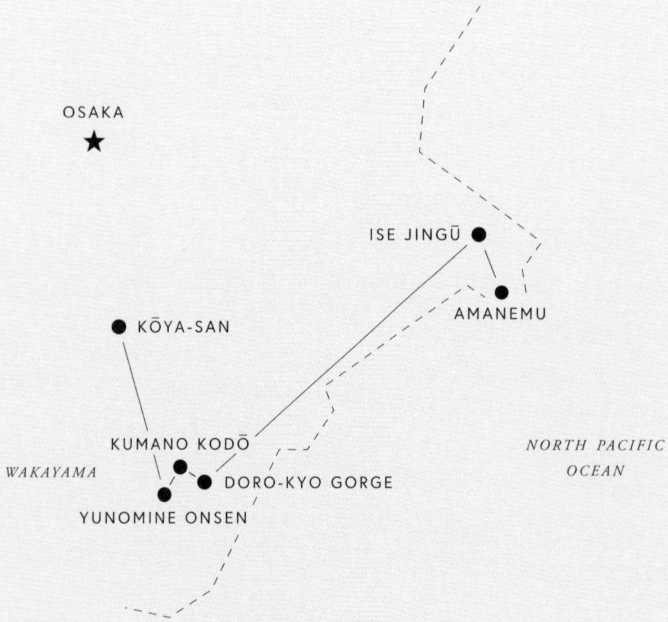

WORDS & PHOTOGRAPHS BY LIZ SCHAFFER

ILLUSTRATIONS BY SAARA KARPPINEN

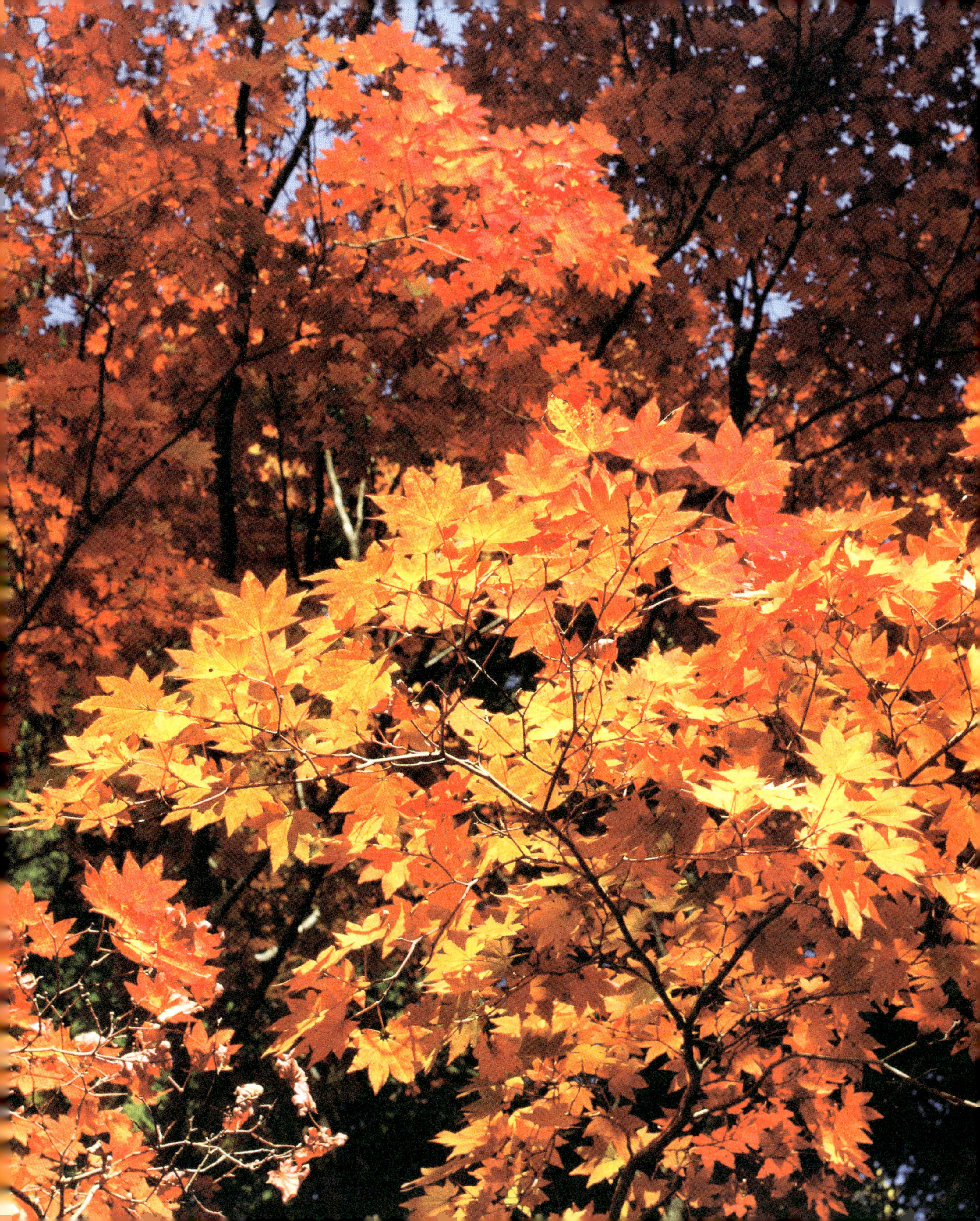

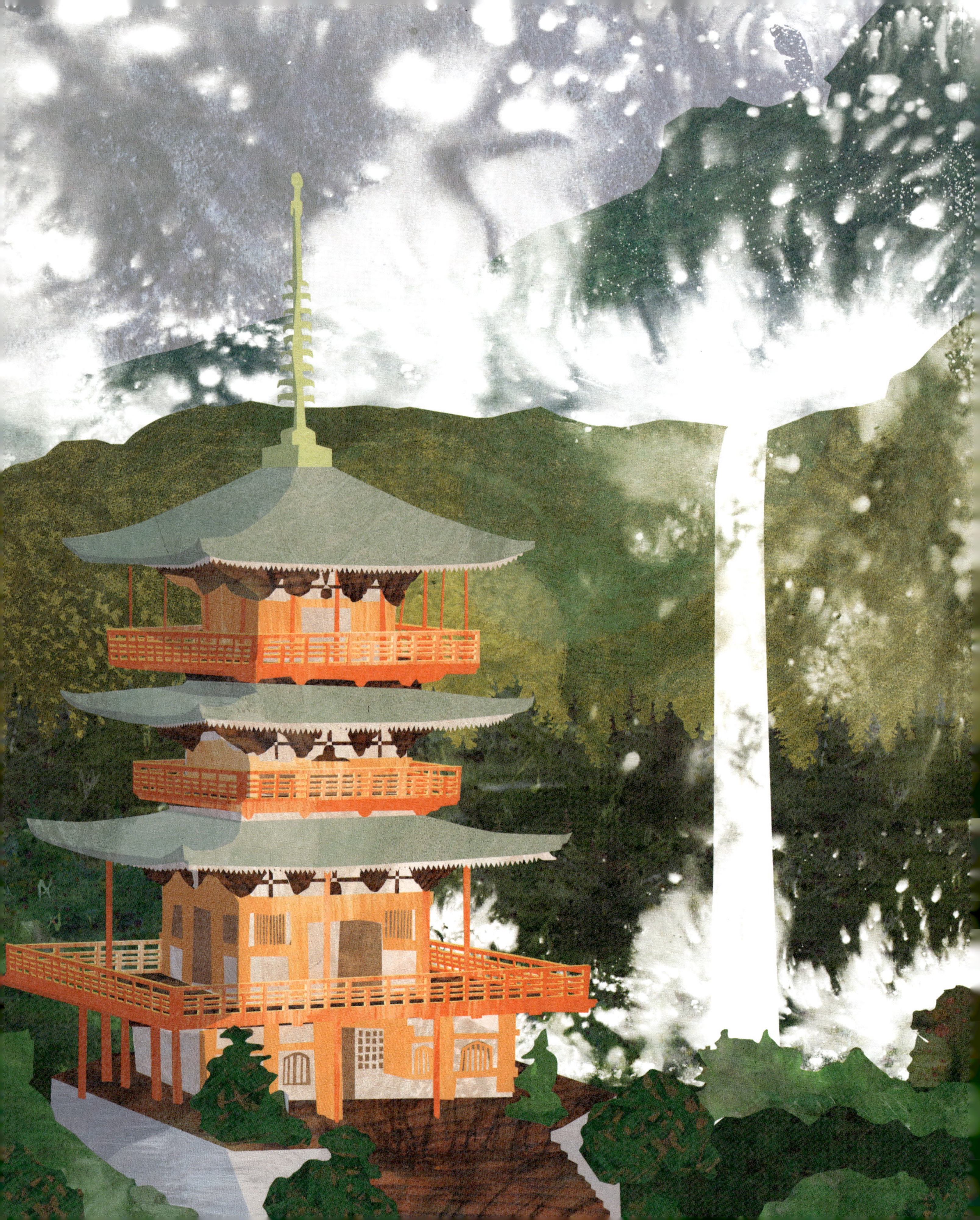

Mountain Spirits

It took me a while to decide what I adored most about Japan, as with its history, politeness, art and food (life is always improved by *takoyaki*) there is much to love. But after venturing into the Kii Mountains in Wakayama Prefecture, I finally figured it out. I was infatuated with nature worship.

It was while scaling these mountains that I had my first encounter with Shintoism, a religion that celebrates nature's might, its divine natural elements embodied by *kami* – deities that can take almost any form and add order to our increasingly chaotic world. Without a set doctrine or founder, Shintoism could be seen as a way of life, one that values honesty, purity and respect. But Japanese spirituality doesn't end there. In the 6th century Buddhism arrived (along with green tea), travelling from India via China. With a philosophical focus, it aimed to eliminate suffering by encouraging followers to discard their desires and aspire instead for enlightenment. Over the years, it mixed with Shinto principles, the two faiths' rituals and practices working in harmony to create a form of nature worship unique to Japan.

For me, travel has always been a reminder of our place in the world; a means of encountering the magnificent – be it the beaches of Okinawa or wilds of Hokkaido – and realising that, while we may be relatively insignificant when compared to such splendour, we are also part of this great, interconnected world. Small and big all at once. Perhaps it was a need to feel this again (and a desire to explore its connection to nature worship) that inspired me to head for the Kii Mountains and the Kumano Kodō – a network of pathways that lead the devout and curious to three of Japan's most sacred sites, known collectively as Kumano Sanzen. These are Kumano Hongū Taisha, Kumano Hayatama Taisha and Kumano Nachi Taisha, which is found by Nachi no Taki waterfall, said to link the spiritual and human realms and worshipped long before the establishment of the Kumano Kodō.

Tackling only a small section of the trail, my 12 day experience took me from forest to farmland, summit to sea and wilderness to village. I passed persimmons drying from rafters, moss-covered stone steps dating from the 11th century and the foundations of tea houses known to promise pilgrims their last stop for miles when in reality a competitor was just down the road. There were stone statues called *Jizō* – believed to protect children and travellers – and mountaintop clearings that revealed peak after peak cascading into the distance, their hues shifting with the sunlight.

Sections of the Kumano Kodō can be long and steep, but there are less exhausting experiences on offer too. Indeed, it is possible to lie upon beds crafted from fallen branches and let the world fall away as you stare into the canopy, listening to birds chirp and a forest therapist play her bamboo flute. It is also worth pausing at the shrines that line the path. Should you wish to pray, bow twice, clap twice and bow once more – this allows you to show respect, call up divine energy and make your wish.

Regardless of the pace you choose (and though it technically isn't upon the Kumano Kodō), it is worth beginning your Wakayama adventure in Kōya-san – especially if it's a spiritual encounter you seek. Bordered by eight peaks thought to mirror the flowering lotus – a traditional symbol of enlightenment – Kōya-san is a sacred city created by Kōbō-Daishi (founder of the Shingon School of Buddhism) as a place where followers might attain peace and happiness through meditation and study. While the natural backdrop may change throughout the year (there's the yellow bamboo of spring, hydrangeas of summer and autumn's reds and oranges), Kōya-san's structures seem untouched by time. Here you can spin prayer wheels that mirror the rhythm of the universe, understand the meaning behind Buddhist architecture and pass through the ancient Dai-mon Gate, guarded by two warriors in statue form who represent the beginning and end of everything. And then there is Okunoin, a cedar-filled cemetery containing around 200,000 grave stones and monuments to departed souls and the mausoleum of Kōbō-Daishi, who remains in eternal meditation.

There are several Japanese words that do not have an English counterpart and one of the most beautiful is *komorebi*, a term that describes the way sunlight filters through foliage. Aware of this phenomenon while wandering Okunoin's paths, and passing a particularly moving memorial dedicated to the Australian, Japanese and Burmese soldiers lost during the Second World War, I began to comprehend the ancient power of this place. So, humbled by my surrounds, I felt the time was right to try my hand at meditation. Alas, despite my good intentions, I was uninitiated in the practice so spent most of my hour-long guided session struggling to find a comfortable position, but did notice that time became a little elastic. Perhaps I will find a way to empty my mind yet.

Should you not wish to walk the Kumano Kodō – and be warned, this walk is far from easy – it is possible to enjoy Wakayama's beauty travelling by road and river. There's the 31 kilometre long Doro-kyo Gorge, famed for its rock for-

There were stone statues called Jizō *– believed to protect children and travellers – and mountaintop clearings that revealed peak after peak cascading into the distance, their hues shifting with the sunlight.*

mations, near-turquoise water and spring-time azaleas, and hotels like Infinito Hotel and Spa where you can admire the sunset from a private onsen, the sea and sky an ever-changing kaleidoscope of pastels. This latter experience is enhanced by the promise of a good meal, with Infinito's Italian restaurant showcasing the country's love for fine foreign fare. Or there's the sulphur-scented Yunomine Onsen, which boasts a UNESCO-listed public onsen (the oldest in Japan) and over 1,300 years of history. Known to change colour as the day progresses, the water flows at around 90 degrees – making it hot enough for peckish visitors to cook eggs and sweet potatoes in.

However you travel, Amanemu should be your final destination. This luxury resort, framed by Ise-Shima National Park and the waters of Ago Bay (renowned for its pearls and seaweed), is where you can restore aching limbs, forget city life and begin to unwind. Built from wood and stone, Amanemu's spacious design seems to be inspired by nearby Ise Jingū, Japan's most sacred Shinto site where the central shrines Naikū and Gekū are rebuilt every 20 years; a centuries-old process that allows new generations to learn ancient skills while honouring the natural world where life is cyclical and nothing is permanent.

Although there are numerous indulgent activities on offer – from lengthy meals (breakfasts are unmissable) to beauty treatments you're unlikely to forget – one of the most meaningful encounters you can have at Amanemu is with an Ama diver.

Swimming around 400 metres off the coast, Ama divers descend to depths of up to ten metres in search of lobster, abalone and other sea-dwelling delights. Having once provided seafood for the Imperial Court and viewed by many as Japan's first career women, they're an inspiring group who happily share their 2,000 year history as visitors devour freshly-caught crustaceans cooked over burning coals. There is no training programme, so divers, almost all of whom are female, learn from their family and peers as they always have.

While there are countless pathways to explore in Japan (and there is much to adore), it was my journey over the Kii Mountains that remains the most vivid. Indeed, even as I write this in the heart of gloriously overcast London, all I must do is close my eyes and I'm back on that light-dappled path, which has been trodden by so many over the centuries, feeling small and big all at once. ⋆

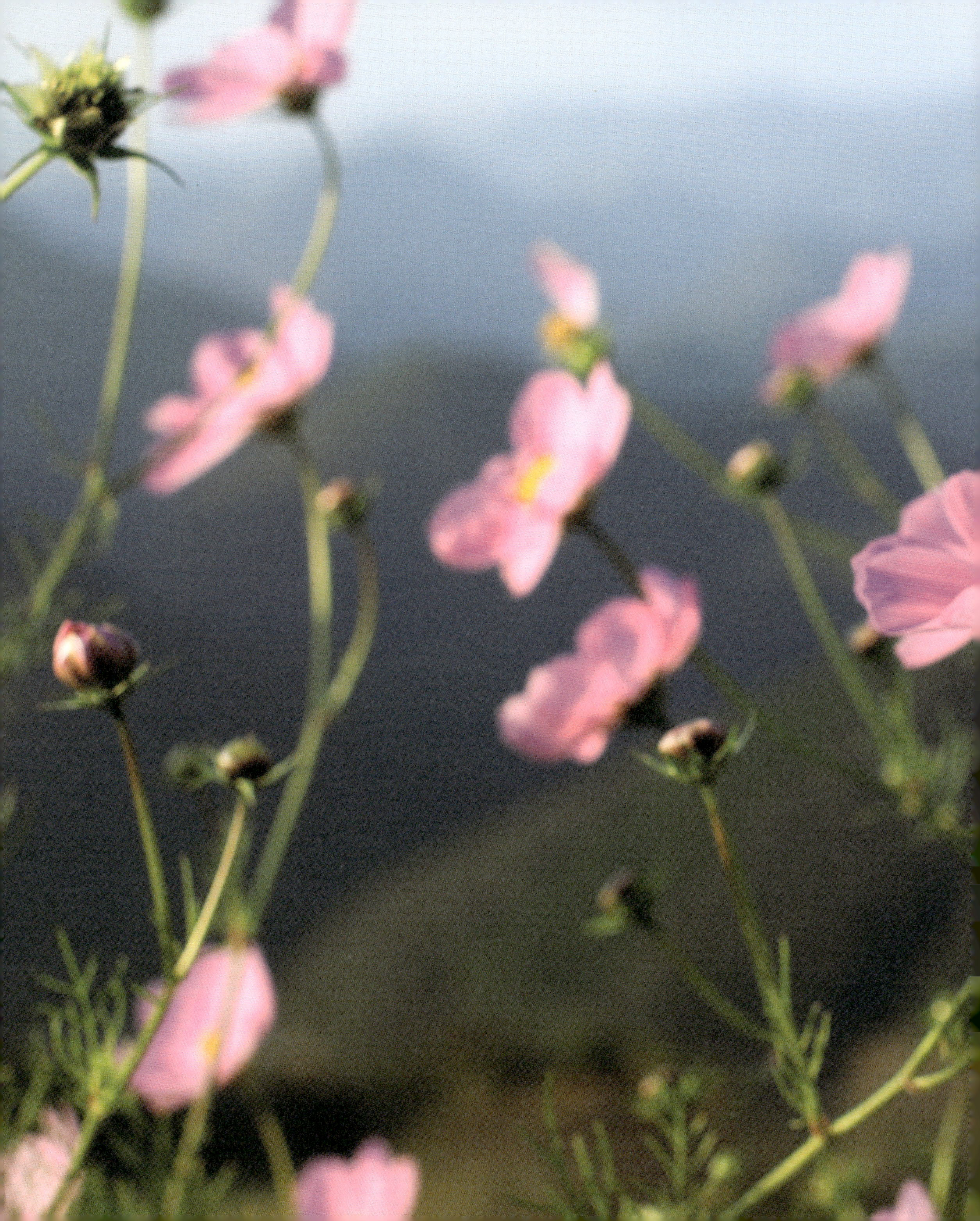

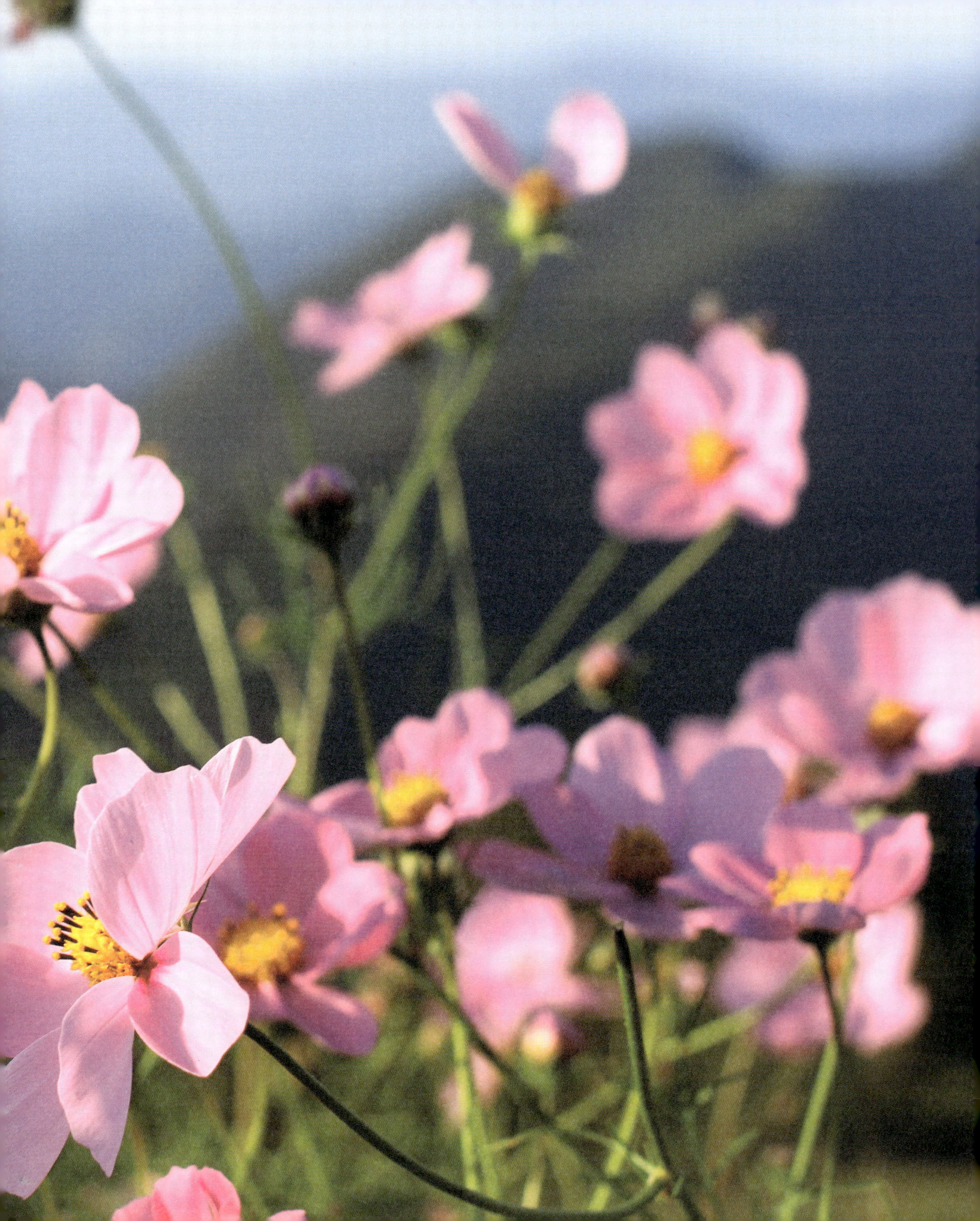

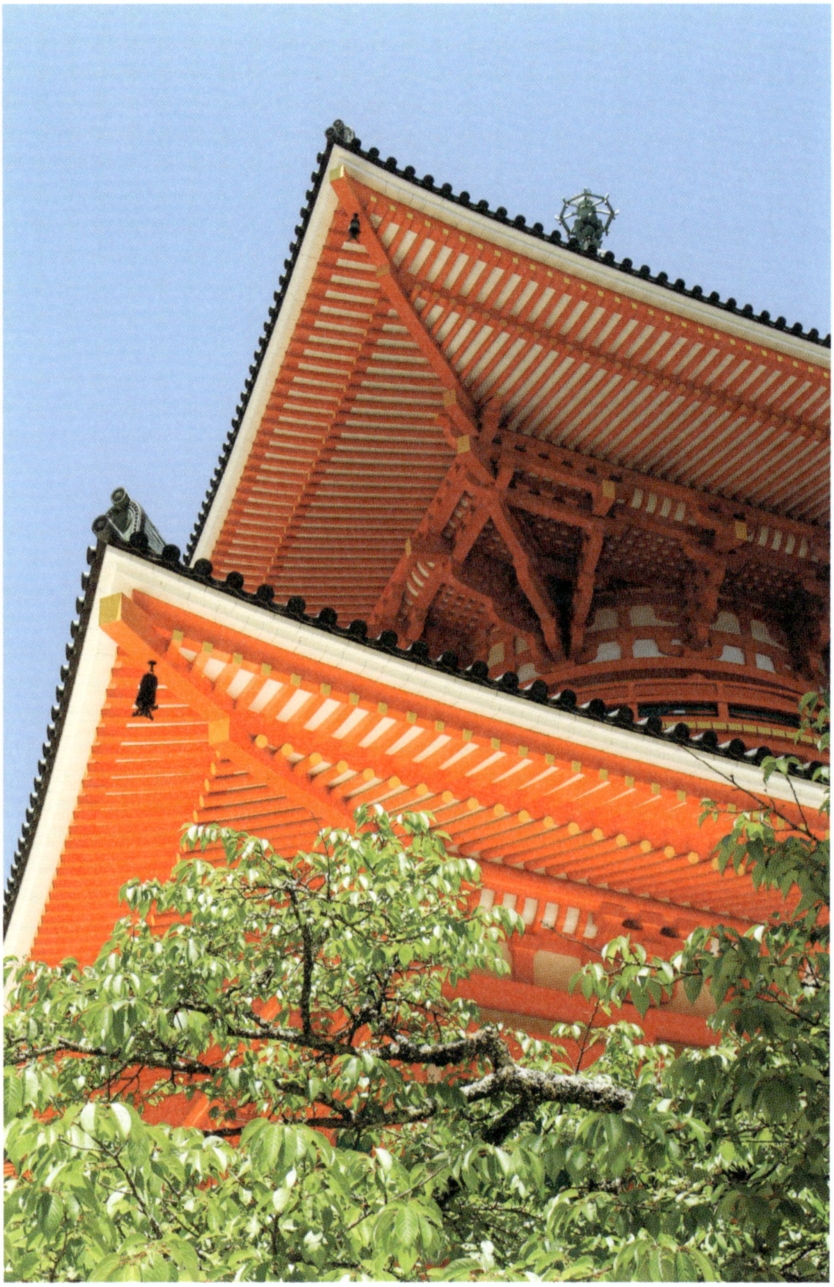

The wonders of Kōya-san, where the colours change with the seasons.

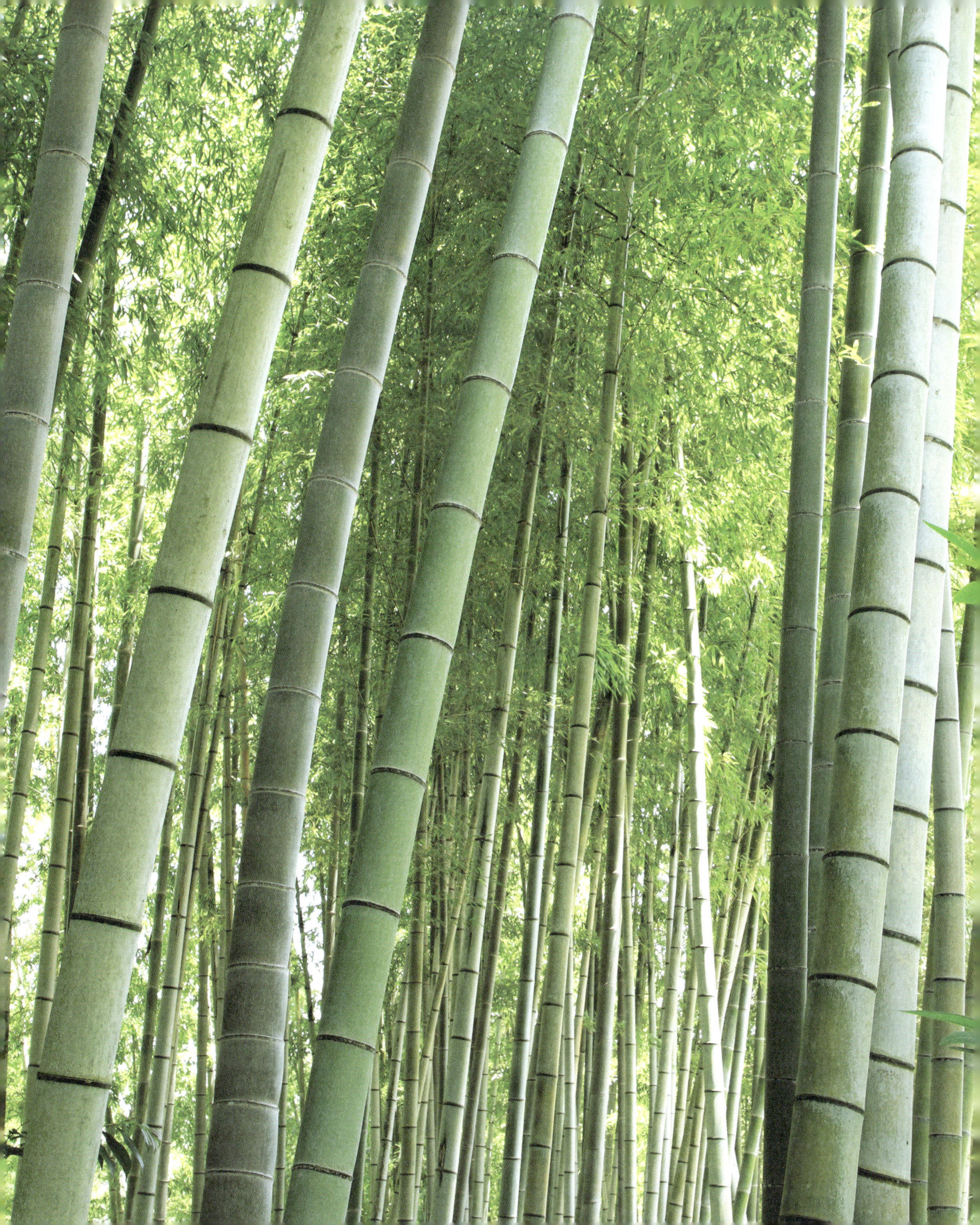

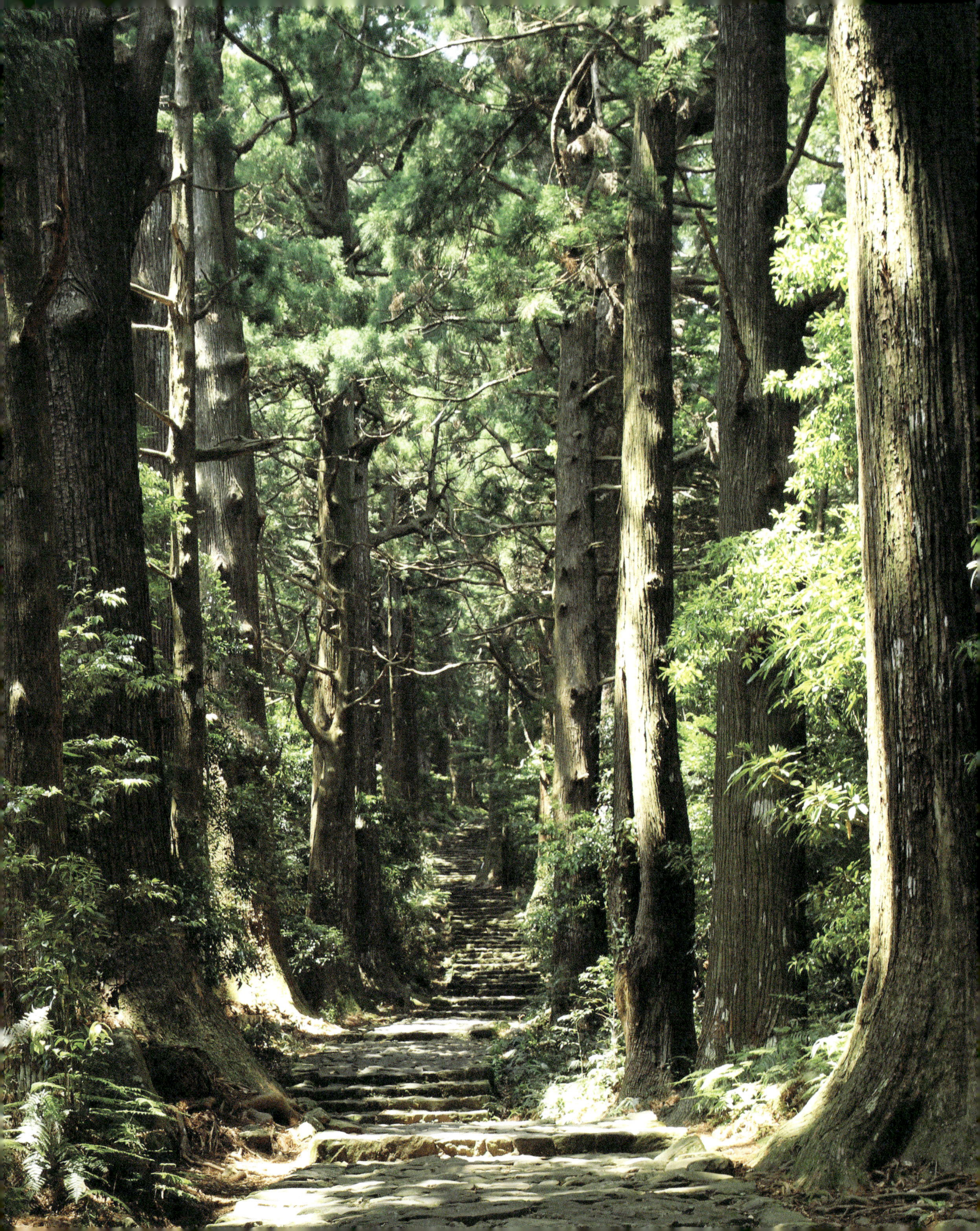

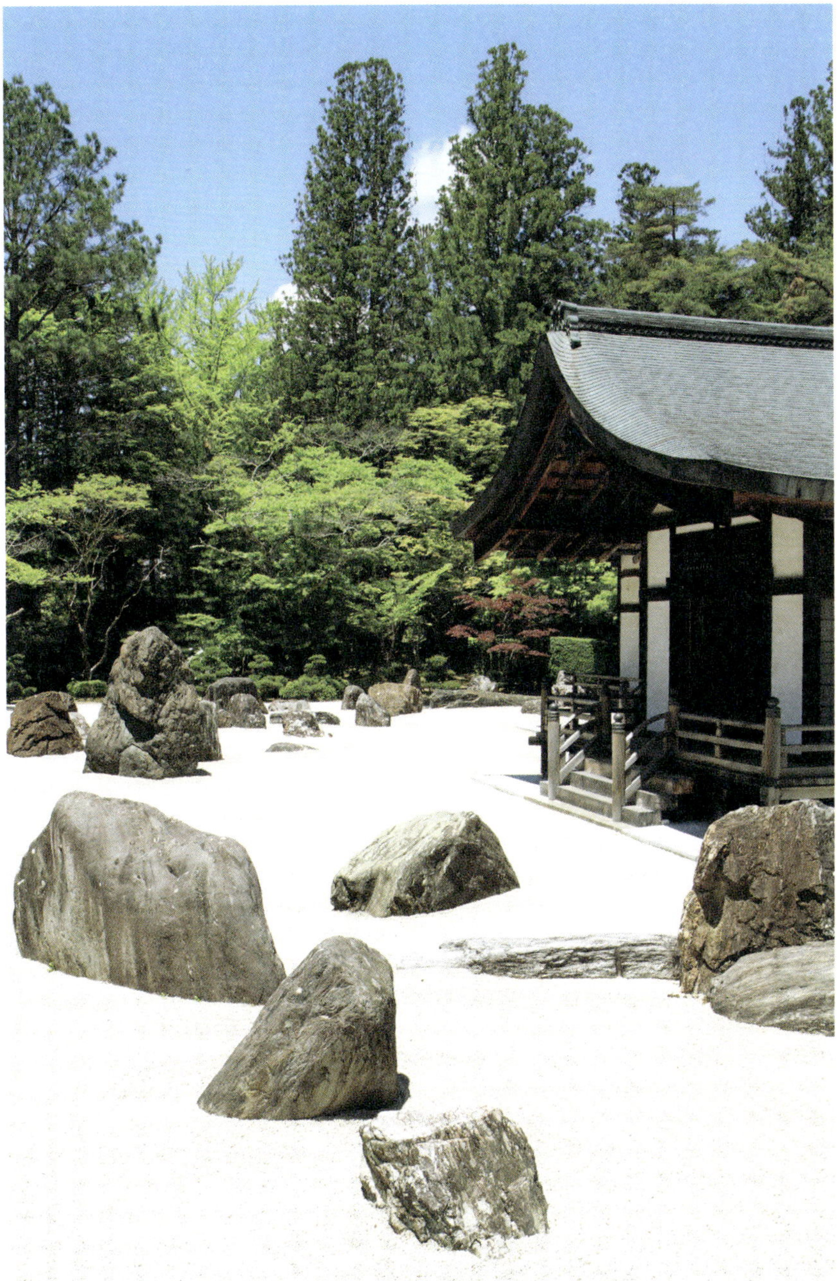

In search of solitude upon the Kumano Kodō. (left)

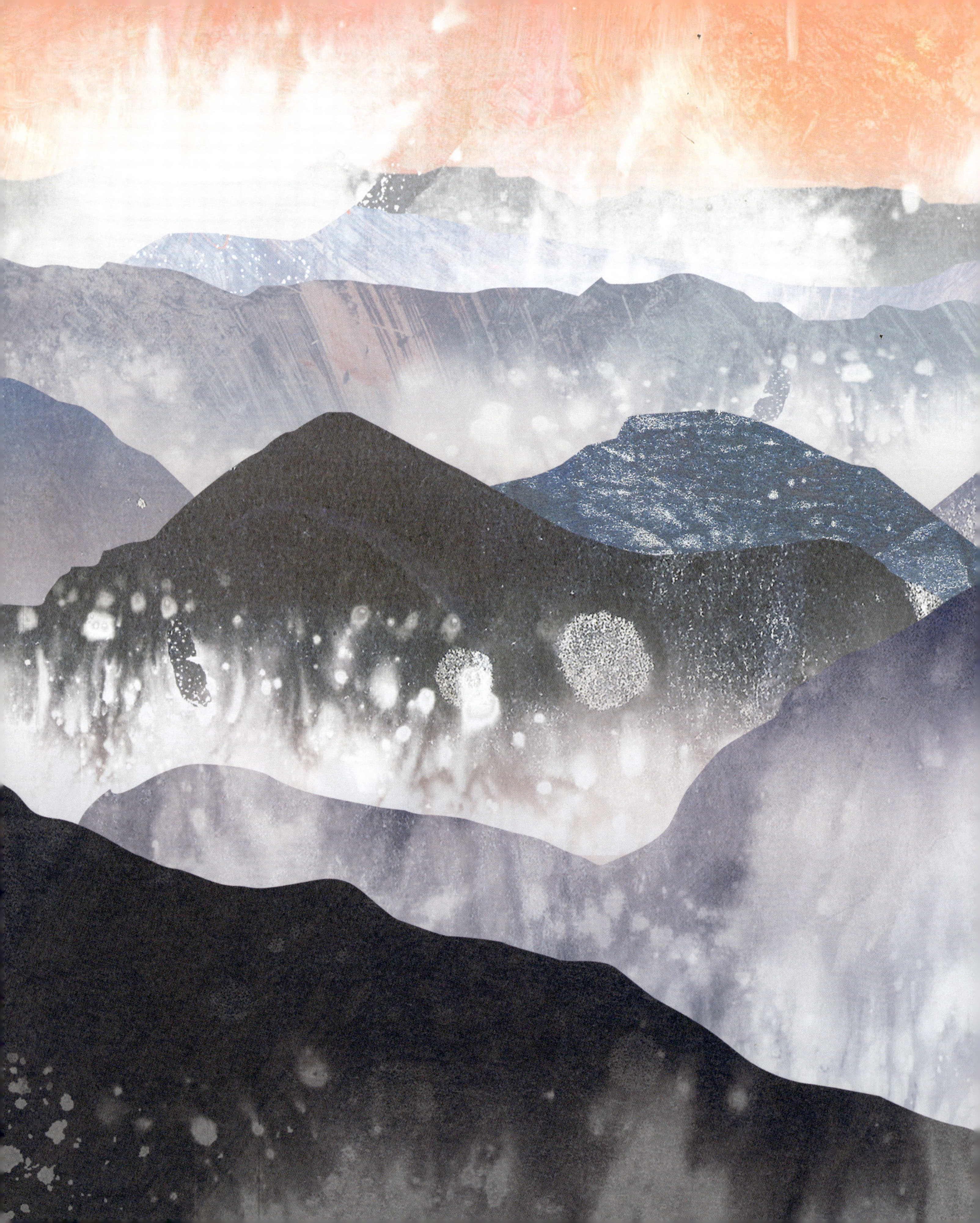

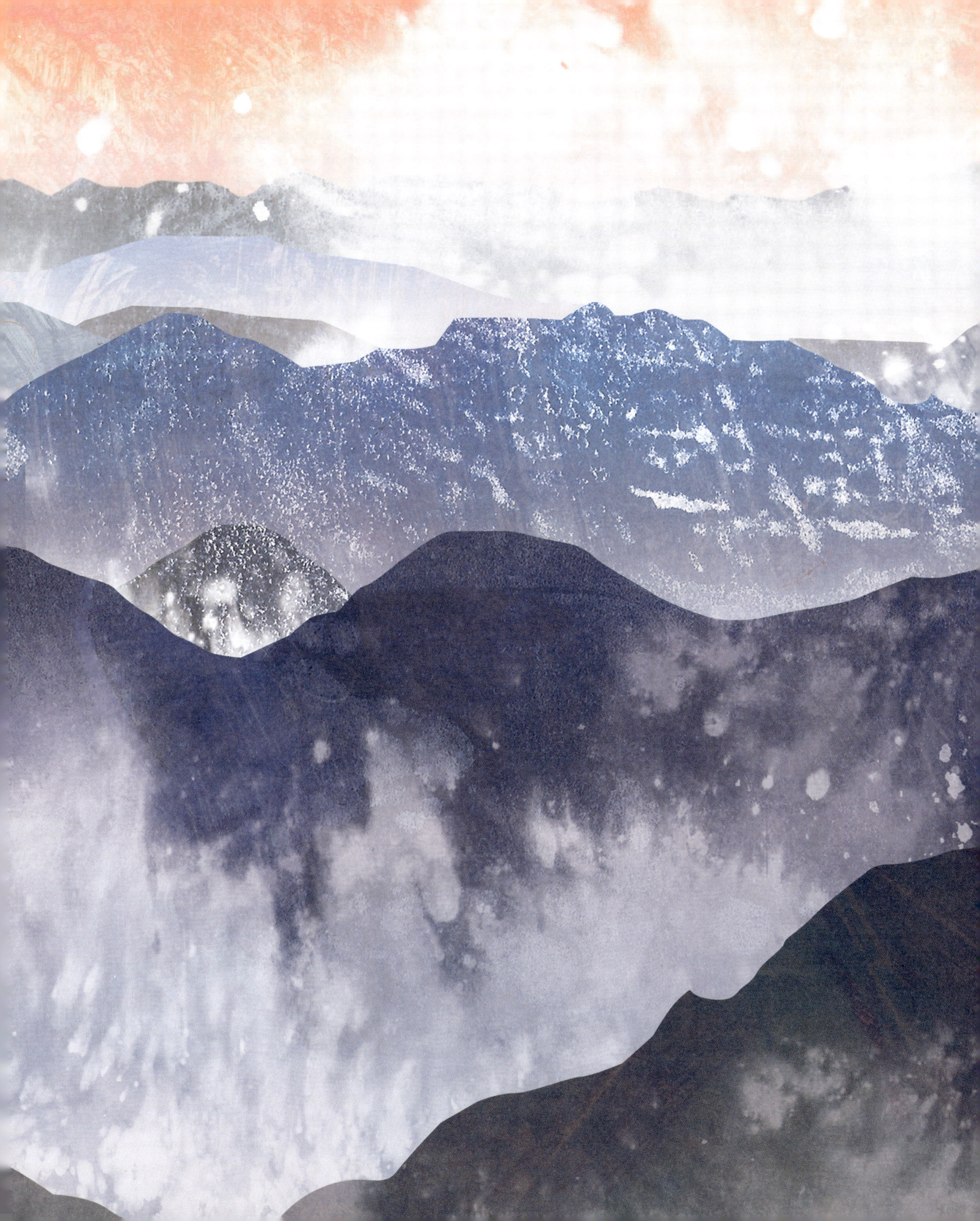

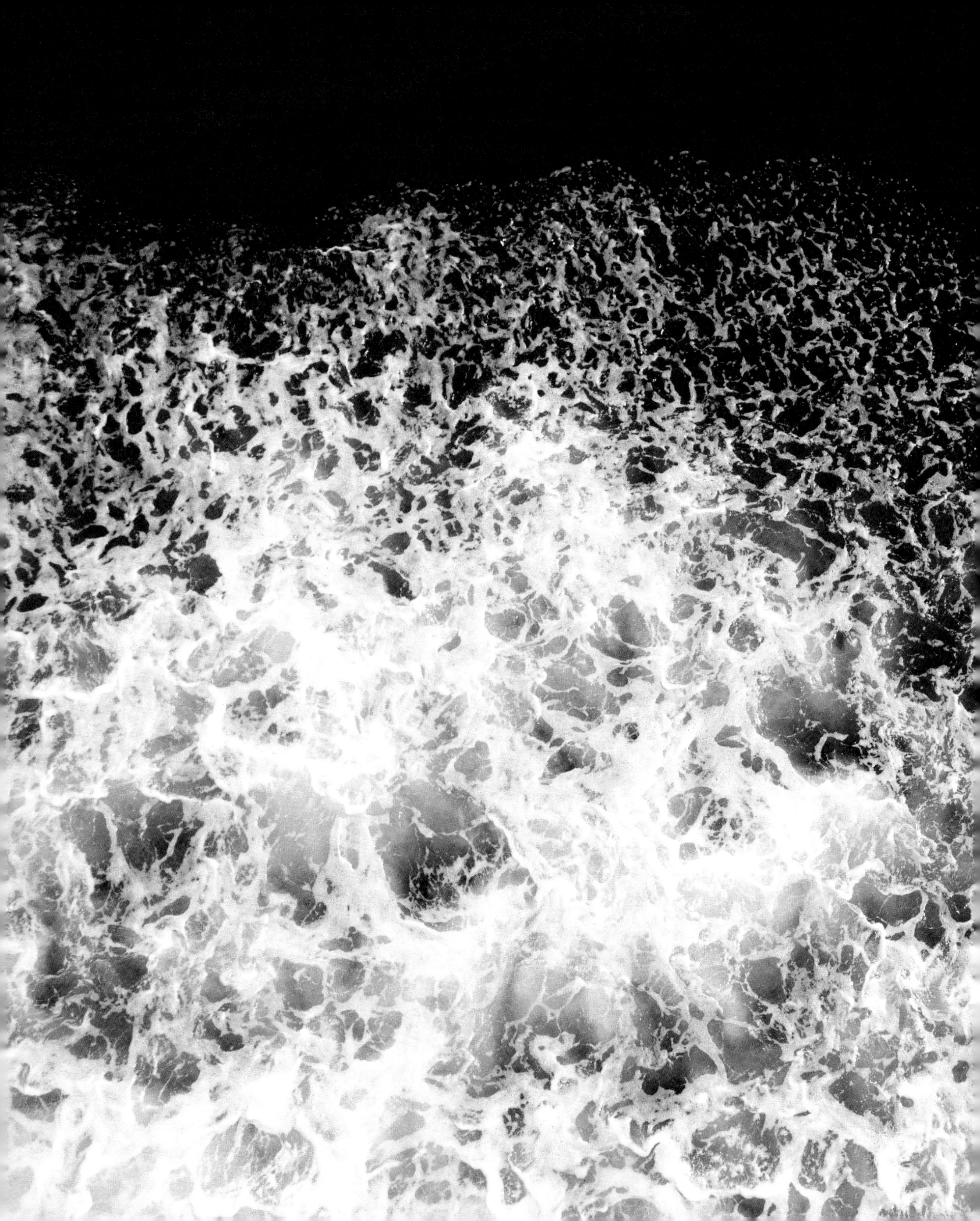

NEW ZEALAND

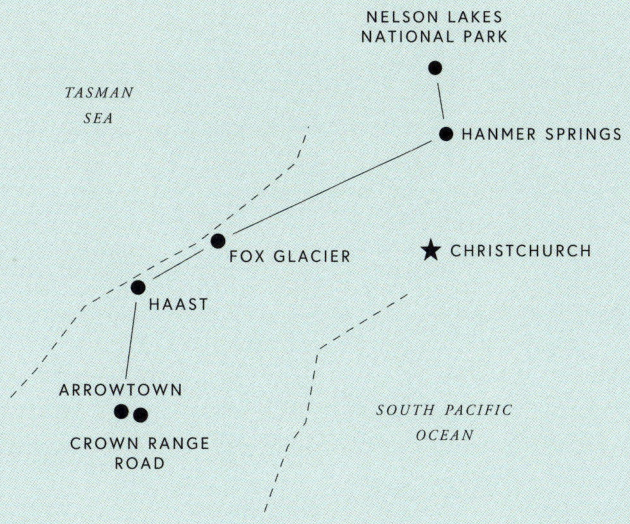

WORDS BY CLAIRE NELSON

PHOTOGRAPHS BY GEORGINA SKINNER

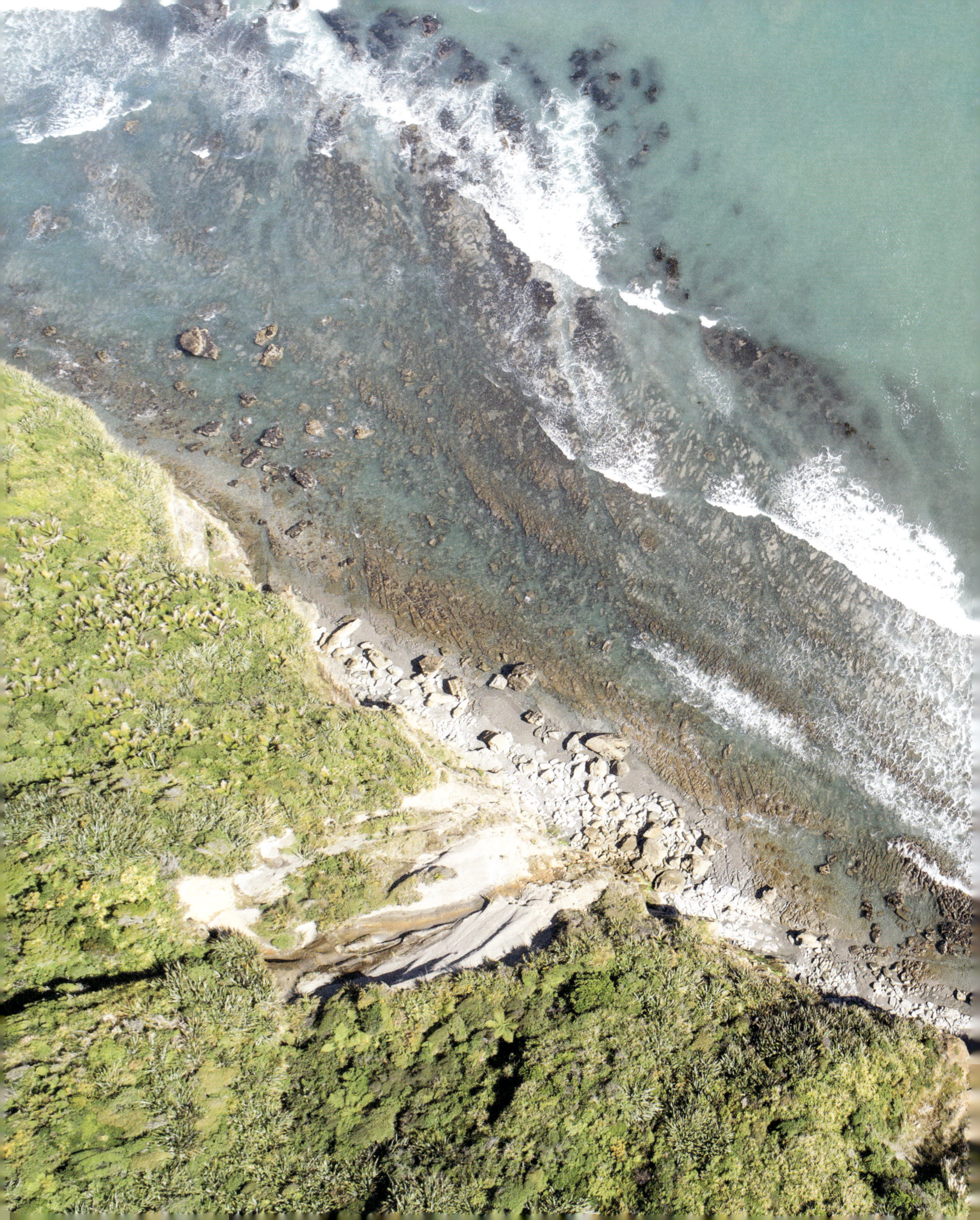

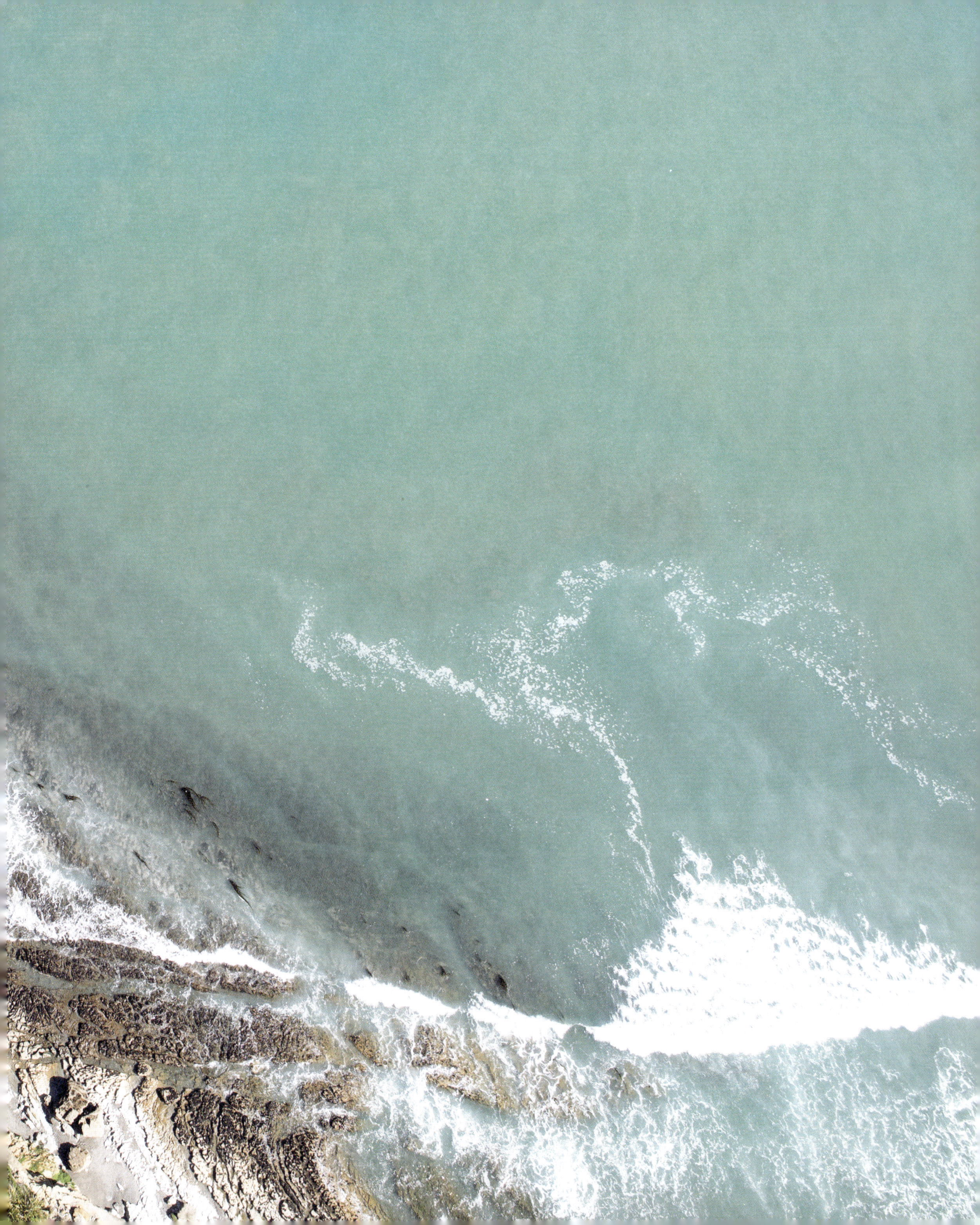

Letters From Home

Everyone knows the grass is always greener on the other side of the fence. This applies even if your grass grows in New Zealand, often considered the greenest of paddocks. As a child who was Auckland-born and Wellington-raised, I'd seen plenty of the North Island, but barely touched the South – instead, I wanted something more. Nursing romantic notions of overseas, I journeyed to England, rather than across Cook Strait, and after a decade of revelling in all things historic and accented I became a British citizen. It was at this point that my mother felt enough was enough. How could I be a certified Brit when I was yet to fully know New Zealand? She had a point. I flew back to Wellington, Mum packed up the Mazda and together we hit the road south.

The West Coast of the South Island is famous for whitebait and weather, and sure enough we arrived to cloudy skies and heavy rain. Somehow it only amplified the beauty of this untamed coast; all wild sea, mist-cloaked hills and roads flanked by nīkau palms – more *Jurassic Park* than *The Lord of the Rings*. In a haze of drizzle we rolled into the township of Fox Glacier at the foot of the Southern Alps, the peaks cloaked in cloud. It was looking ominous for the heli-tour we'd scheduled the next morning; in fact, helicopters hadn't been up for days. By some miracle then, we woke to blue skies and kept our date with the glacier, hovering along the great sweep of ice with my jaw glued firmly to the floor of the tiny cockpit. It dawned on me that I was now a tourist in my own country; a realisation made all the more humbling by the fact nature almost turned me away.

Having encountered enough weather, Mum and I went in search of that ultimate Kiwi delicacy: whitebait fritters, fresh from the pan, served on no-frills, generously buttered white bread. In Haast we came upon a corrugated iron cart on the side of the road serving classic whitebait sarnies, on which we inelegantly gorged as the proprietor rested her elbows on the counter and told us how she parks here for the summer. "My kids are playing over there somewhere," she says, waving an arm towards the park as the barefoot, tree-climbing nostalgia of a Kiwi childhood flashed before my eyes. "They'll come back when they're hungry," she shrugged. I wished we could do the same.

Our route veered inland across the Alps, through beech forest and rugged schist ravines, and we emerged into what looked

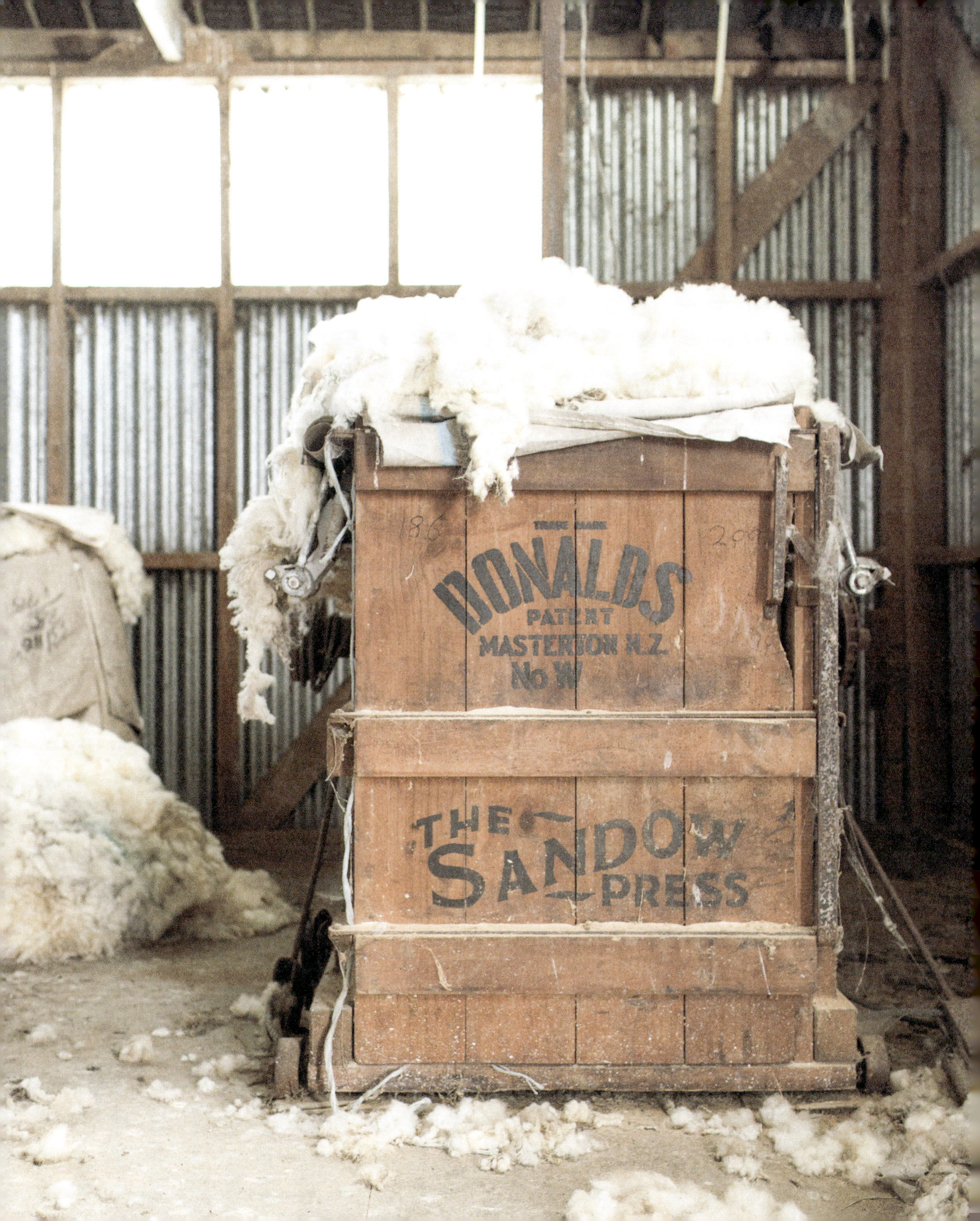
TRADE MARK
DONALDS
PATENT
MASTERTON N.Z.
No W
THE SANDOW PRESS

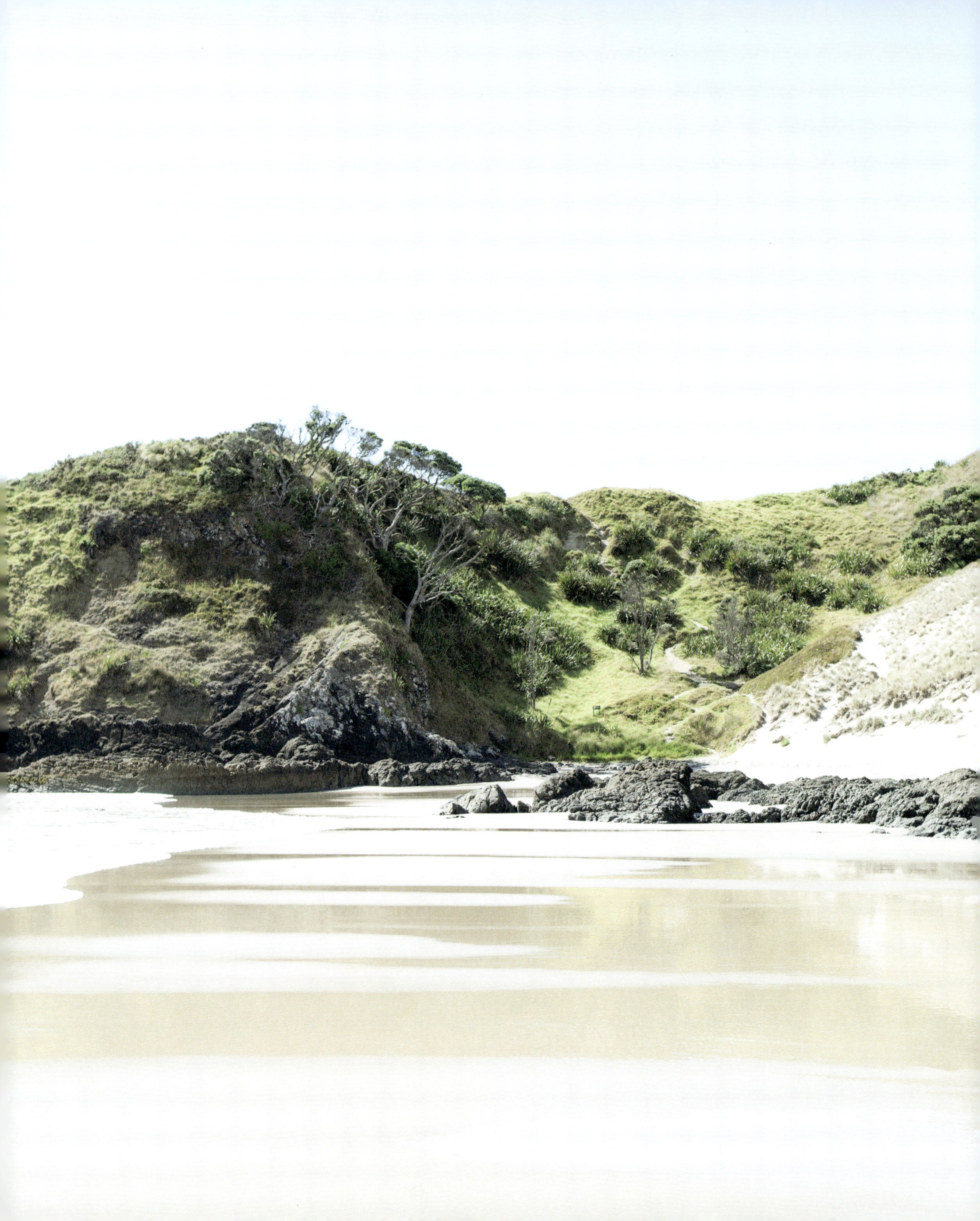

like an entirely different country. Here the moody greys and greens of the West Coast were replaced by pale browns and the striking blues of Lakes Wanaka and Hawea. Continuing on, we tackled the lofty heights of the Crown Range Road with its winding, heart-in-your-mouth hairpins – which by rights deserved a cold drink at the Cardrona Hotel along the way. This iconic coaching inn dates back to 1863, which has nothing on archaic English pubs but, given New Zealand was only founded in 1840, is pretty bloody old.

We spent a couple of days in Arrowtown, a welcome distance from the summer crowds of nearby Queenstown. Retaining its gold rush charm, the main street is a cluster of heritage-style shops and original miners' cottages, making it easy to imagine the lives of families who emigrated here to make their fortune panning the Arrow River for gold. New Zealand may not have seen the rise and fall of empires or had the likes of Shakespeare walk its streets, but our country has an intrepid history all its own, something I was only now beginning to appreciate.

The southern landscape was really showing off its startling range as the Mazda delivered us into lake country. Here the road hugged the curves of Lake Aviemore, where 'freedom campers' congregated in their laundry-draped vans, then eye-wateringly blue Lake Pukaki, and Lake Benmore beyond, born out of the colossal hydropower dam. We spent that night in a tiny cabin on the edge of Lake Tekapo, part of a UNESCO dark sky reserve – perfect for stargazing.

Our journey was supposed to take us on to Kaikoura and lunch at the iconic Nin's Bin crayfish van, but our plans were dashed by the devastating earthquake of November 2016, which closed access roads and heaved up the seabed (decimating the crayfish with it). Such natural disasters, as heartbreaking as they may be, almost seem like common occurrences in a country that straddles an irascible fault line, and New Zealanders are champions at simply 'getting on with things'. We too did just that, resetting our course to Hanmer Springs; this ancient oasis of geothermal hot springs offering steamy mineral pools ideal for soaking weary bones and car-contorted limbs. With one hand nature may taketh away but it giveth back with the other.

On our final morning Mum and I hit the road early, the peaks of the Southern Alps striking against the pale sky, and stopped for fuel and flat whites in Springs Junction; the only place to benefit from the quake, it was fielding the rerouted traffic and local business was booming. As I juggled takeaway coffees a smiling, tattooed truckie held the cafe door open for me and I felt a long-overdue surge of affection for my little country and its people, grateful it had so warmly welcomed back its prodigal daughter.

We paused one final time in Nelson Lakes National Park by the shores of Lake Rotoiti, where I wandered barefoot to the end of its creaking wooden jetty and felt the sun warm my skin. And it was here that I finally got it. There really is no place like home... I'd just had to venture to the other side of the world and back to get here. ⋆

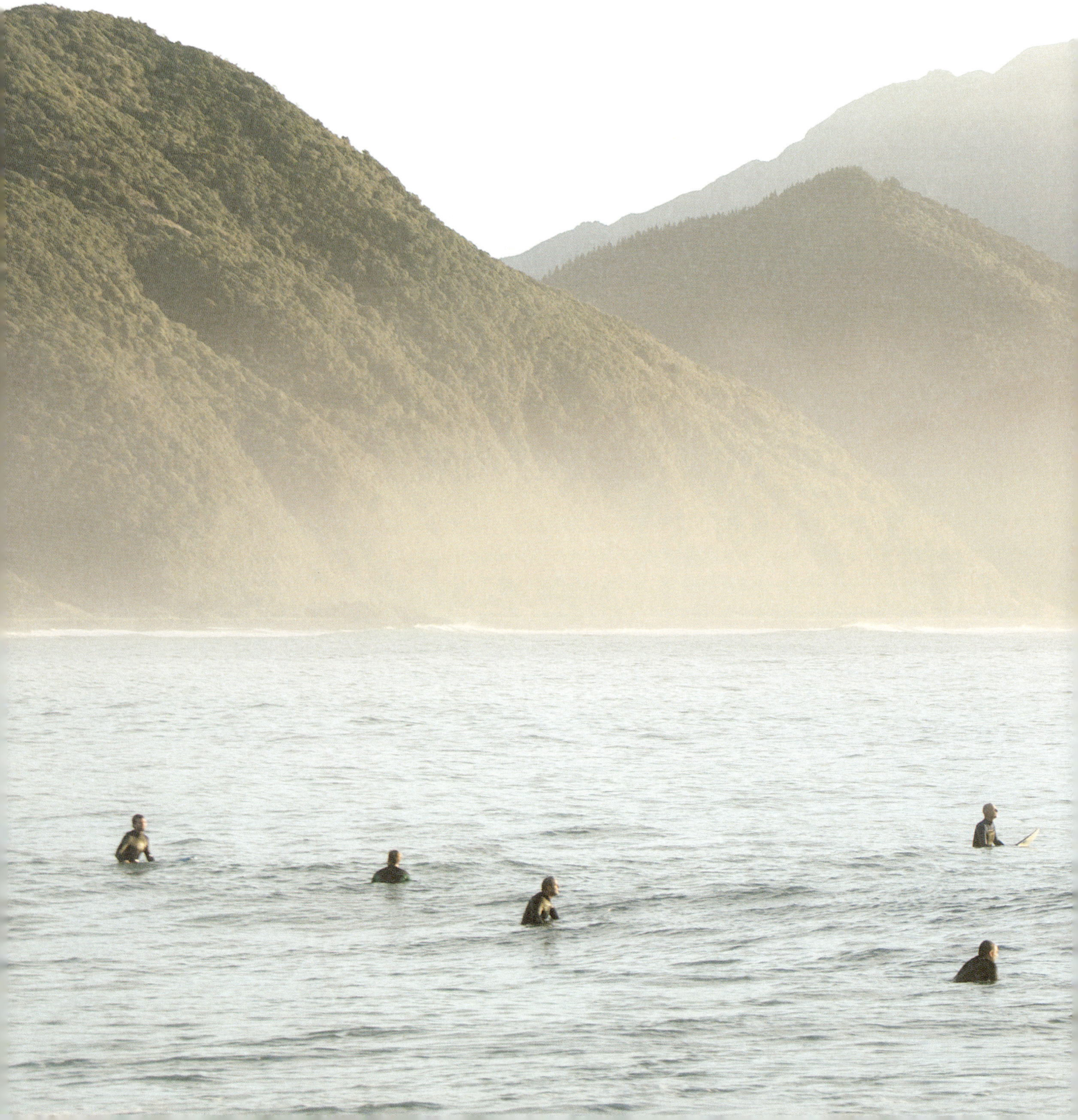

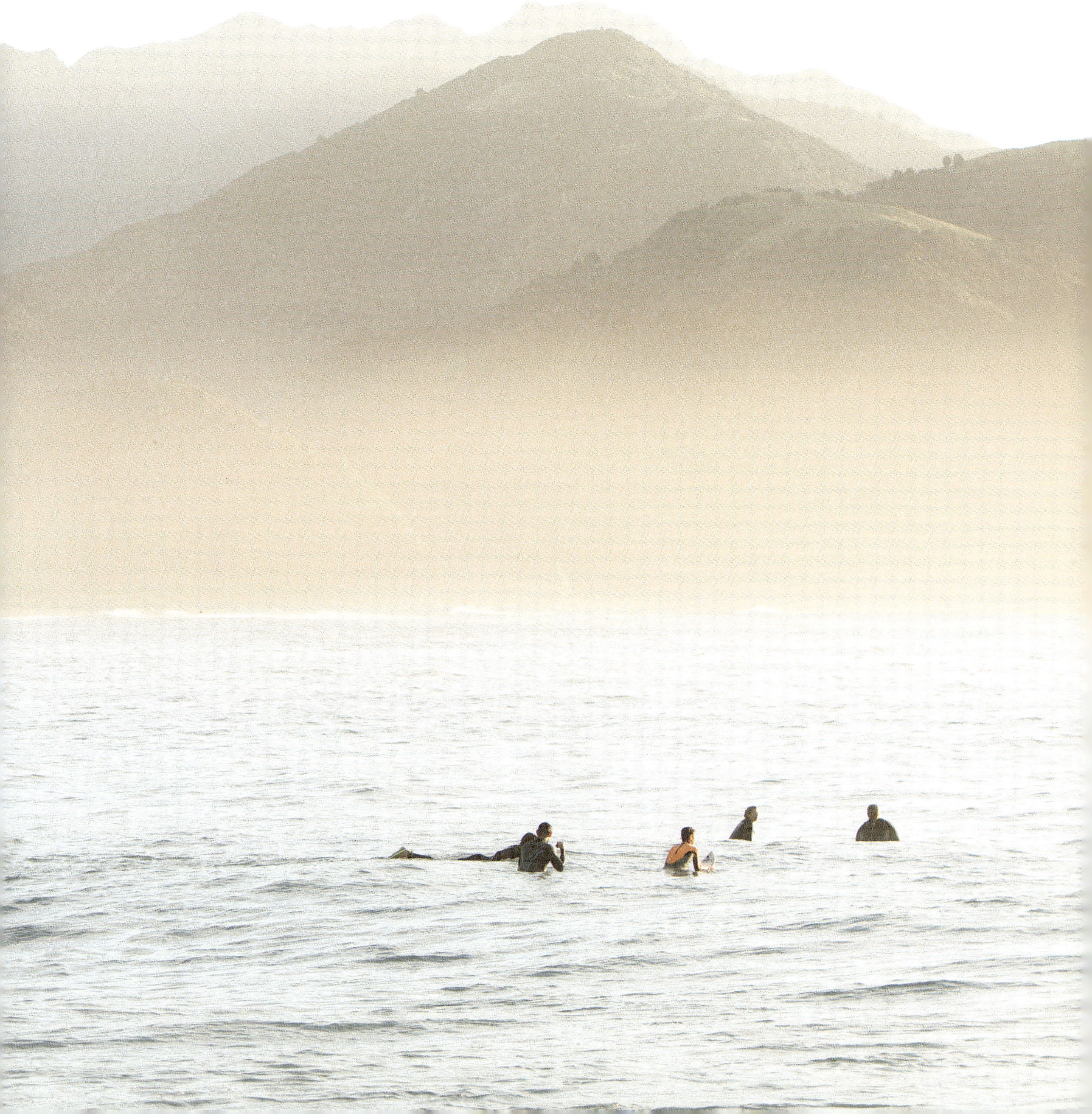

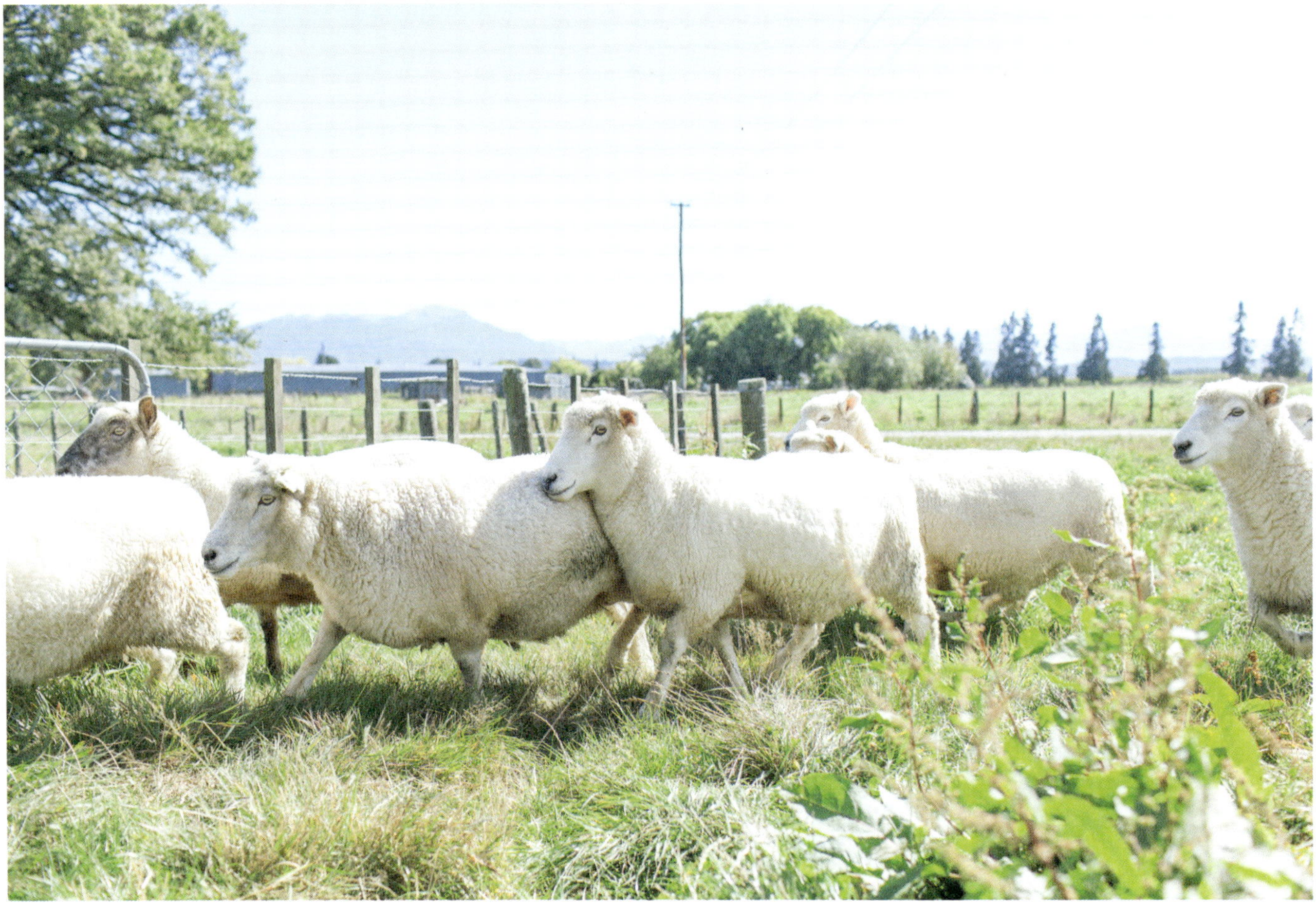

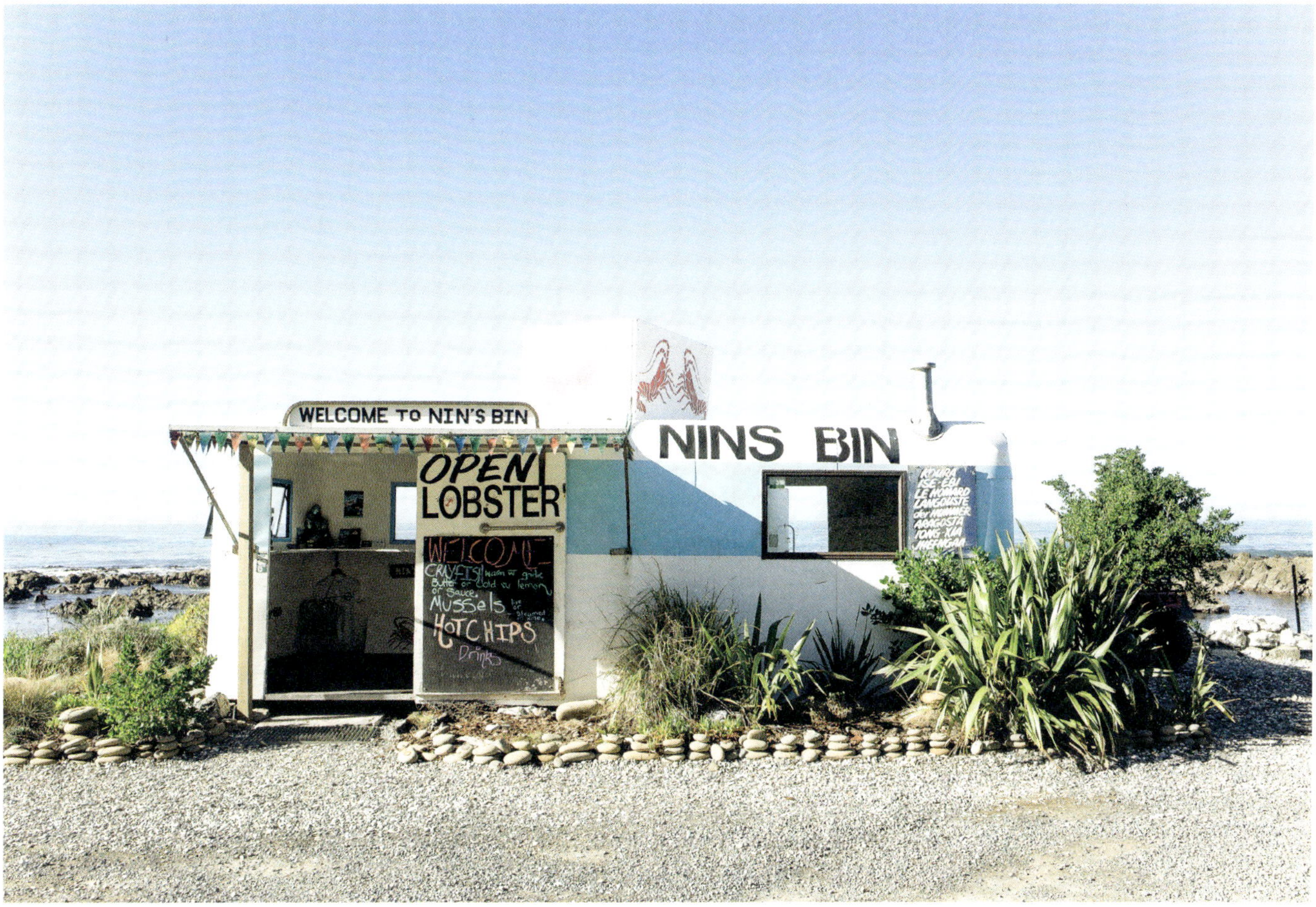
WELCOME TO NIN'S BIN
NINS BIN
OPEN
LOBSTER
WELCOME
CRAYFISH
Butter or Cold w lemon
or Sauce.
Mussels
HOT CHIPS
Drinks
KOURA
ISE-EBI
LE HOMARD
LANGOUSTE
der HUMMER
ARAGOSTA
LONG XIA

New Zealand may not have seen the rise and fall of empires or had the likes of Shakespeare walk its streets, but our country has an intrepid history all its own, something I was only now beginning to appreciate.

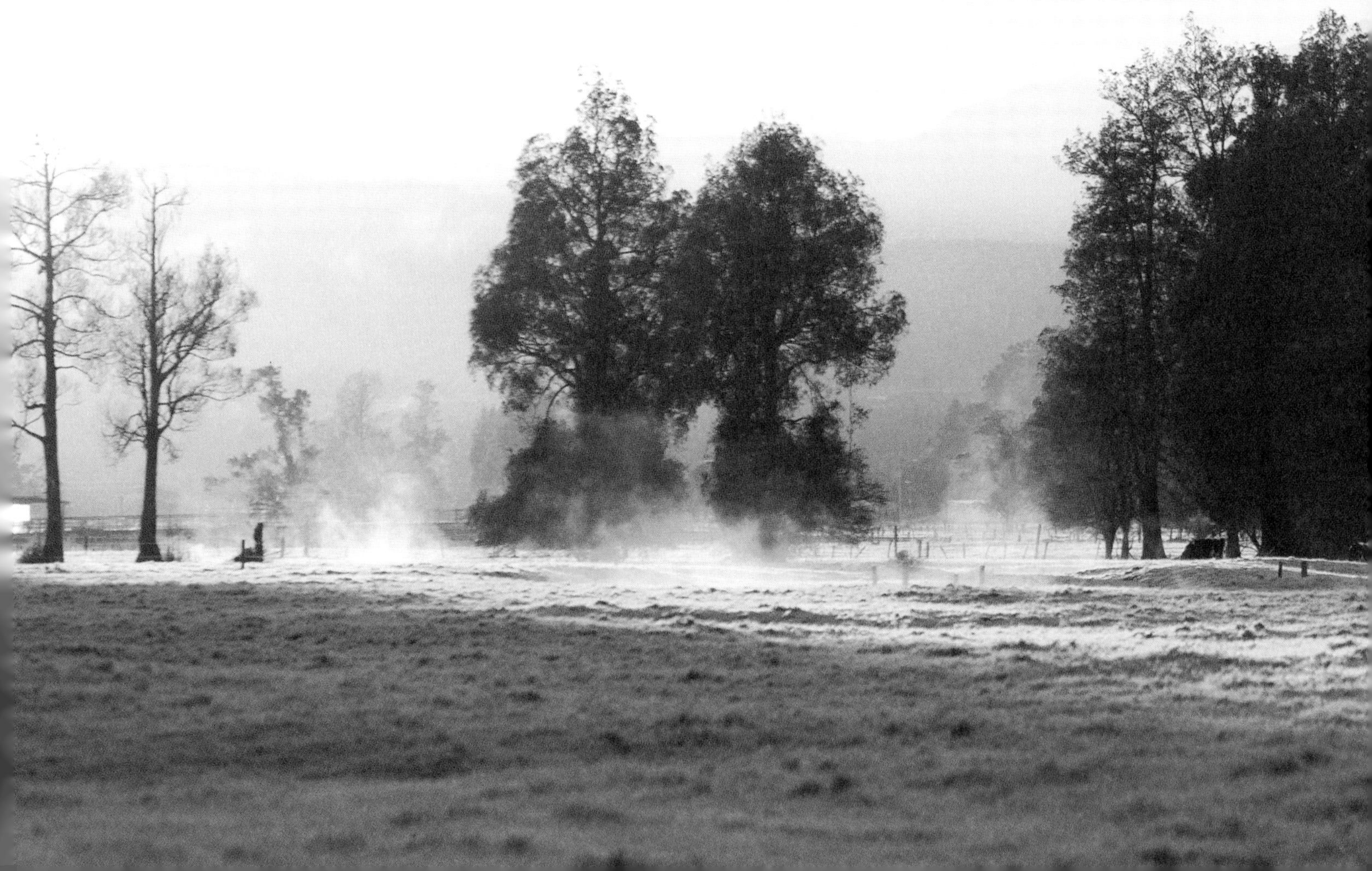

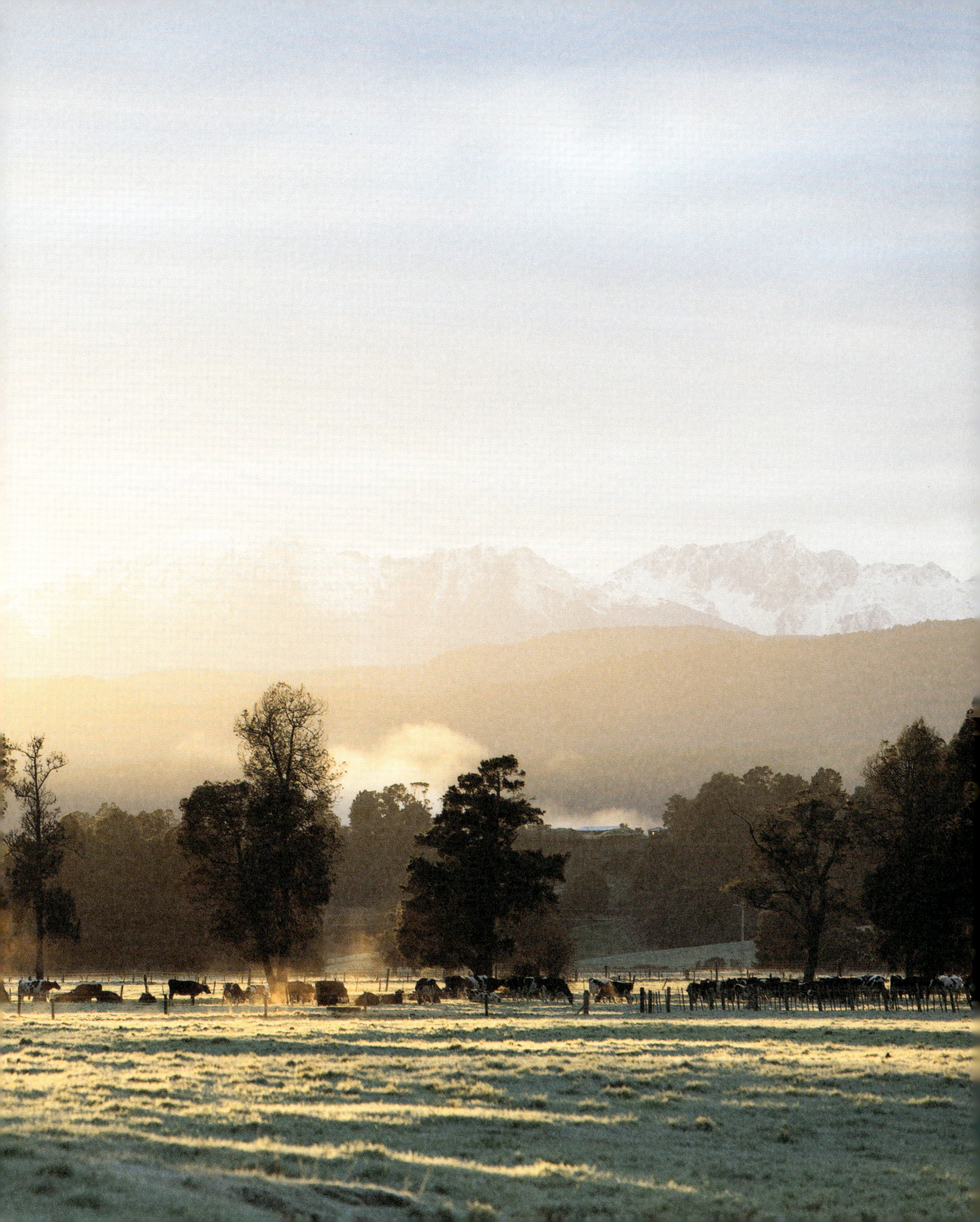

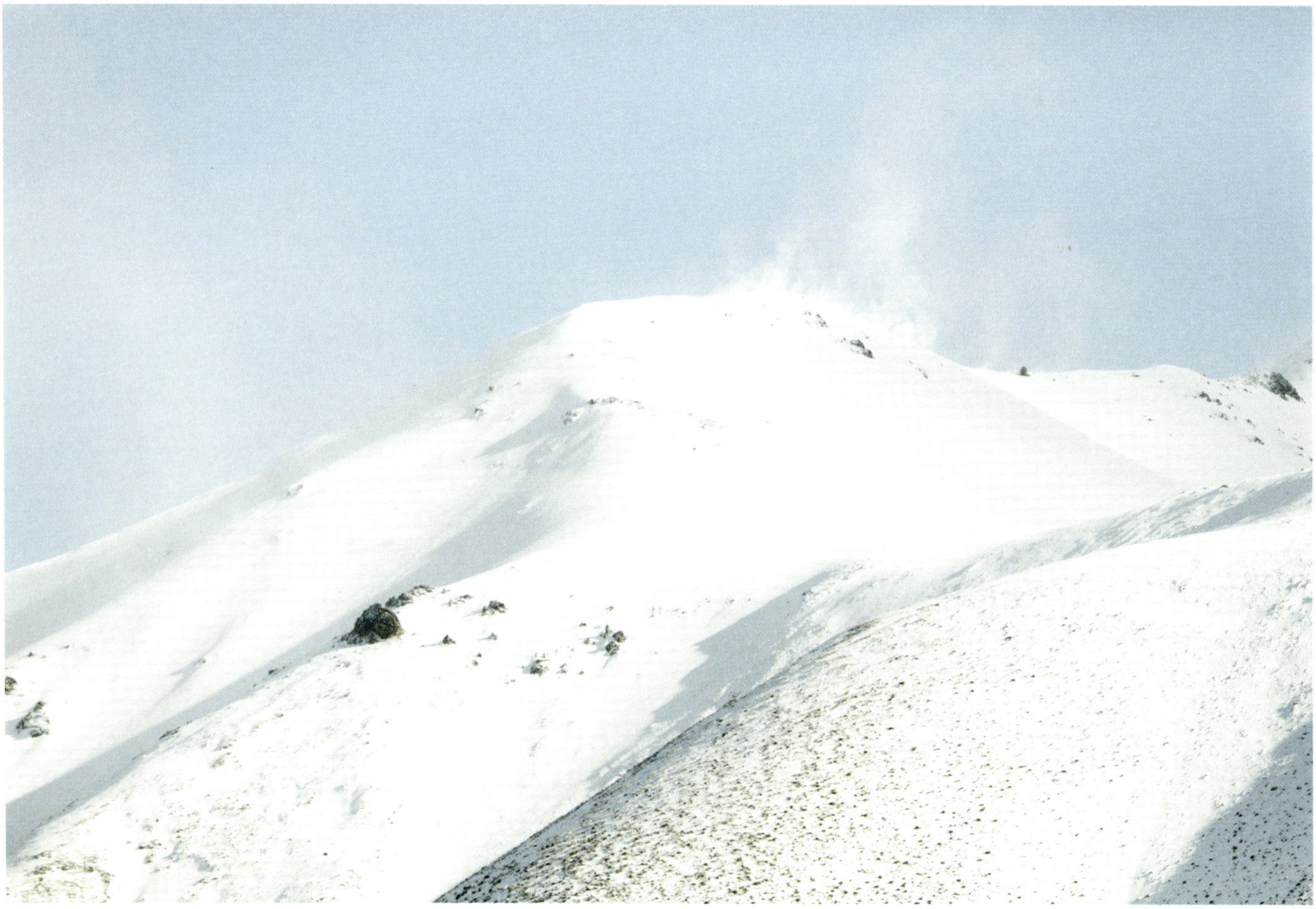

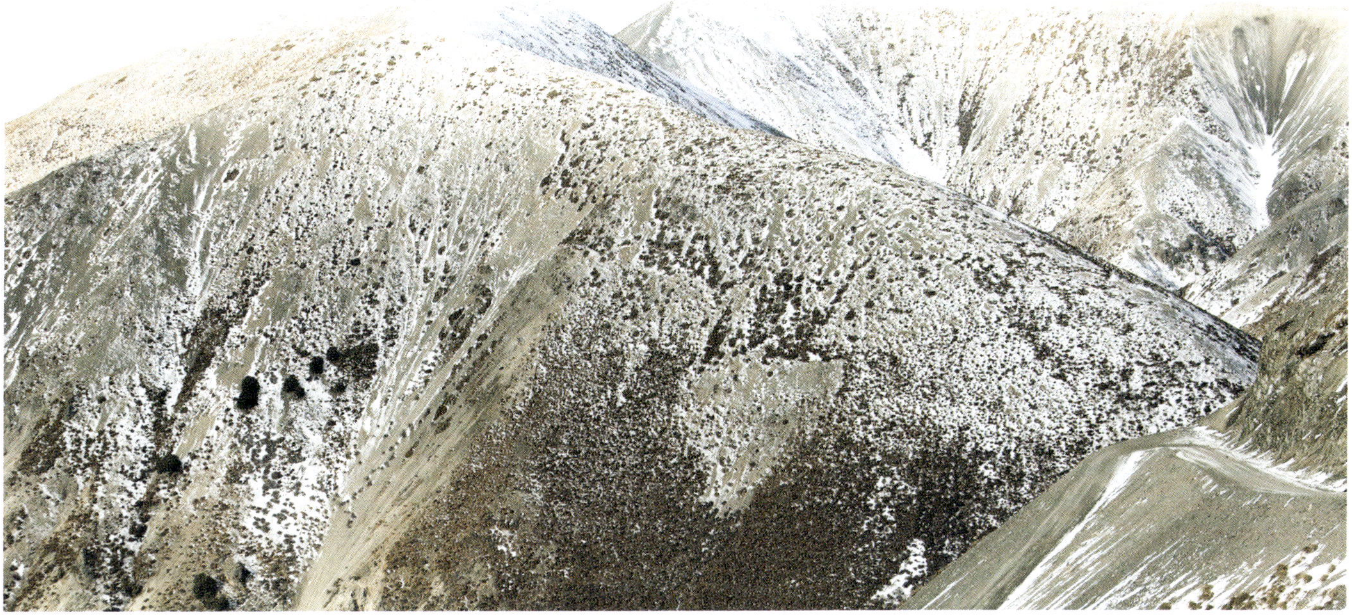

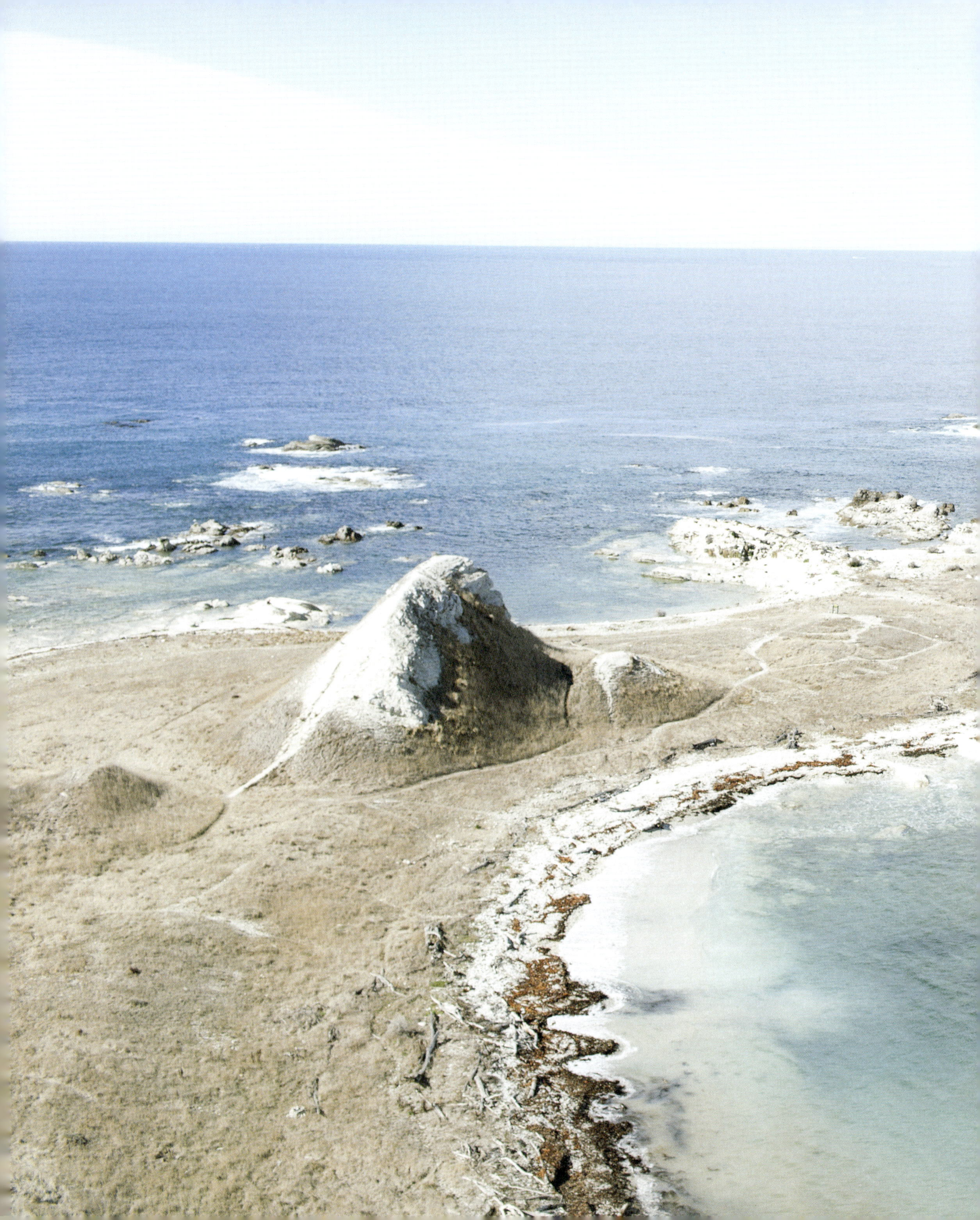

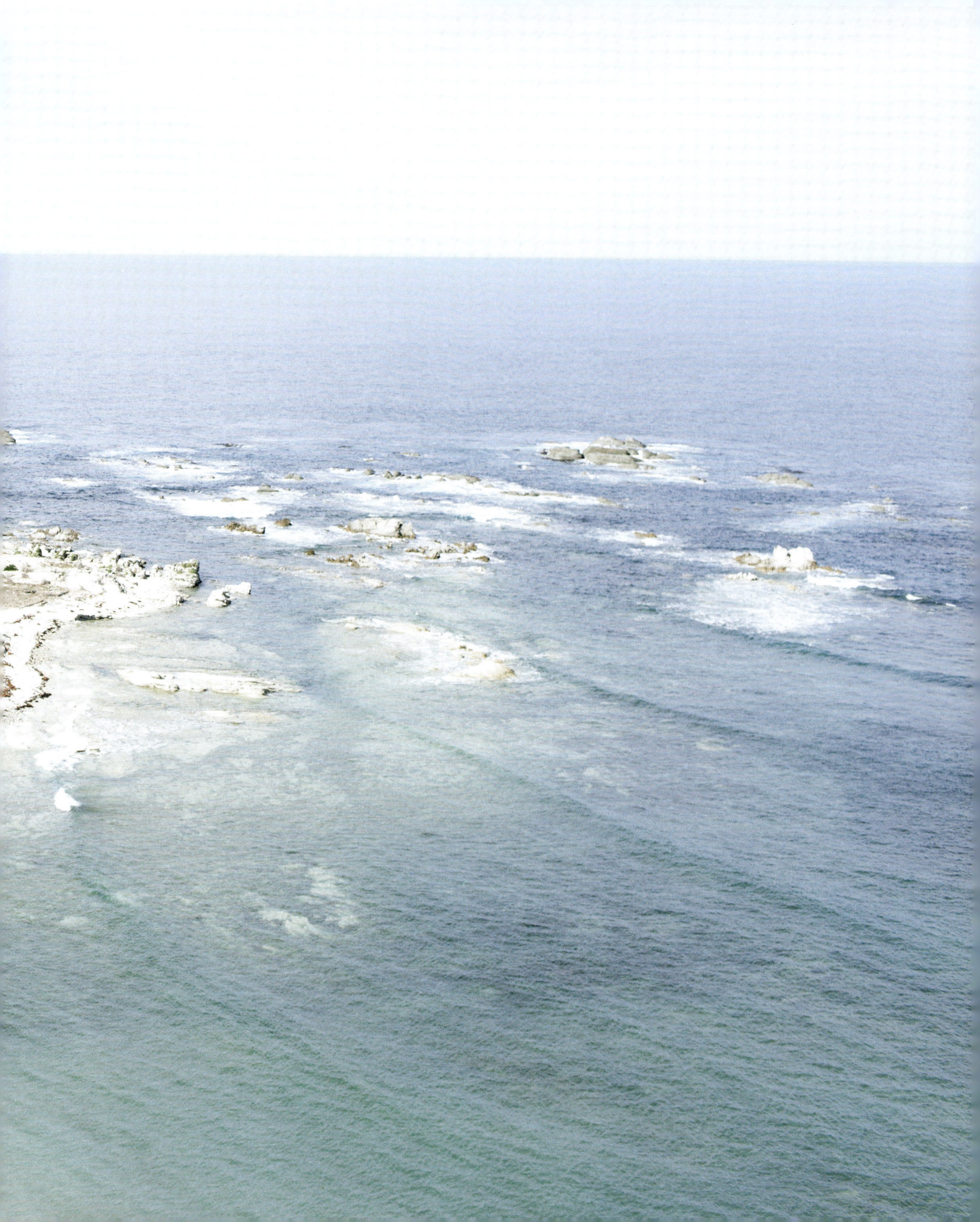

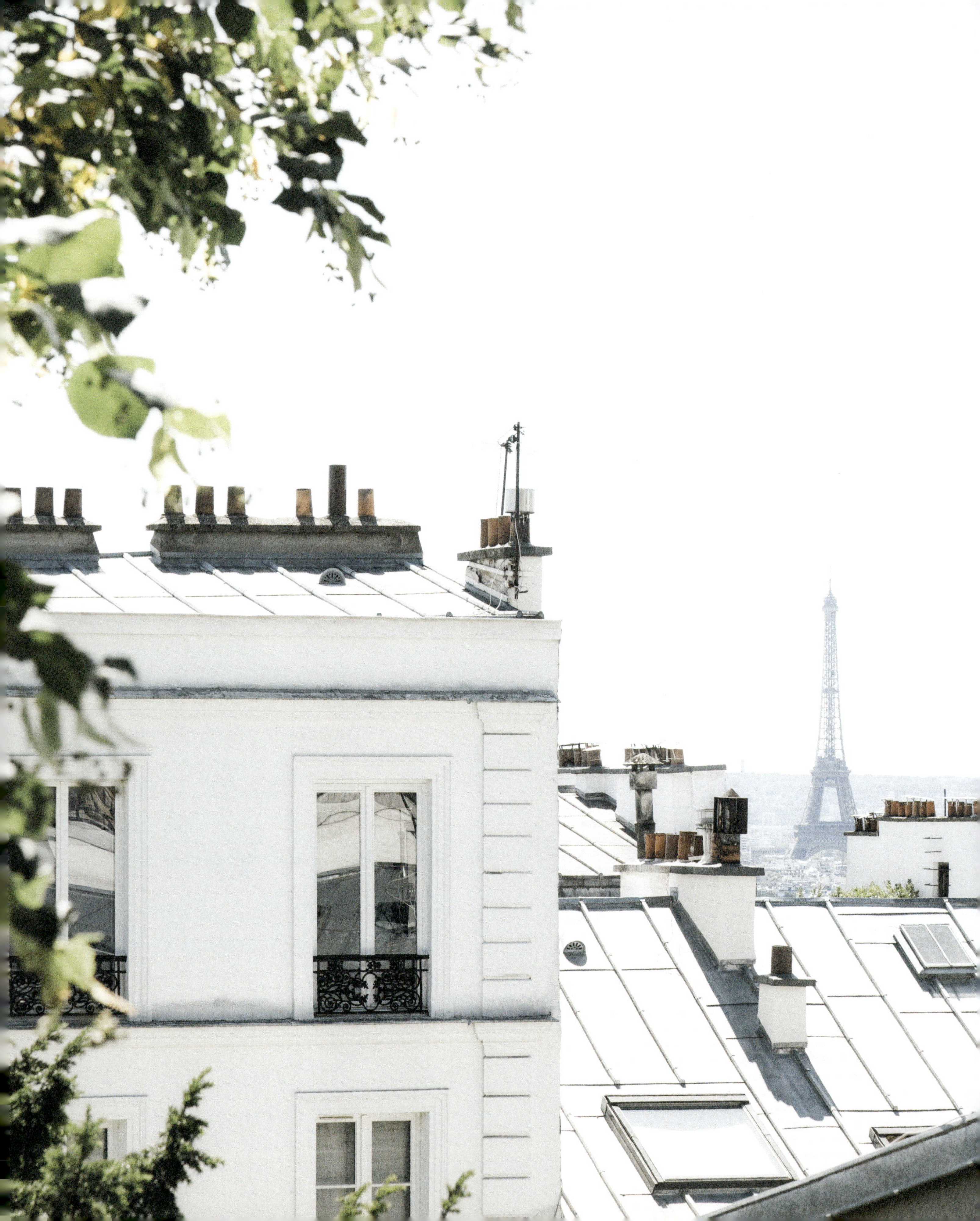

FRANCE

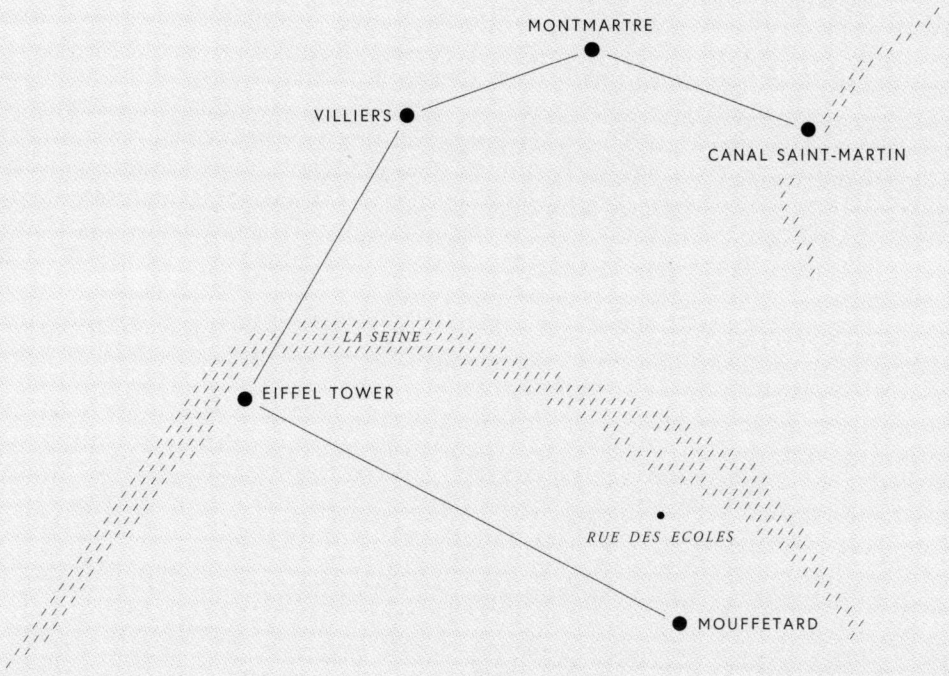

WORDS BY FRANCOIS LE BLED

PHOTOGRAPHS BY MATT PORTER

ILLUSTRATIONS BY PHOEBE ATKEY

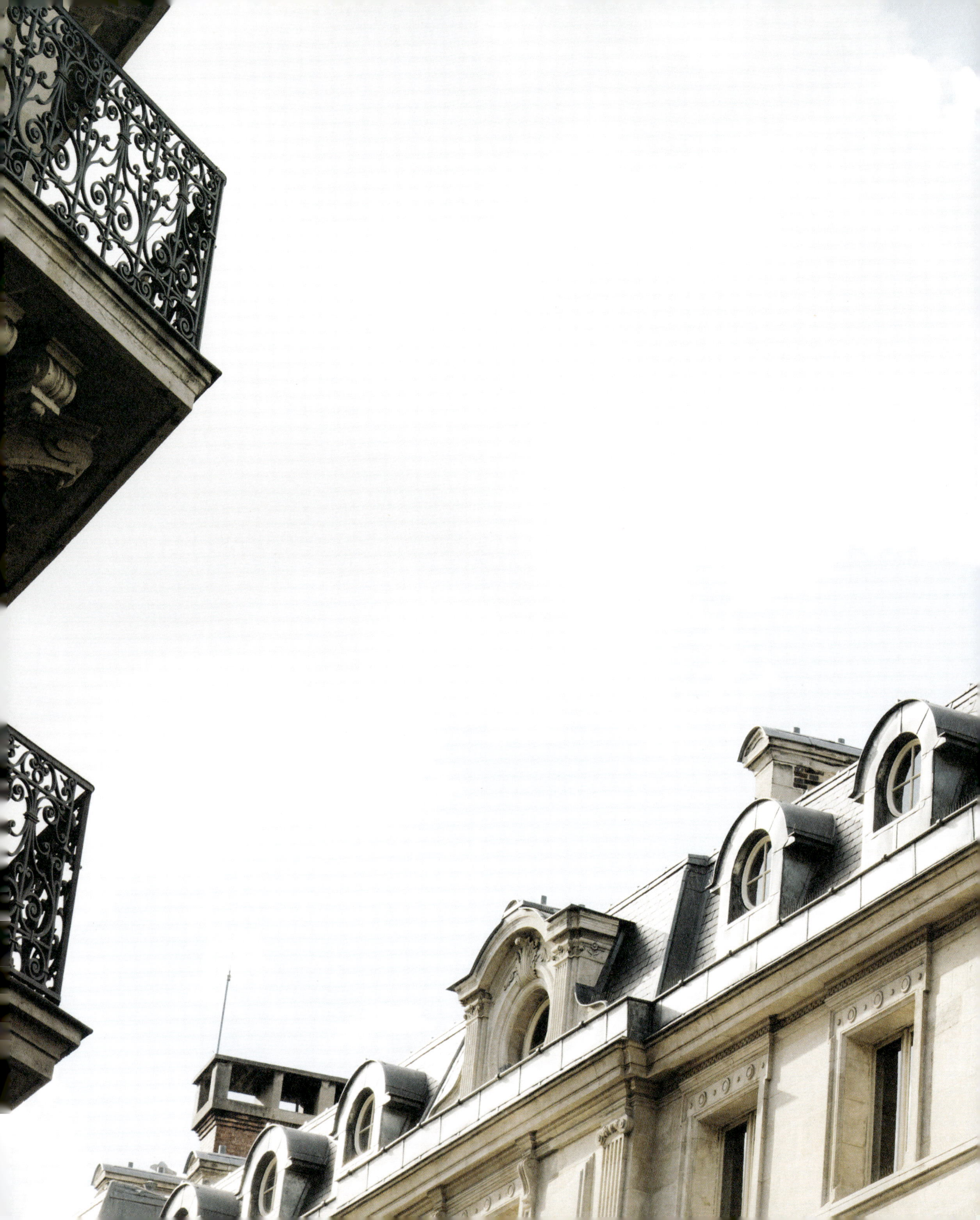

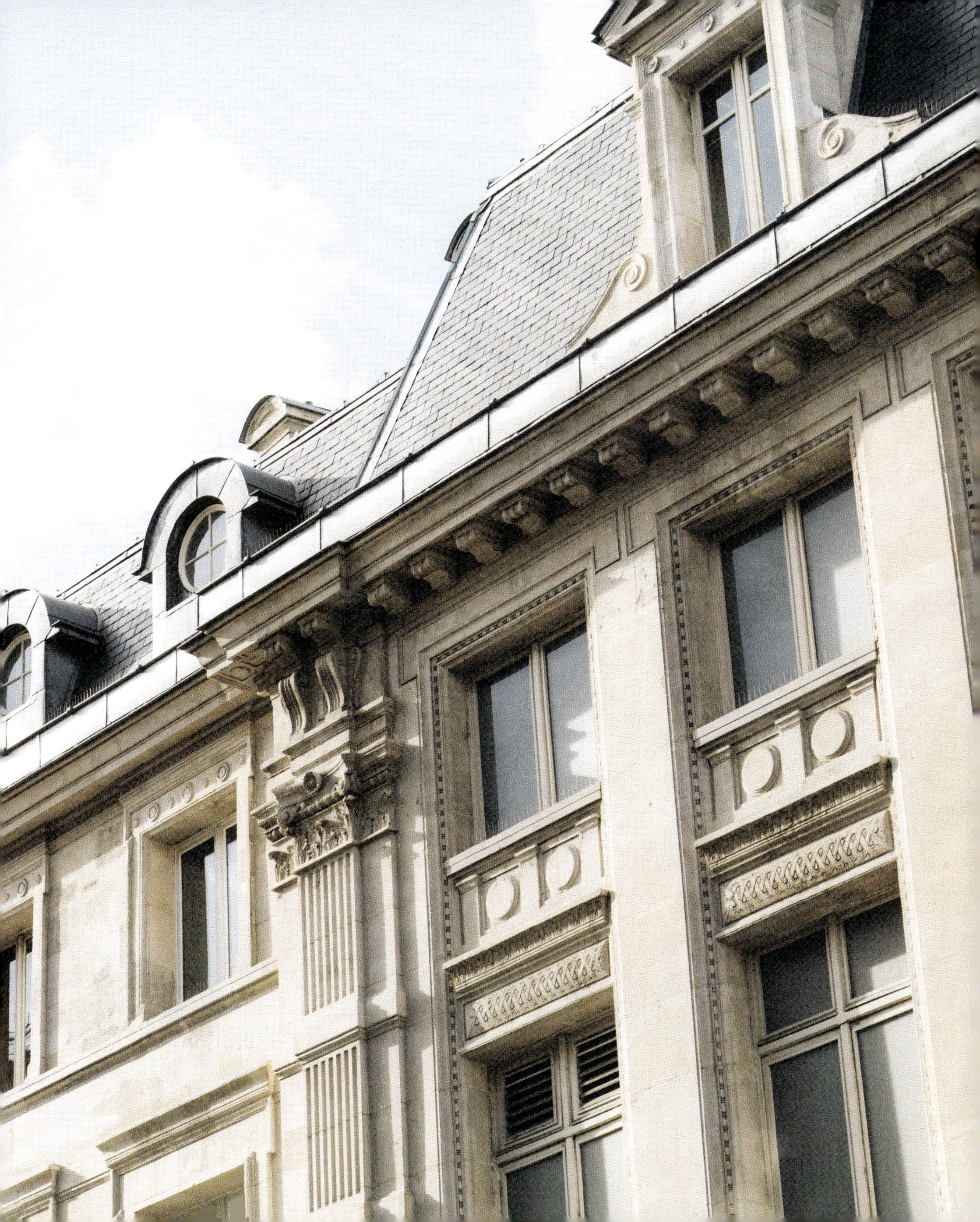

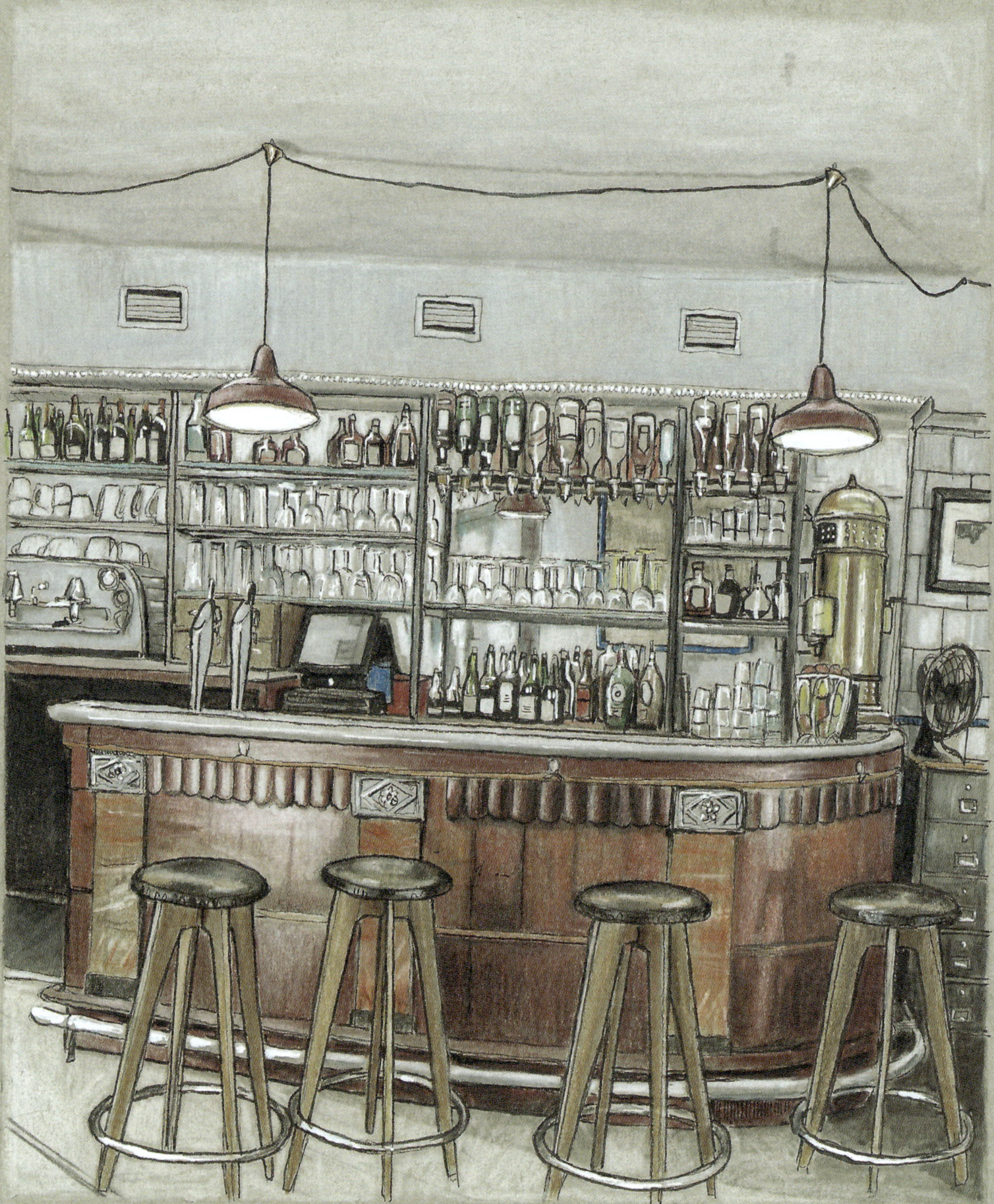

A Moveable Feast

Being a foodie in Paris comes easily. In fact, the French capital offers so much in the way of culinary experiences that narrowing down your choices can become a bit of a problem – albeit a delicious one. So, when my photo-taking companion and I embarked on a weekend-long culinary odyssey through Paris, we challenged ourselves to unearth typical and not so typical food establishments alike. There was no fixed route, no overly-planned itinerary, just comfortable shoes and big appetites.

At 7 a.m. on a quiet Saturday morning, Paris was nearly lifeless – for this is a city fond of summer lie-ins. But behind the Art Deco exterior of 78 Avenue de Villiers, *pâtissier* Kévin Lacote and his team were already bustling away in their kitchen. Cake tasting, just moments from the Champs-Élysées, was to be our introduction to this place of culinary artistry. Since earning his reputation as a top pastry chef, Kévin's KL Pâtisserie is never empty, and we joined the customers queuing at the doors, eagerly waiting for the opening hour to strike.

Everything in Kévin's kitchen is done with purpose and it was a joy to observe the energy and meticulous precision he displayed when producing his award-winning creations, the most iconic being the Kara Damia (a mix of coconut biscuit, caramelised macadamia nuts, sweet dough and milk chocolate mousse). Watching this delicacy take shape next to the zesty Jaune Limone and vibrant Framboise Piper was salivating stuff and as the cakes were set out in their boutique display cabinet, they became more than just artistic sweet treats – they were instead tempting testaments to time, rigour and talent.

Kévin's approach reflects the way food habits and produce accessibility are changing. While Paris is seen by many as the culinary capital of the world, the approach to French cuisine has shifted in recent years. Restaurateurs such as Alain Ducasse and Joël Robuchon still capture the essence of what French cuisine is/was, but TV stars and food bloggers are now also bursting onto the scene. Yet that's one of the great things about food – it evolves. Not just in terms of practitioners, taste and techniques, but also the ways in which we enjoy it, with pop-up cafes, food trucks and festivals growing in popularity. Sinking our teeth into Kévin's pastries, it was clear that our hedonistic wanderings would be leading us far and wide.

Paris is best explored on foot and traversing its many tree-lined avenues (heads turned upwards to appreciate the intricate architecture) we soon found ourselves in the lush garden of Hôtel Amour. Situated in the 9th *arrondissement*, steps away from Moulin Rouge, the hotel offers a tranquil scene made all the more serene by the endearingly gaudy backdrop. Fresh, vibrant salads and a crusty baguette suited the calming atmosphere perfectly and, while feasting on our colourful meal, we plotted our next gourmet destination. But our minds were repeatedly drawn back to the plates before us. Each ingredient was singing out, the flavours both unique and gloriously complementary. And suddenly it clicked – why not make our own dinner? We had the food markets of Paris at our door, a thirst to create and an apartment to boot.

In Paris, food pilgrimages don't just take in restaurants – they also lead you to market stalls and specialist producers, allowing you to experience ingredients first hand while living and shopping like a local. With this in mind, our own pathway led us to Marché Mouffetard, a well-known market on the Left Bank praised by Ernest Hemingway. Our baskets full of fish and other epicurean delights, we sought vegetables from Au Bout Du Champ, a small distribution chain sourcing their fare directly from the farms around Paris. We then called in at La Belle Hortense in Le Marais for wine. This was an inviting, curious place; a bar, wine shop and book store all in one, opened in 1987 by self-proclaimed food activist Xavier Denamur, who champions small restaurants serving all things fresh and local. Taking our time and sampling at least one glass of wine was essential.

Back at the apartment (having taken a detour along Canal Saint-Martin where cinematic darling Amélie freed her goldfish), we let the ingredients speak for themselves; our Parisian dinner comprised of monkfish, cherry tomatoes, asparagus, burnt butter sauce and Burgundy wine, and finished with an apricot and honey pie. What better reminder could there be that the beauty of food in Paris is not just found in restaurants, but in cooking with the bounty of ingredients on your doorstep? People say the best way to discover a city is to aimlessly wander. The same is true with food; walk, buy the ingredients and then improvise at home.

Sunday morning: our goal, after procuring a coffee and croissant, was to have a hamburger from the Le Camion Qui Fume. Recommended by Sebastien Batard from fine food retailer FOOD Y VINO, Kristin Frederick's two mobile food trucks have been making burgers "the American way but with French produce" since 2005 (those after a more conventional meal can head to her specialist meat restaurant in the city centre). The queue at the food truck before it even opened – parked by the National Library François Mitterrand – was proof enough that Kristin's creations are already an institution for Parisian carnivores.

Burger consumed and umami taste buds satisfied, our adventure took us to Bar à Bulles, a brunch spot back in the 9th. Filled with an eclectic mix of modern and vintage furniture, Bar à Bulles is famed for its 'station based' brunch. Your main dish is picked up directly from the kitchen, coffee is taken from where it brews on the zinc counter and a bar station is dedicated solely to bread and butter. From their eggs and bacon to the raspberry cheesecake, brunch here is worth the hype. But be warned, booking is mandatory and your name will be checked at the entrance … if you can find it. Located on a small street, you climb a flight of stairs (that could lead anywhere) to discover a tranquil rooftop garden that feels worlds away from the hullabaloo below.

It was here, basking in the summer sun and in awe of the setting, that we pondered the Paris we'd seen and the food spots that had left us full, content and, if anything, a little lethargic. As we prepared to leave this wondrous city a final coffee was clearly in order. Café Kitsuné in Galeries du Palais-Royal (former residence of the writer Colette) met all our requirements – quintessential Parisian architecture, a great espresso and a warm smile from the barista. Could there have been a more atmospheric end to our French foodie adventure? ★

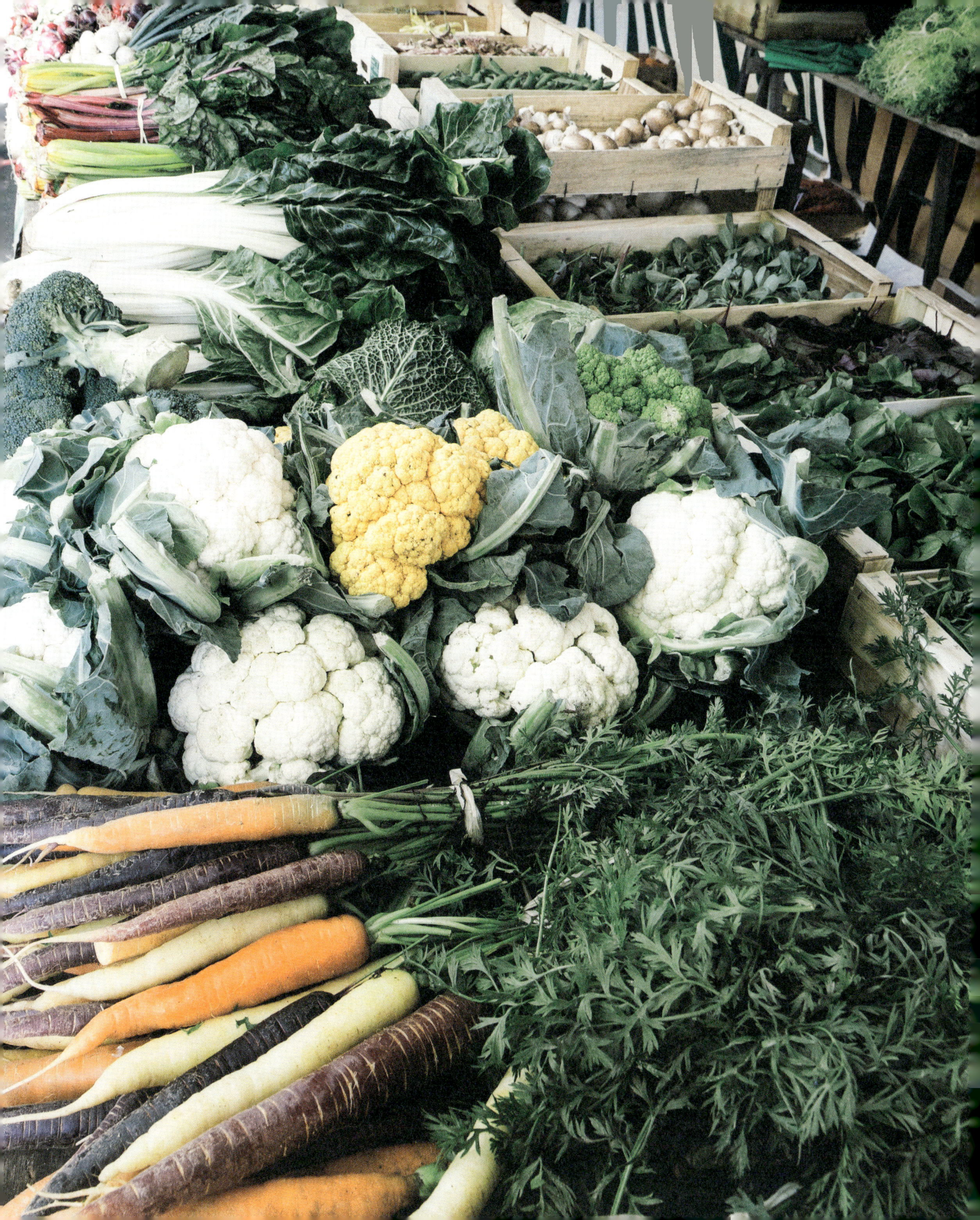

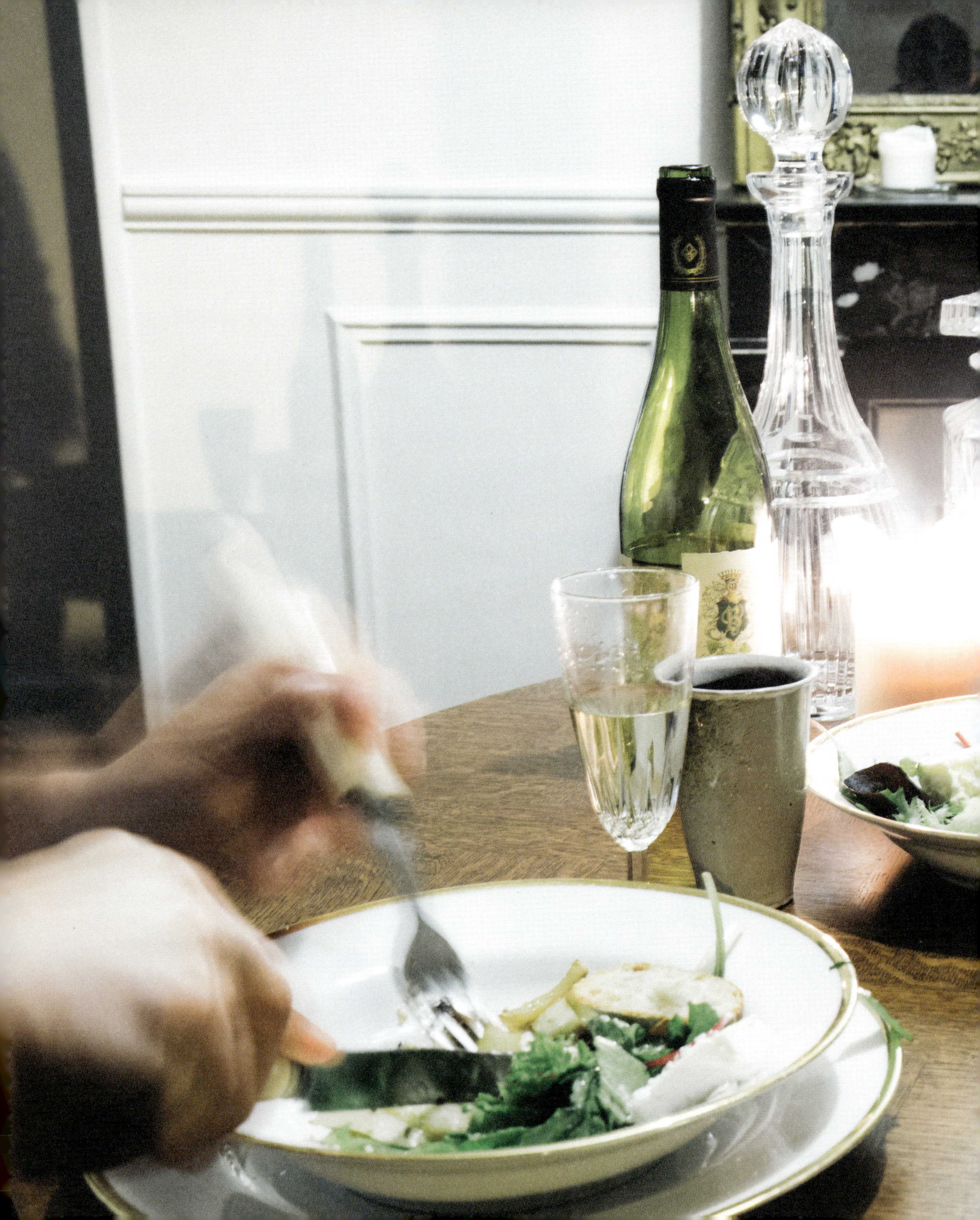

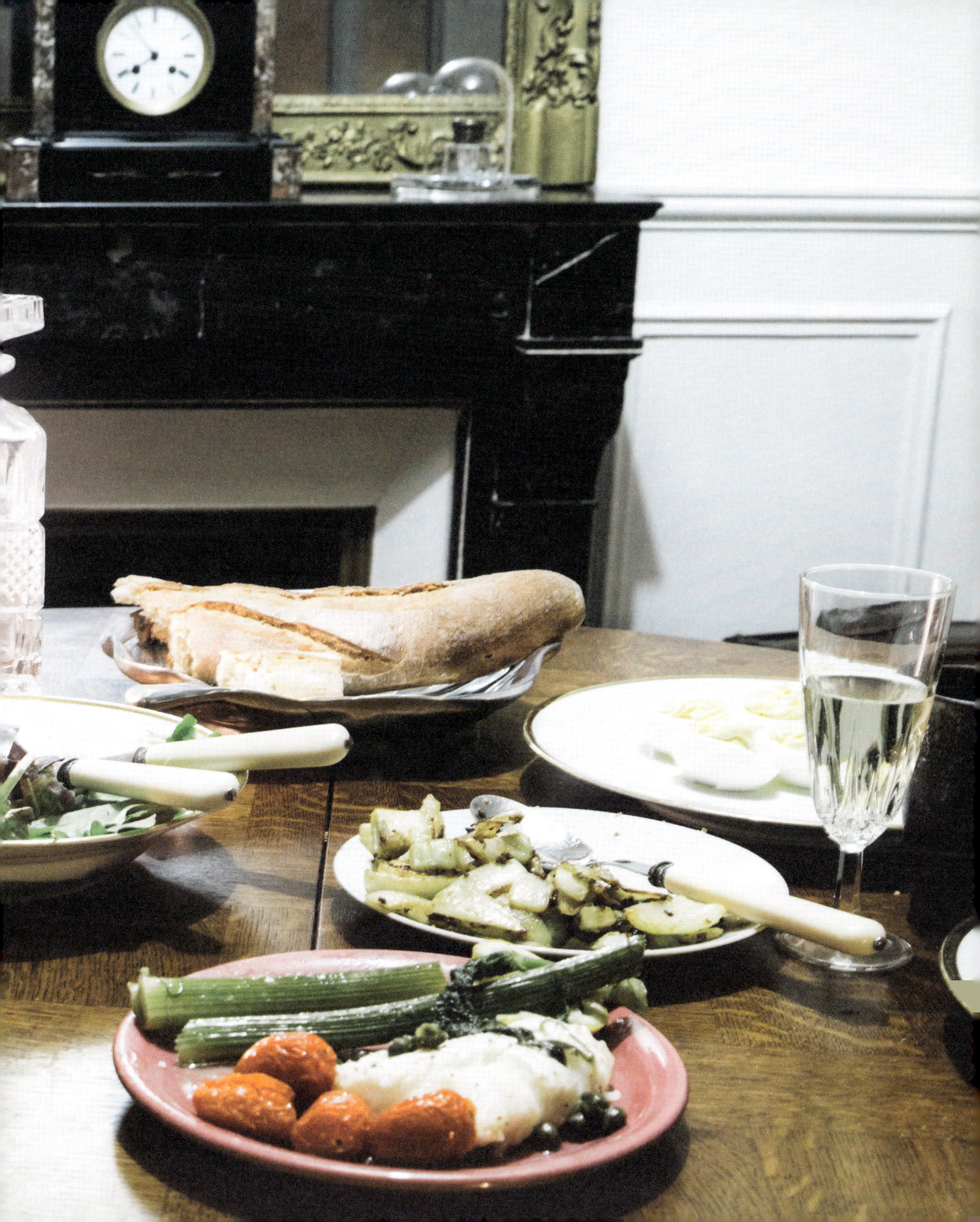

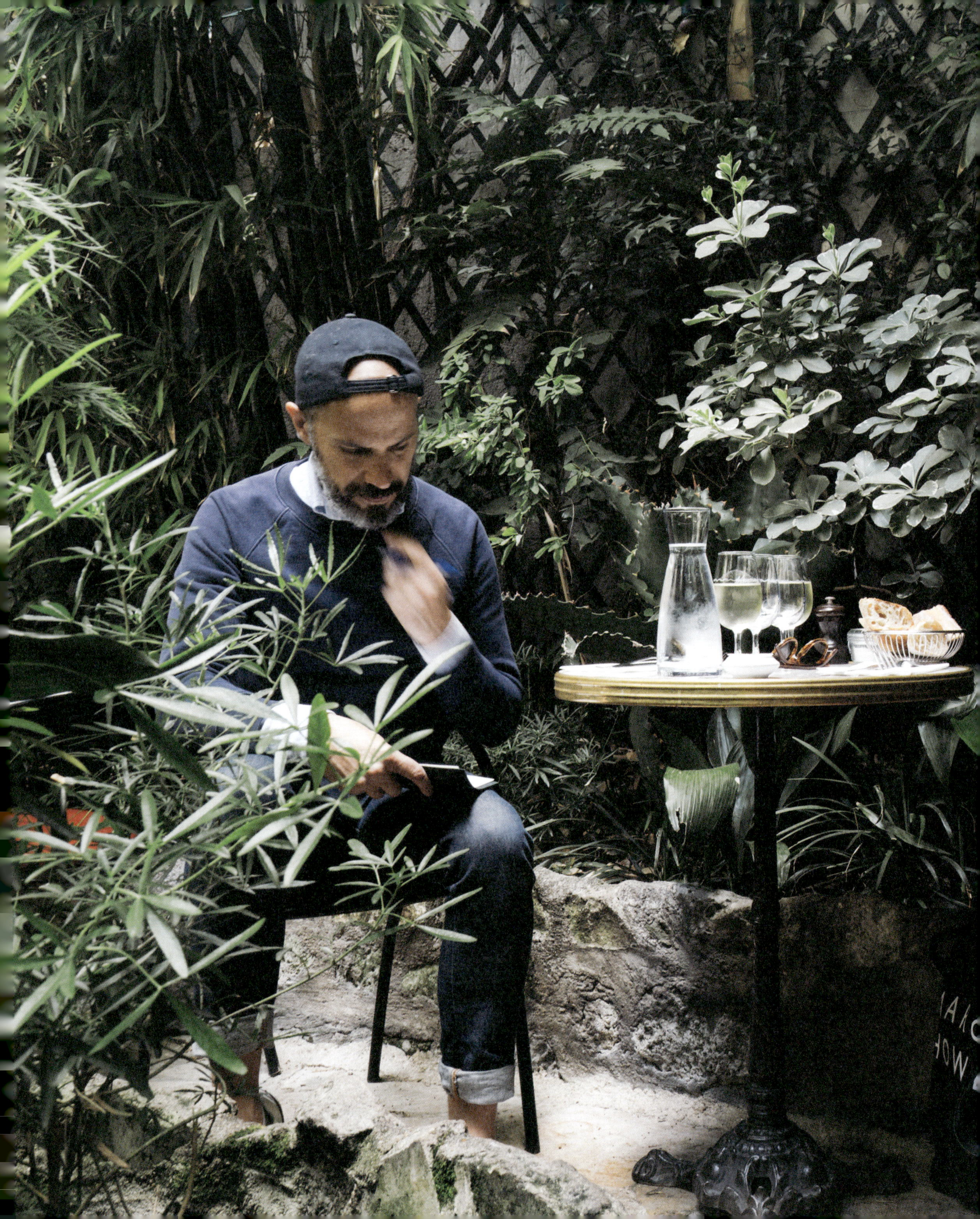

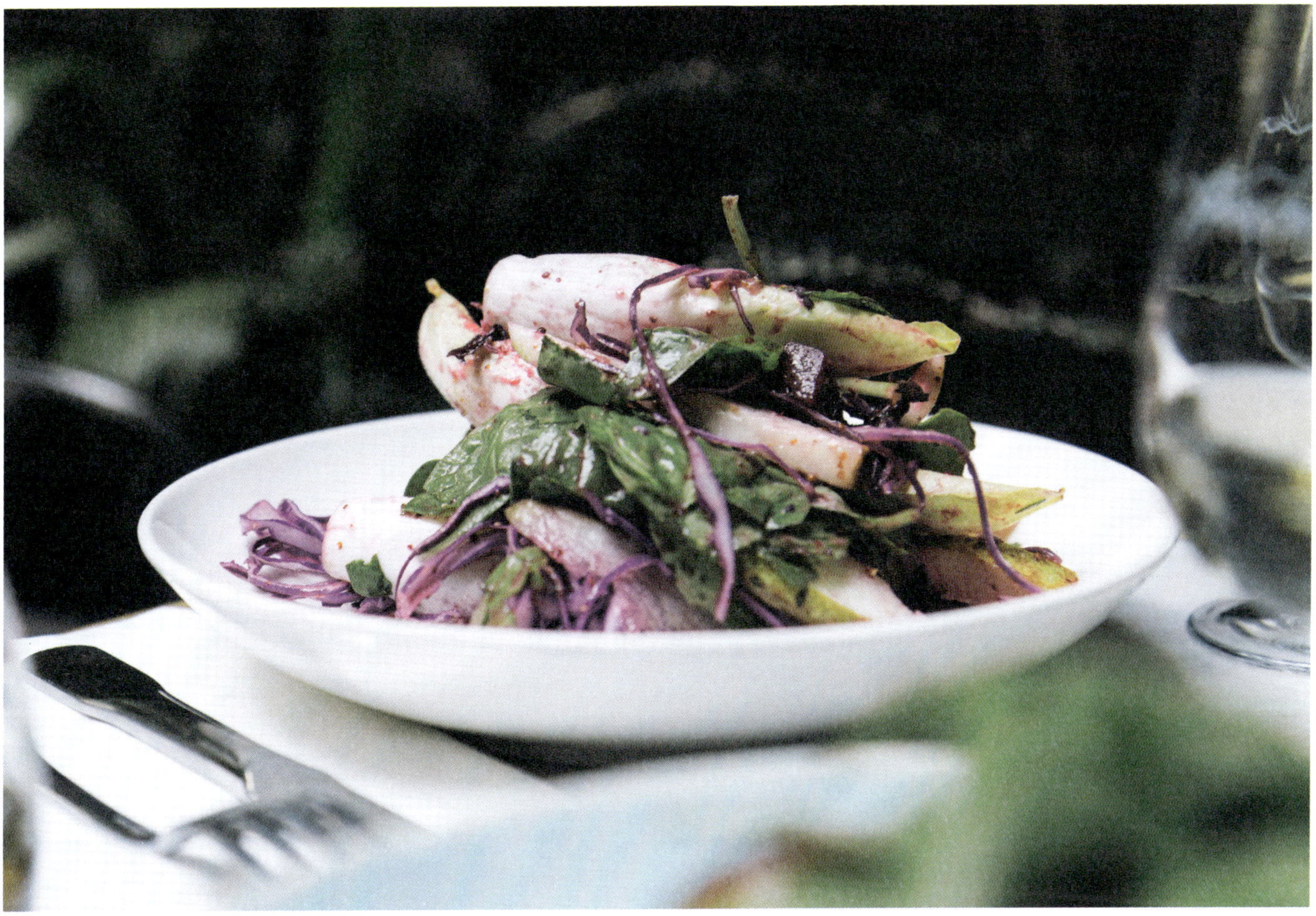

Savouring the vibrant fare served at Paris' Hôtel Amour.

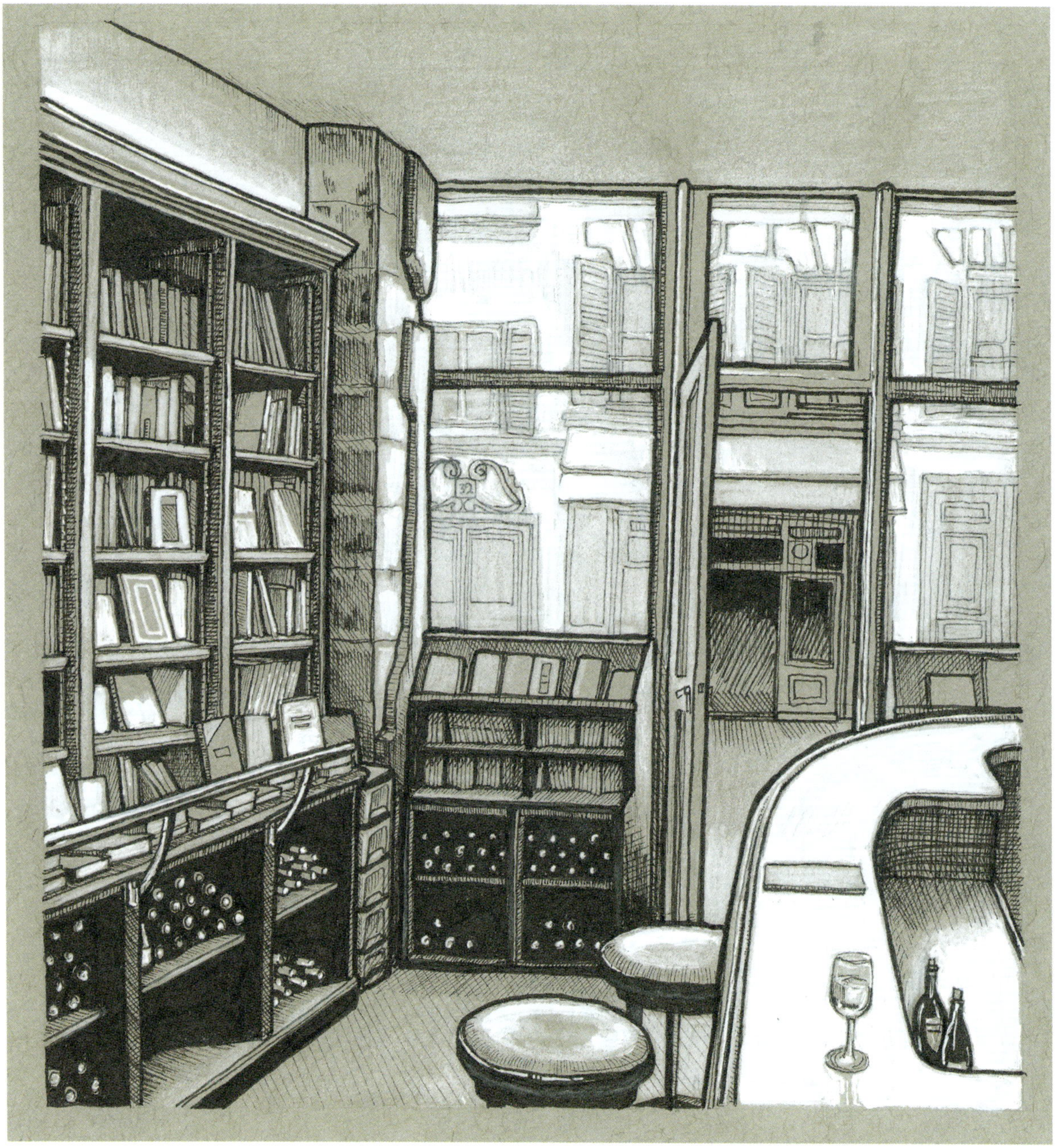

In fine company (with wine and books) at
La Belle Hortense in Le Marais.

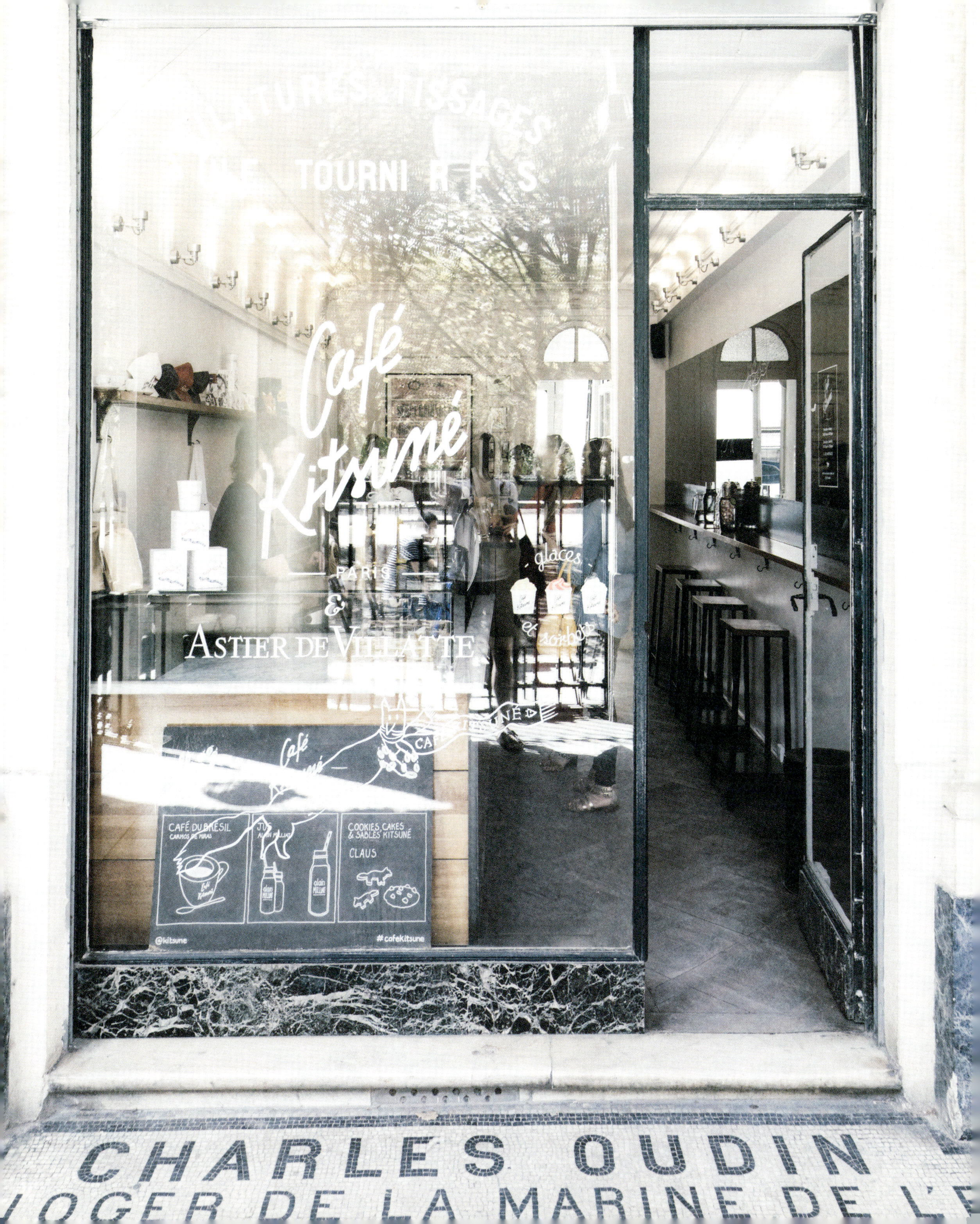

Café Kitsuné
PARIS
&
ASTIER DE VILLATTE
glaces et sorbets
CAFÉ DU BRÉSIL
COOKIES, CAKES & SABLÉS KITSUNÉ
@kitsune
#cafeKitsune
CHARLES OUDIN

USA

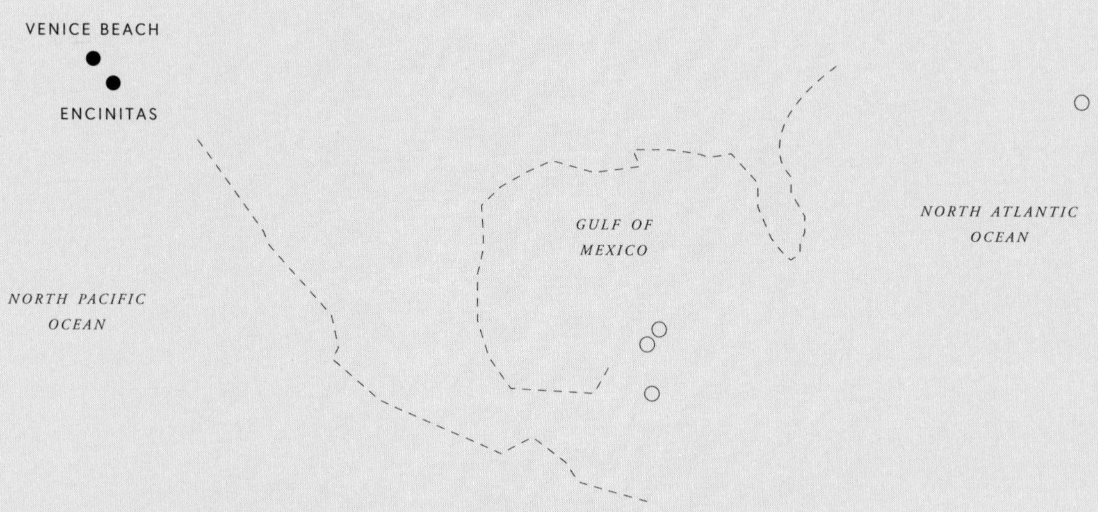

WORDS BY YVETTE EDWARDS

PHOTOGRAPHS BY VIRGINIA WOODS-JACK

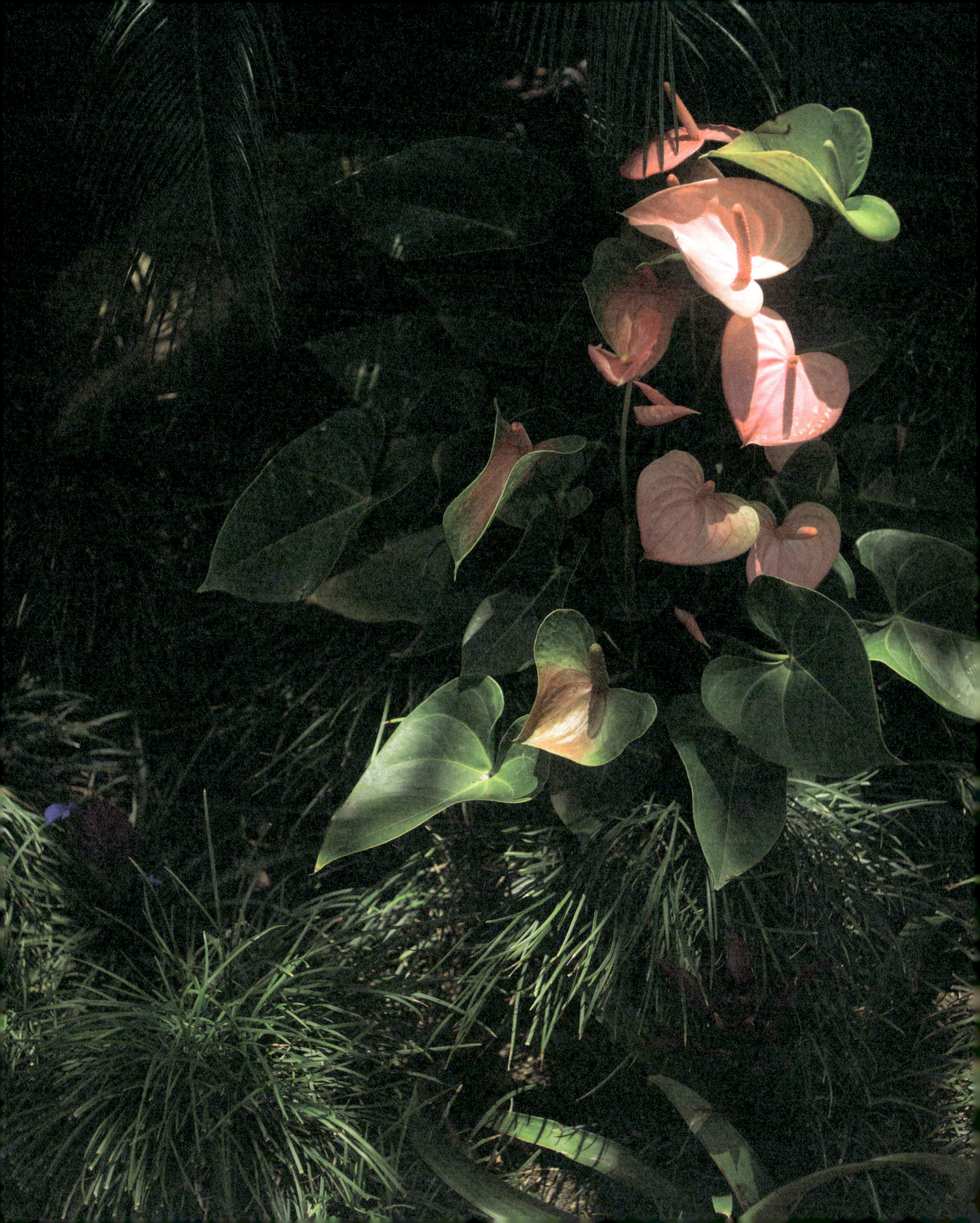

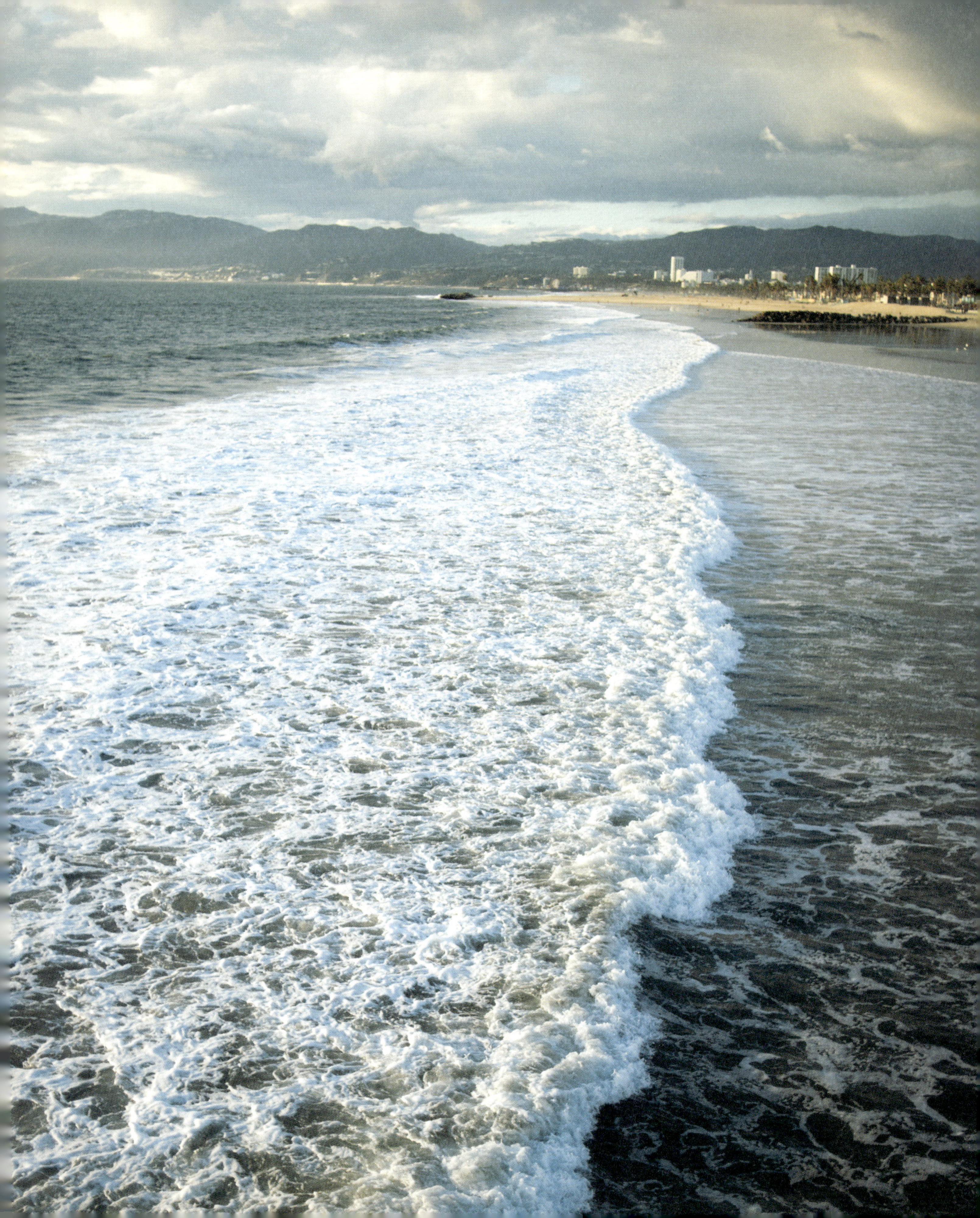

Back to the California Coast

Enamoured with foreign landscapes and the promise of escape, it is difficult to resist the romance of distant shores. Some of these yearnings may remain idle, little more than wanderlust-infused daydreams, while others are enough to see us journey into the unknown. Yet, as glorious as the new and undiscovered may be, once we have explored a destination (living like a local and venturing beyond the tourist trail), it's not uncommon to find that there are certain spots we can't help but return to. While first encounters are marvellous, following a pathway back to the familiar can be just as inspiring.

Photographer Virginia Woods-Jack has visited the Californian coast on many occasions, enthralled by its natural wonders and soulful inhabitants. Seeing her depictions of Venice Beach, with its laid-back surfing vibes, and the mellow scenes of the Encinitas area, it's not difficult to imagine why.

From her first visit to these glowing shores, Virginia felt like she was coming home; somewhere she hadn't been for a while that was familiar nonetheless. With the beauty of the scenes and the calm of the people observed remaining constant, each visit was a reminder of that first encounter – a chance to once again capture smiles, soft light and rolling waves. However, Virginia's lens was also drawn to the subtle changes in the landscape, the shifts in mood and colour that arose with the turning seasons. Over time these changes helped bring the setting to life, elevating it from mere 'holiday destination' into something alive and ever-evolving. And so, with each return Virginia asked herself the same question – what would life be like if this was truly home?

It is by revisiting certain destinations that we are able to reflect on the pathways we have chosen: where we find ourselves, where we have been and who we wish to be. From here, far from the constraints of the everyday, we can do more than recall fond memories or sate our inner vagabond. We can instead focus on the minute, appreciate the altering patterns and perfection of nature and plot future journeys surrounded by a setting that remains strangely familiar. We know the scenes around us will transform before we return, and we might too, but it is this sense of possibility that remains forever promising. ⋆

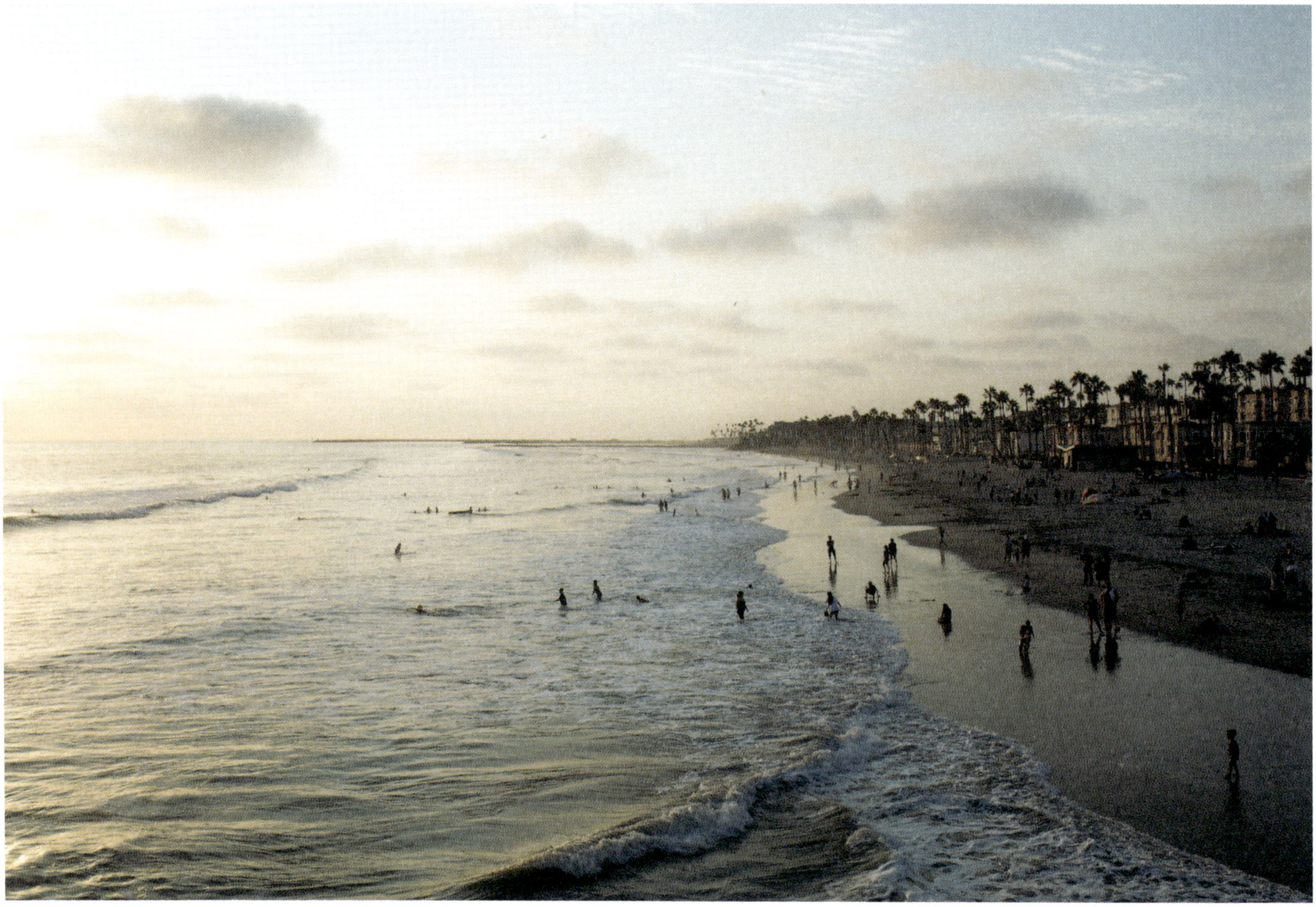

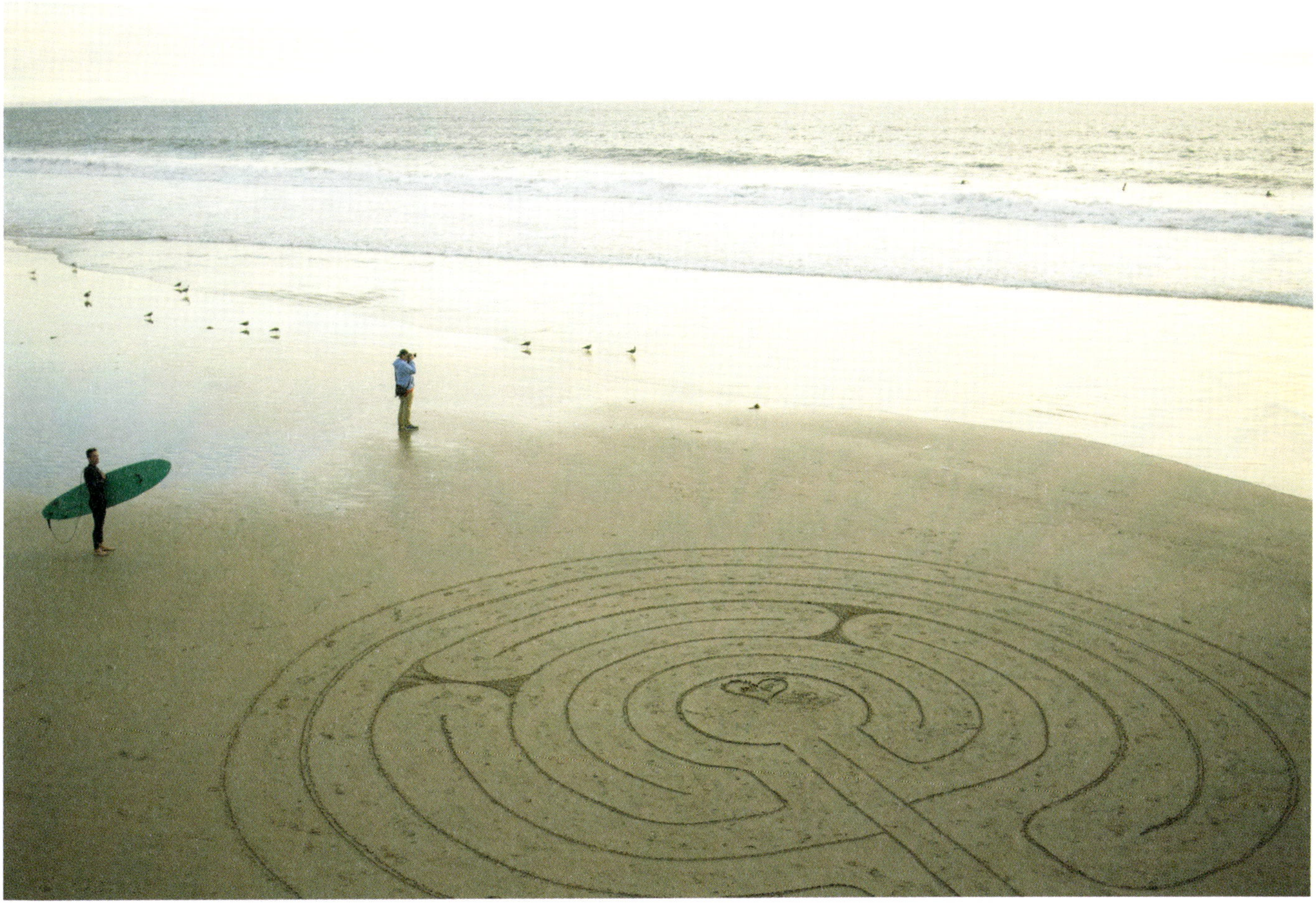

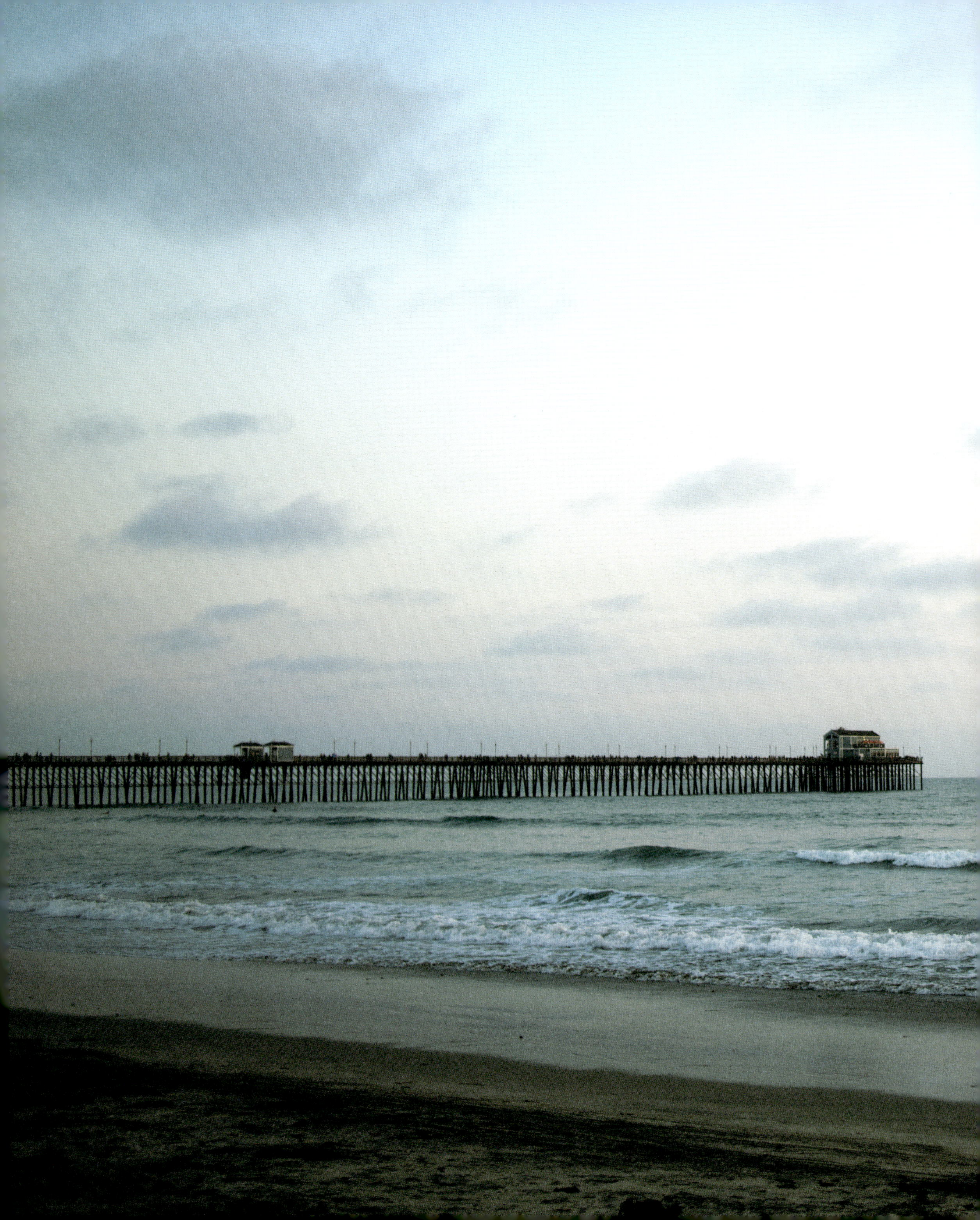

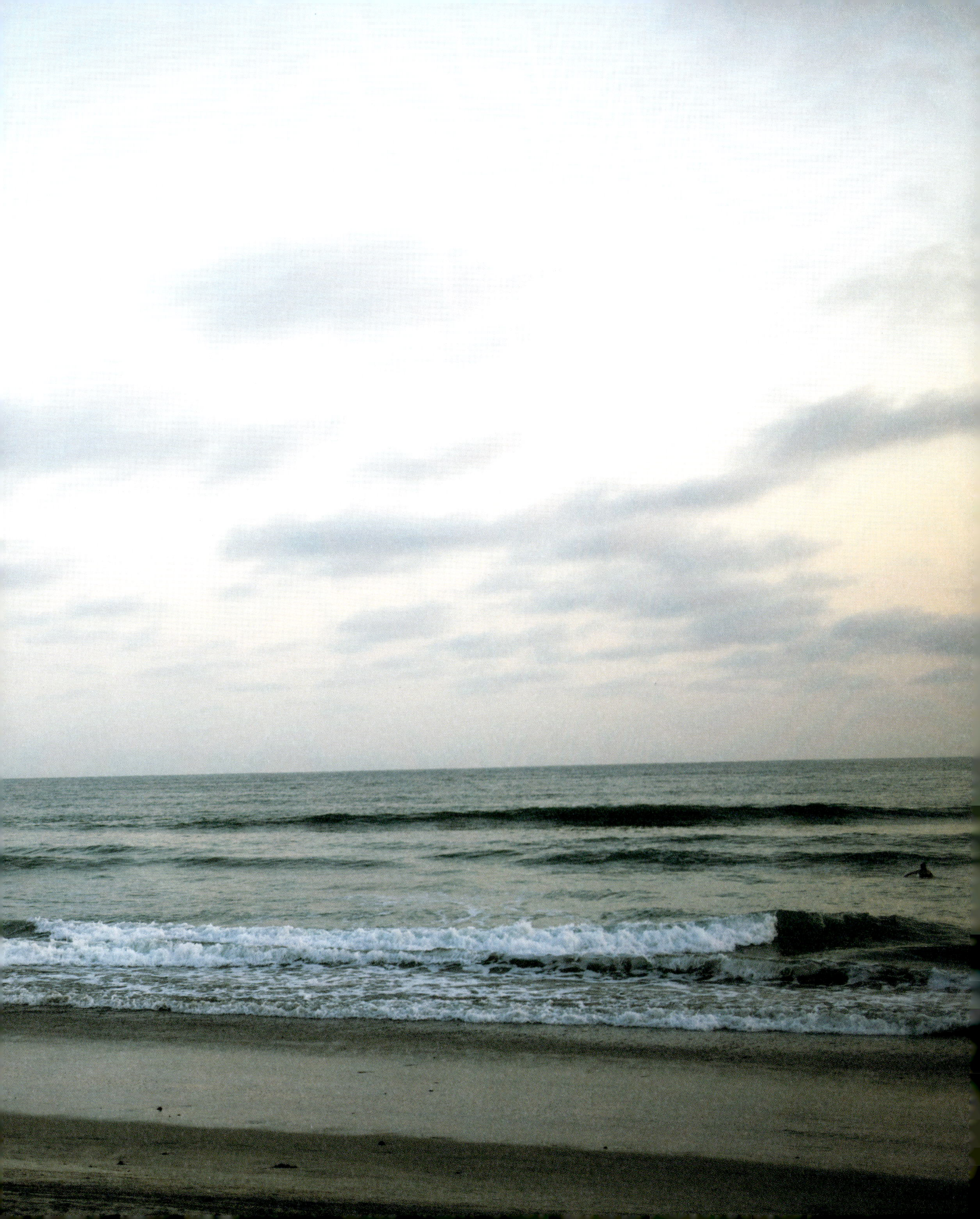

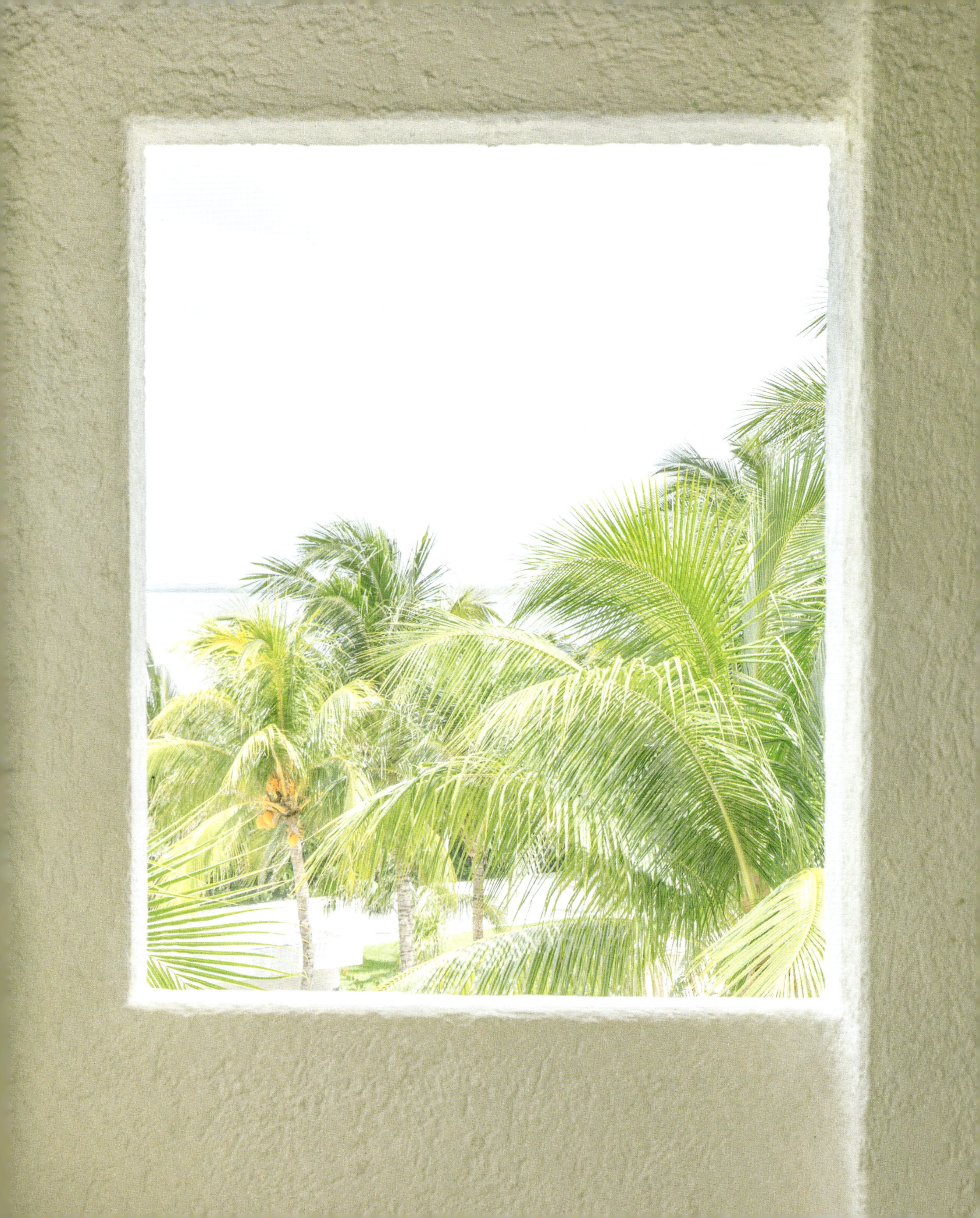

MEXICO

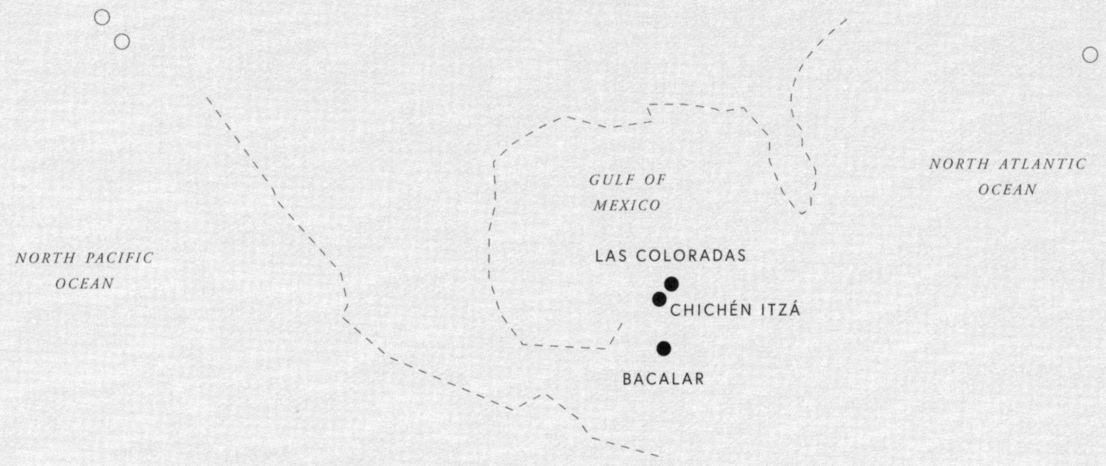

WORDS BY LIZ SCHAFFER

PHOTOGRAPHS BY MARIOLY VAZQUEZ

Captured Colour

No matter how long you live in a country, it's never possible to see it all – something that becomes painfully apparent when you exchange the home you grew up in for a new one across the seas. Living continents away from a place you once knew, it's the scenes unseen that begin to beckon – the great drives, waterfronts and unexplored history you always assumed there would be time for. And so you sometimes find yourself returning home craving not the old stomping ground, but the locations and pathways yet to be discovered.

For Mexico-born, London-dwelling Marioly Vazquez, this longing was for Las Coloradas in Yucatán, a small industrial town famed for its surreal, pastel-pink salt lake. Marioly wanted to photograph this lake, watch clouds dance upon its rosy surface and feel the sun of her homeland. So, having returned to Mexico for a fleeting family visit, she commandeered a car and drove south from Cancún, "to seek a pretty colour in an unexpected place." Her journey was punctuated by a string of small towns whose buildings were covered in coat upon coat of cracked and peeling paint, like tree bark revealing the layers of time.

One such town was Bacalar, where you'll find Laguna de Bacalar (Lake of Seven Colours), an incredibly clear body of water that changes its hue depending on the depth of the sand and reservoirs below. "The light was perfect for photographing," muses Marioly. "When I moved to the UK I really missed that sun and vibrancy. It's different. I think in the UK you get a more melancholic feeling in the photography and in Mexico you can feel the passion. You get more emotion."

Marioly suspects she will return to Bacalar, but is not so sure about Las Coloradas. The salt lake was everything she imagined, but there is something poetic about it remaining a memory. "It was magical that first time and I will always remember it as magical, something I did that's in my heart. I want to leave it that way. Las Coloradas is not touristy. There are no hotels, no places to eat. You just go and then you leave. You're a passerby. I think that makes it more special because there's something almost ephemeral about it. It's there and then you're gone and you don't know if you're coming back. So you need to enjoy the moment while you have it."

The importance of memory, of treasuring those icons from home we are fortunate enough to see, rang true when Marioly stopped at the Mayan pyramid Chichén Itzá on her drive back to Cancún. She was here to pay her respects to her ancestors, something she hadn't initially planned on doing. "I didn't photograph much because it was my first time there and I wanted to focus on senses other than the visual. All these places are incredibly powerful, there's a certain energy. I wanted to connect with the structure, to feel it rather than photograph it, so I put my camera away and just enjoyed being present."

It's strange how faraway shores can make us long for home, and how home, when we get there, can be the reminder needed to travel further, be in the moment and see a place for what it is. We'll never experience all that our homelands have to offer – time is unfair like that – but wouldn't it be wonderful if what we encountered helped us to pause and appreciate the world's immensity? Even as passersby. ⋆

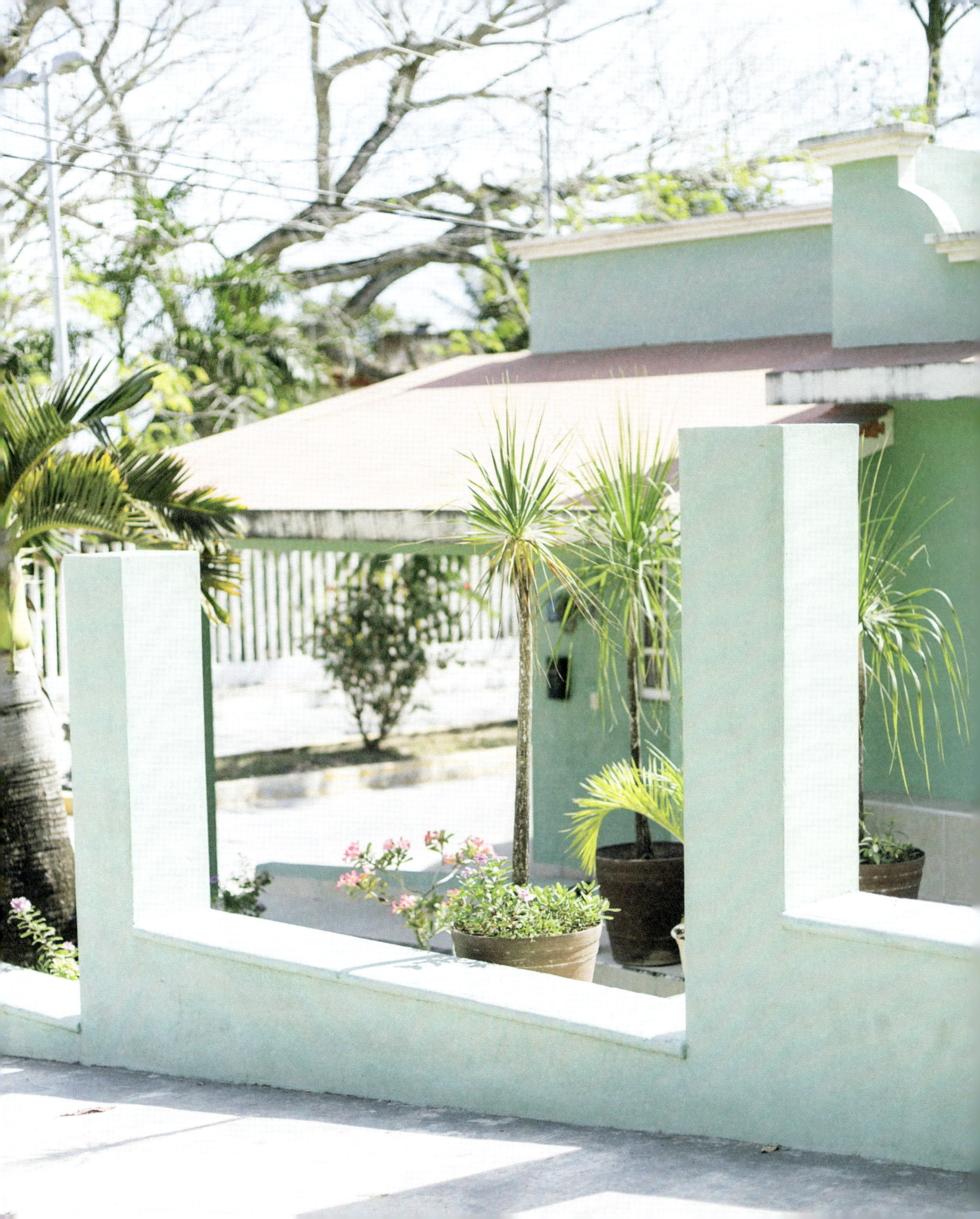

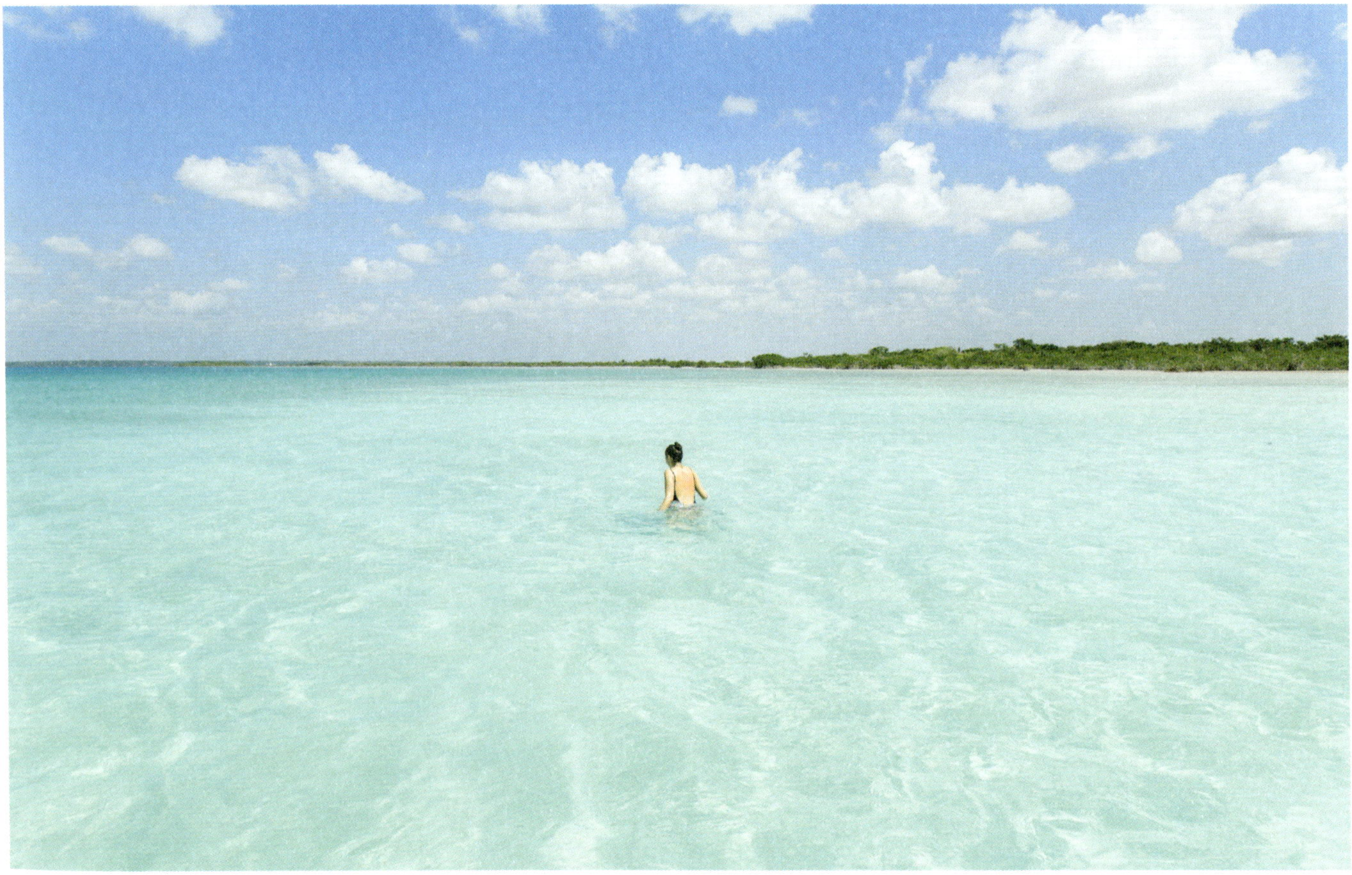

Finding a pristine patch of watery
paradise in Bacalar.

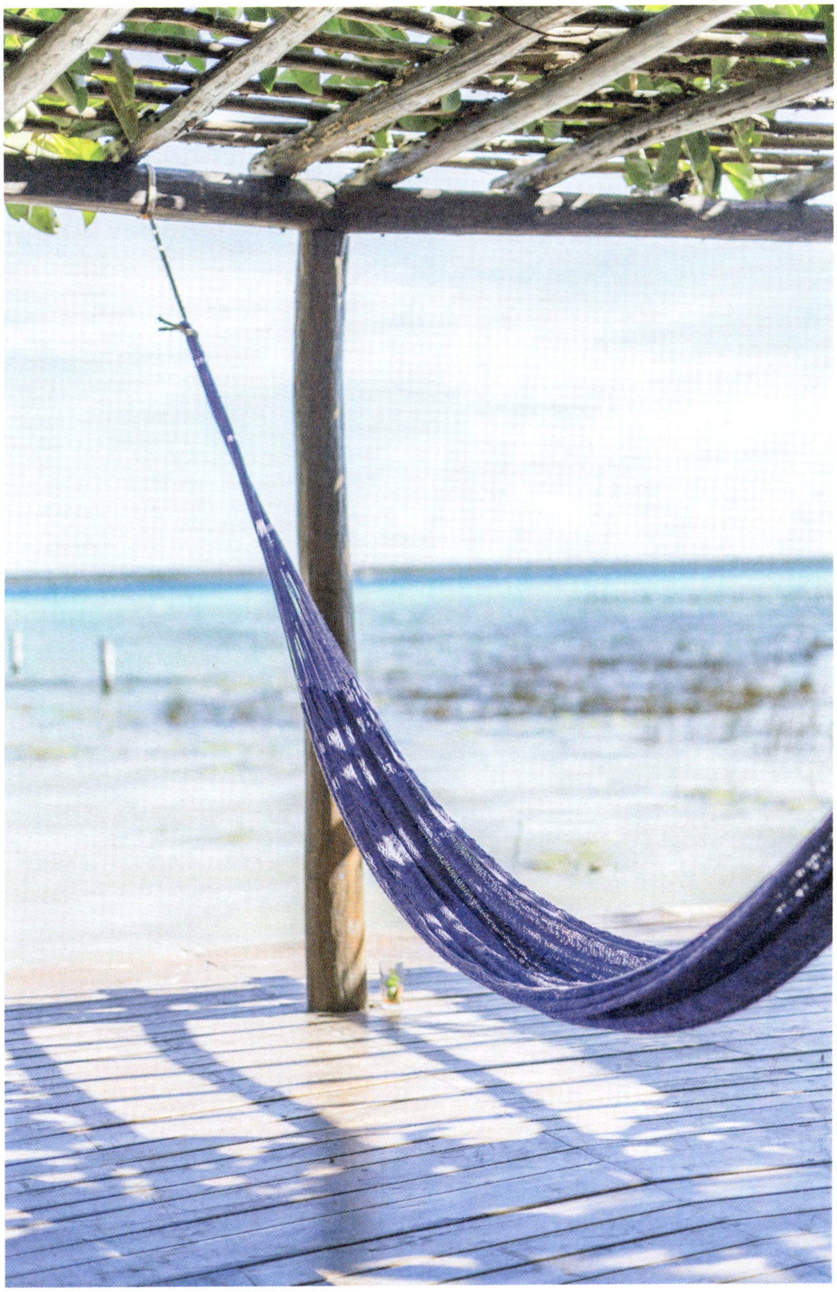

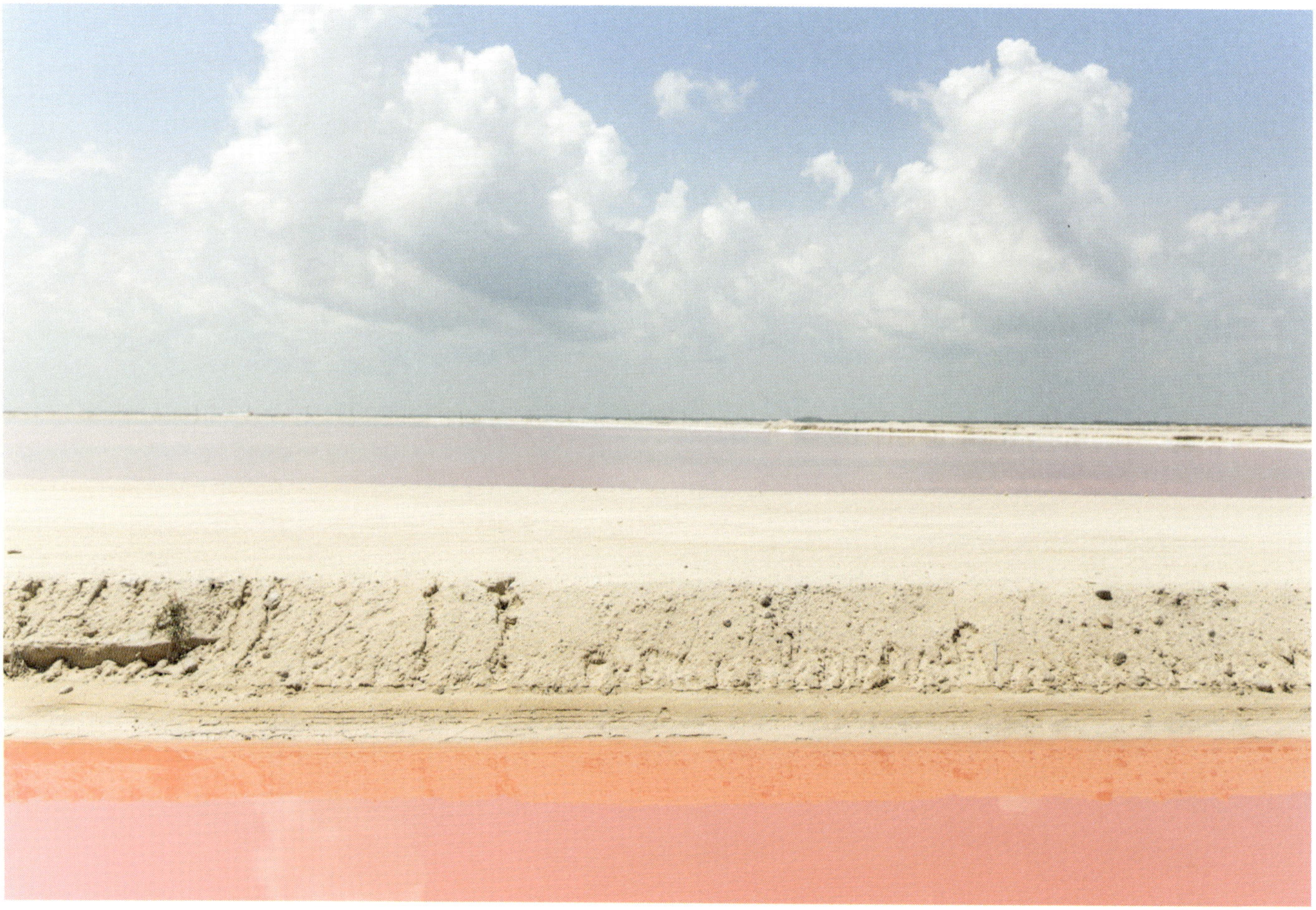

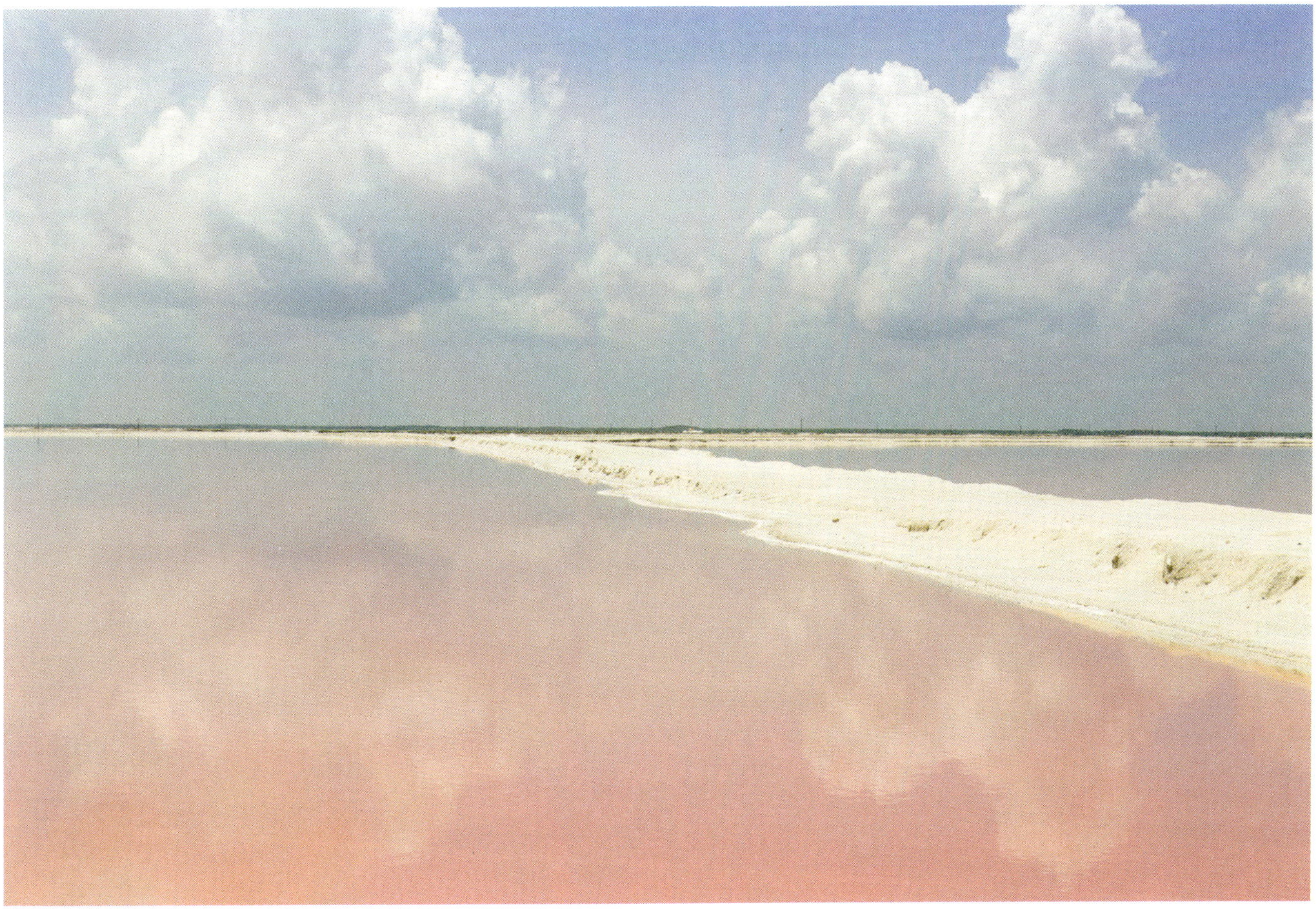

Committing the etherial hues of Las Coloradas to memory.

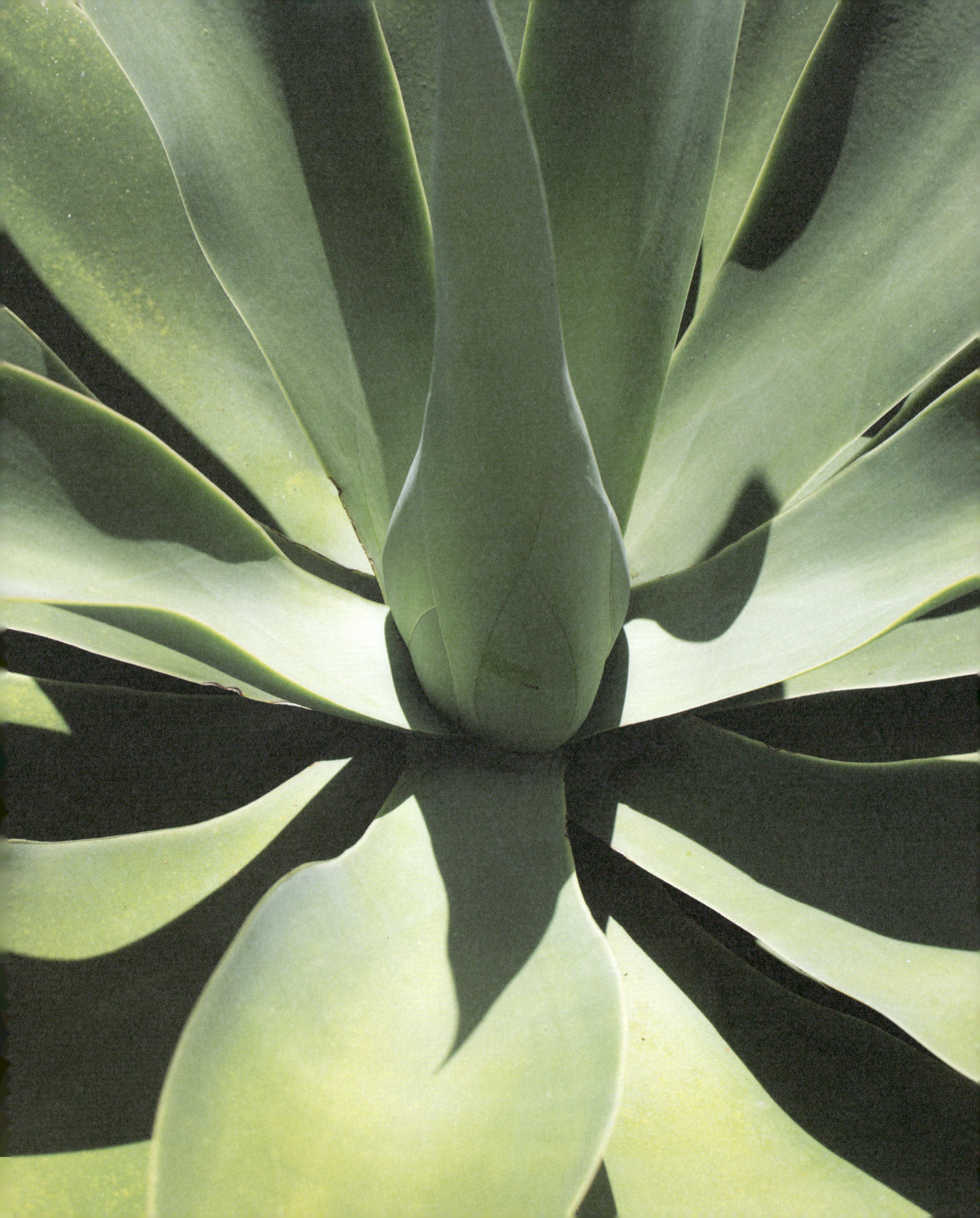

BERMUDA

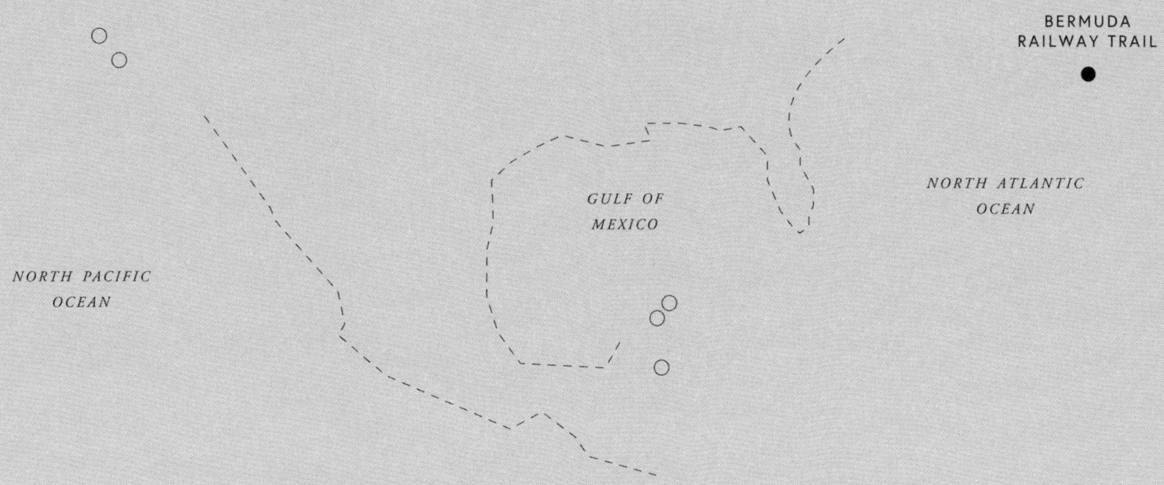

WORDS & PHOTOGRAPHS BY MEREDITH ANDREWS

The Bermuda Railway Trail

Although the Bermuda Railway was only in service for a brief period from 1931 to 1948, this single-track, 35 kilometre line has left a profound legacy on the Bermudian consciousness. But there are physical remnants too. Cut into the island's craggy limestone, the Bermuda Railway Trail, which follows the disused route, is a sub-tropical oasis filled with flora, fauna and memories of a not-so-distant past.

The British colony of Bermuda is one of the world's most isolated inhabited islands but its strategic Mid-Atlantic position saw it develop into a cosmopolitan society with a state-of-the-art railway, one of the globe's most expensive at the time. In its heyday, self-propelled steel carriages would rumble across the length of the island, carrying residents who would have otherwise had to endure the sluggish pace of walking, cycling or horse-powered transport. However, the end of the Second World War and introduction of private cars caused a steep decline in passenger numbers and the railway was eventually decommissioned.

My paternal grandmother's lineage goes back to some of the island's first 17th century settlers, while my grandfather arrived as a British seaman aboard the Monarch of Bermuda. Family lore tells the tale of my dapper, moustachioed grandfather spying my grandmother riding her bicycle down the dockside of Hamilton's Front Street. Picking up the courage, he followed her into the Bank of Bermuda, where she worked, and immediately charmed her. The rest is history. These are the sort of romantic memories that come to mind when I walk the trail today.

Despite human intervention, nature has been the dominant force shaping the trail's contemporary appearance, for the Bermuda environment can be a harsh one. The timber and steel structures are no match for the corrosive power of the sea and in the decades since the railway ran, the salt air has punished the original architecture. In addition, plant life has reclaimed the land, creating organic tunnels and cracking concrete foundations.

Over 1,000 kilometres from the nearest landmass, it's no wonder Bermudian history is rich in the extraordinary. The railway ran predominantly along a coastal path, inhabiting a narrow, curious zone between the comfort of land and the vast unknown of the ocean. At times this sense of isolation is frightening, but a short walk or bike ride along the trail quickly grounds me. With history and beauty ever-present, it's a much-needed reminder of how insignificant we really are.

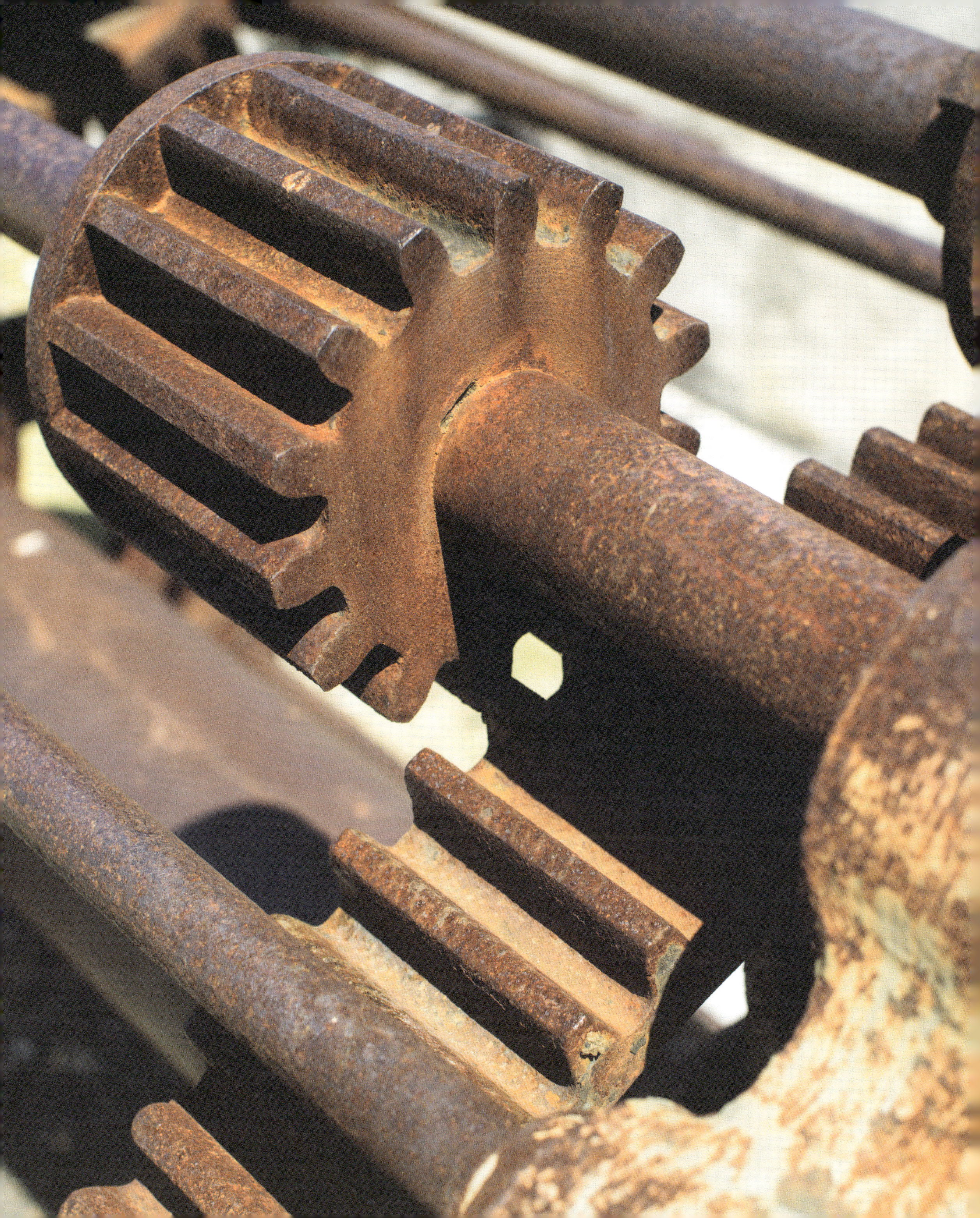

As a photographer I often see my surroundings in visual and geometric ways - the law of thirds, vanishing lines and the captivating infinity of the horizon. Along the trail this is especially true. The sun beats down with hard, uncompromising light for most of the day, while the gently diagonal palm trees create a sense of scale against the merging sea and sky. Naked concrete pylons, upon which the railway's many bridges once sat, remain scattered like solid, vertical sculptures.

The Bermuda Railway Trail is filled with patinated ghosts from its industrial past and personal tales of a simpler, bygone era. For these reasons I cherish it. Although the twists and turns of the path are familiar to me, it is the mental journey that proves most engaging. I look forward to my next walk where I can, once again, get lost in a place I know so well. *

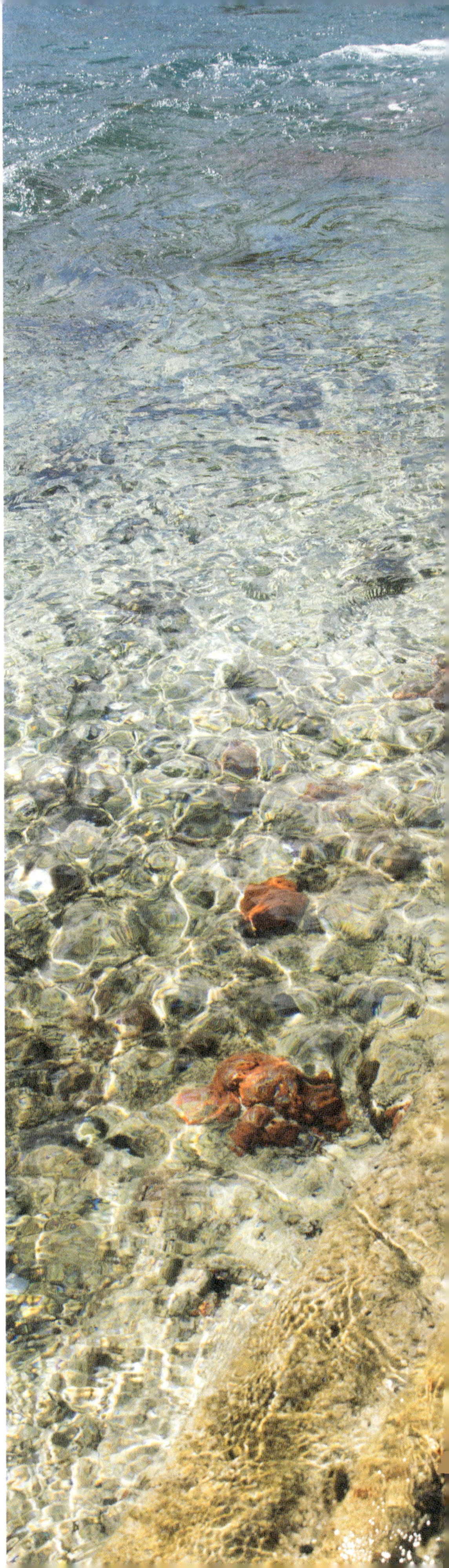

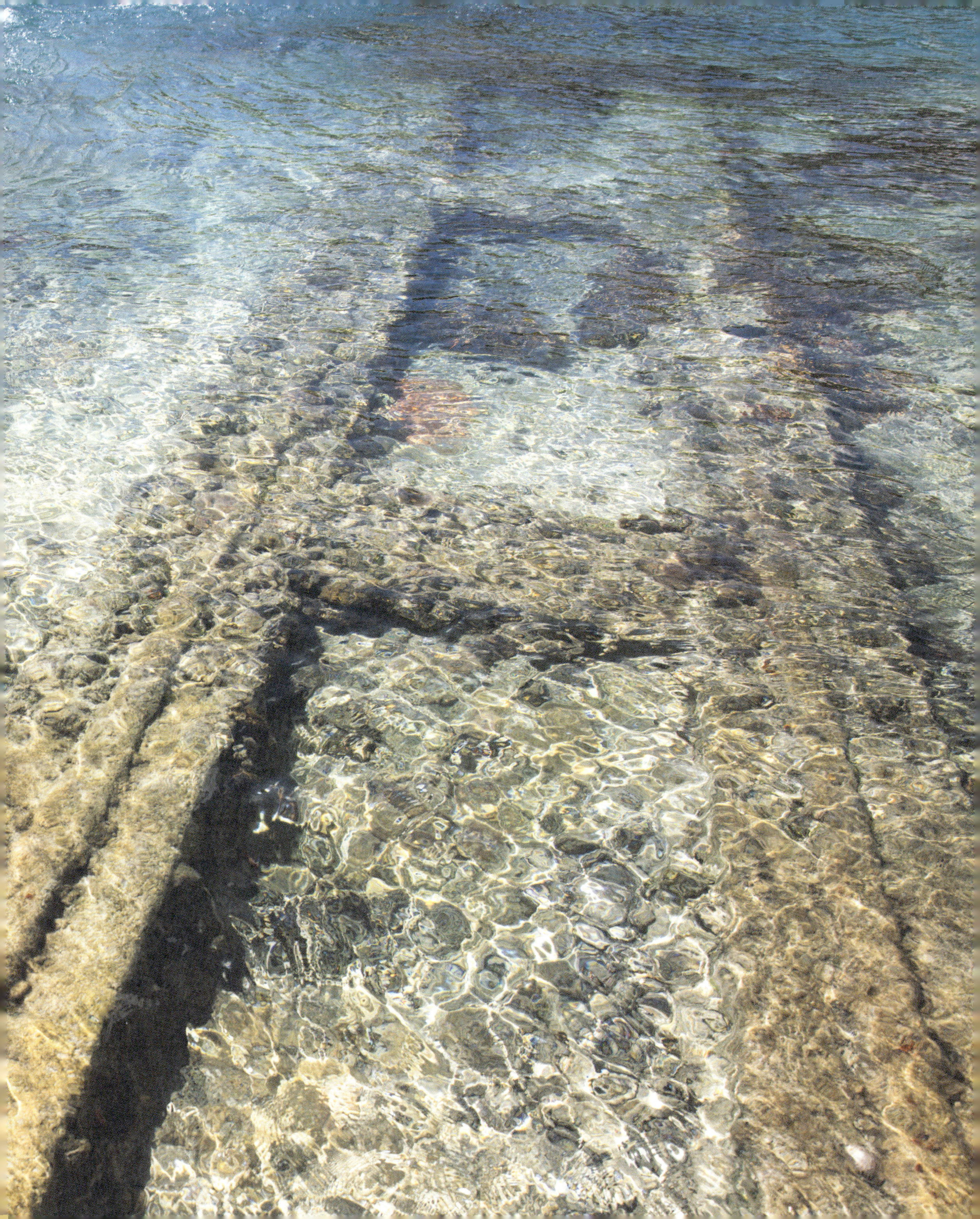

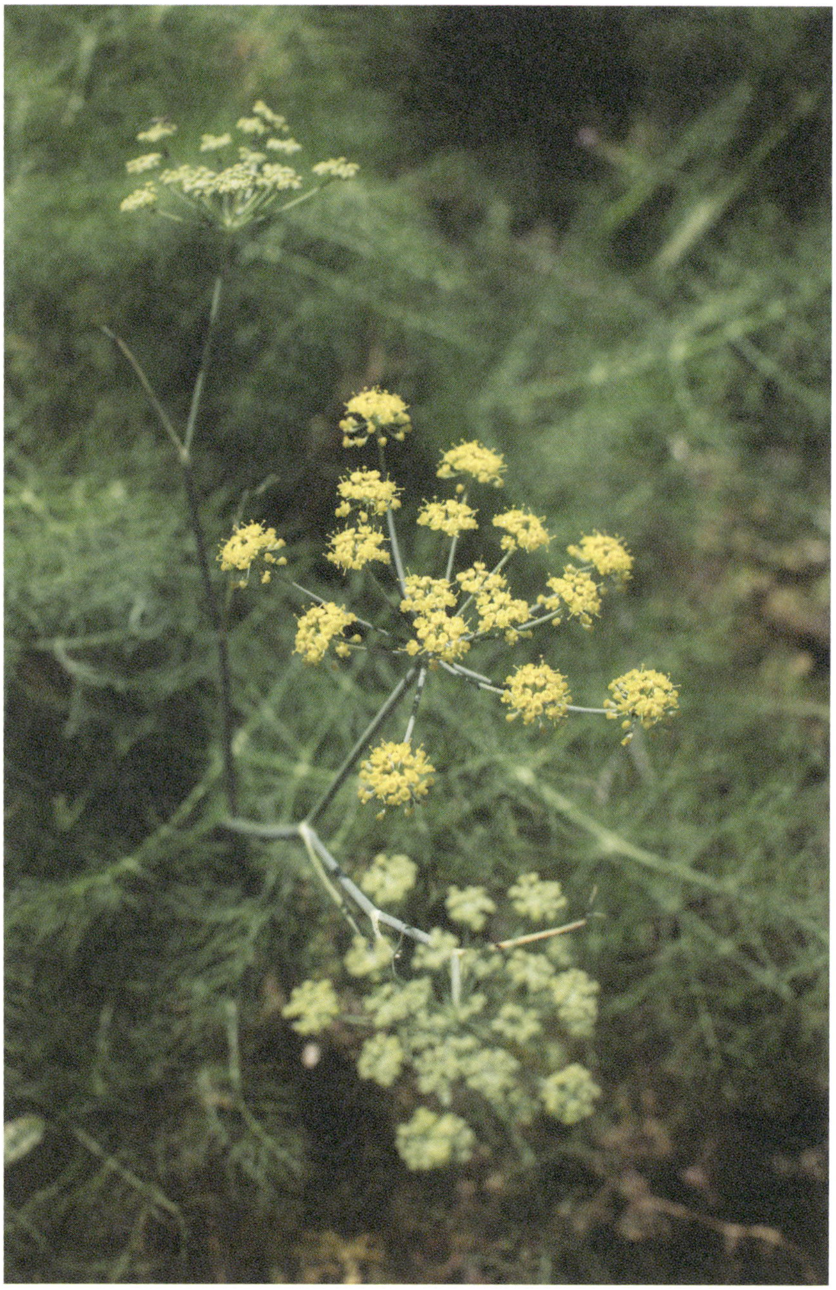

The enthralling scars of time, salt and wind upon the Bermuda Railway Trail.

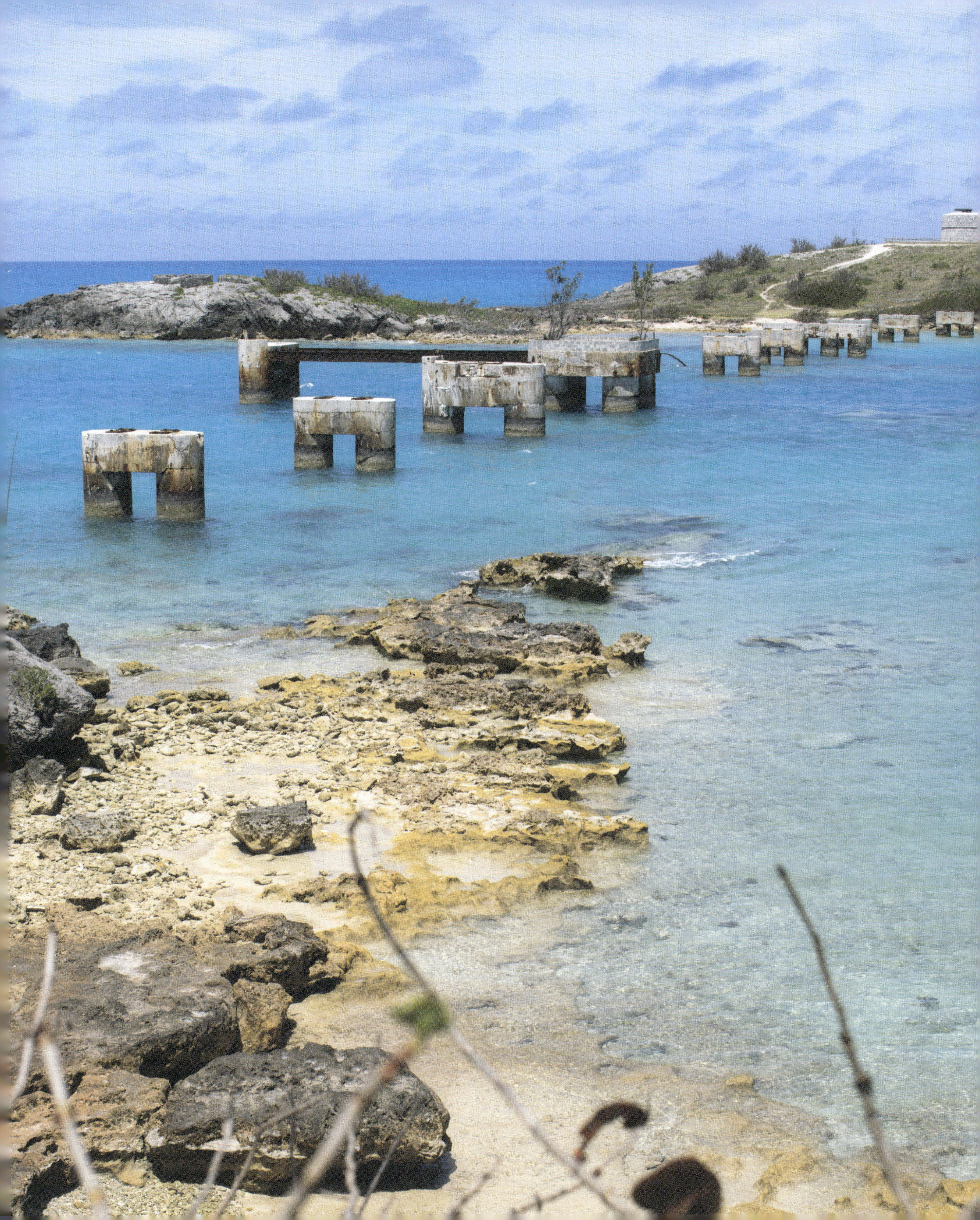

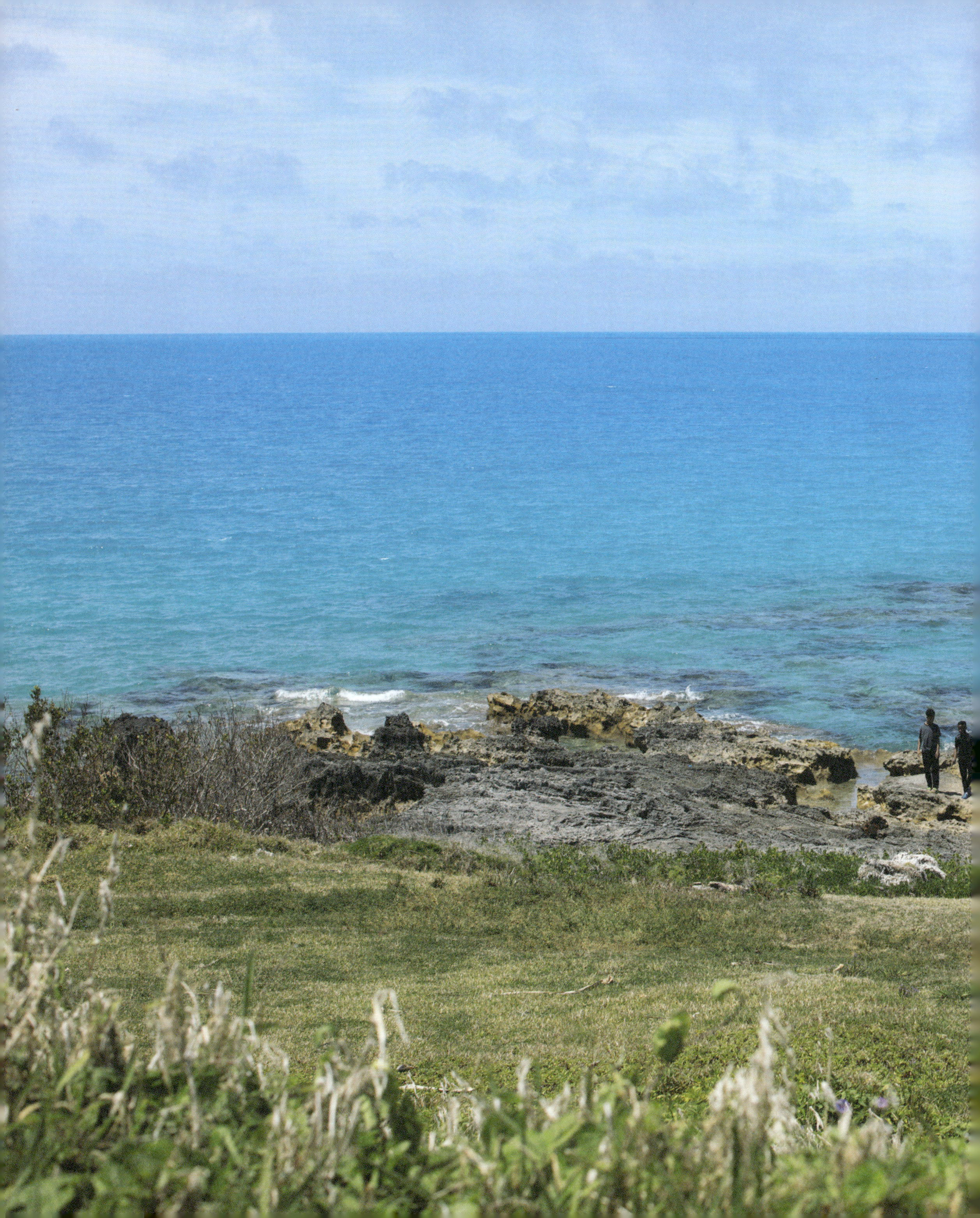

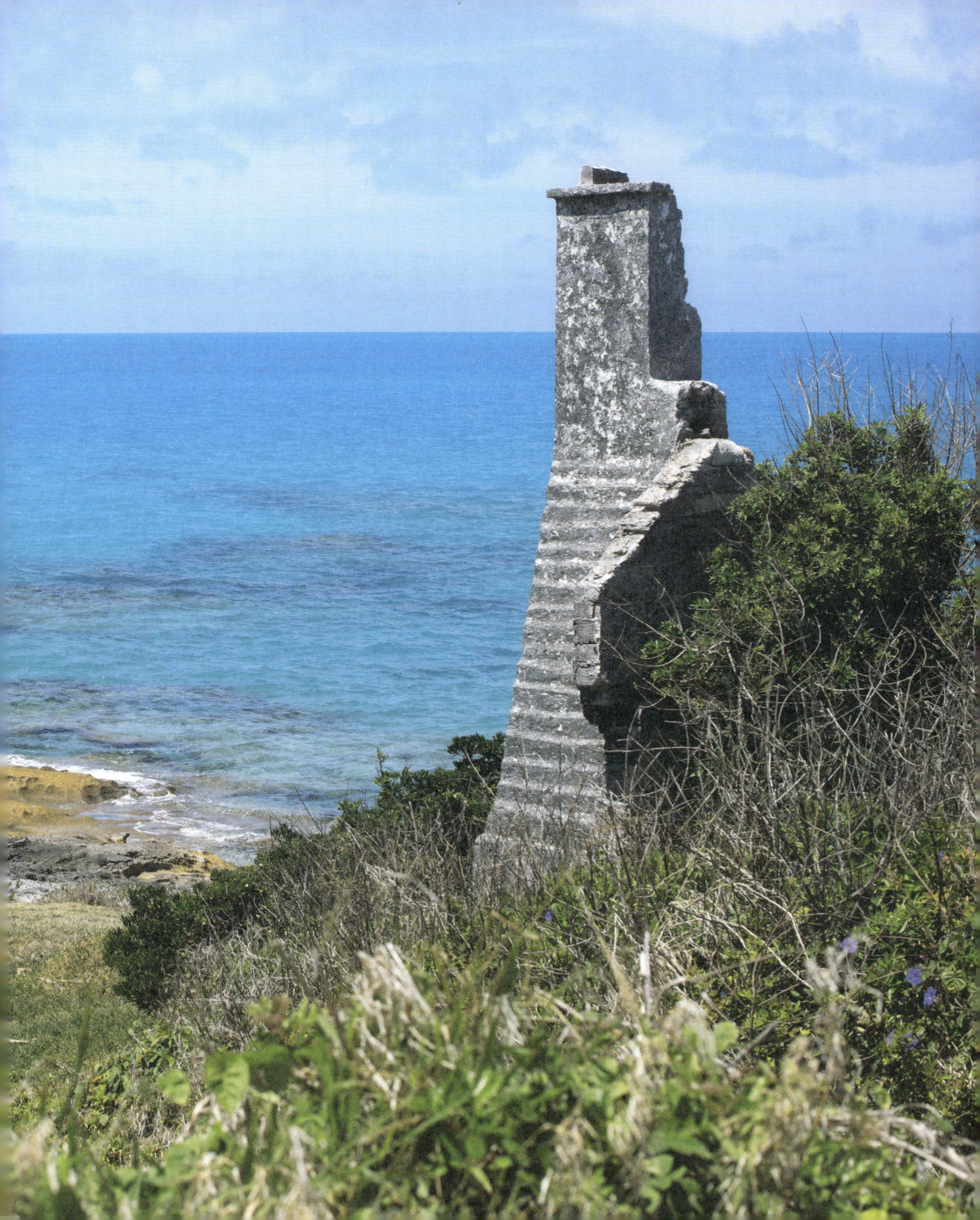

LODESTARS ANTHOLOGY

PATHWAYS

Published by New Heroes & Pioneers

Edited by Liz Schaffer

Creative Direction: Francois Le Bled

Creative Consultant: Matt Porter

Book Design: Daniel Zachrisson

Cover Photograph: Georgina Skinner

Photography:

Meredith Andrews, Tom Bunning, Tania Malkin, Matt Porter, Liz Schaffer, Georgina Skinner, Renae Smith, Beth Squire, Angela Terrell, Marioly Vazquez, Virginia Woods-Jack

Text:

Meredith Andrews, Yvette Edwards, Jen Harrison Bunning, Francois Le Bled, Claire Nelson, Shaun Pett, Liz Schaffer, Angela Terrell, Kieren Toscan

Illustration:

Phoebe Atkey, Saara Karppinen, Marina Marcolin

Portions of the text appearing in the Scotland, Japan and New Zealand chapters have appeared in previous issues of *Lodestars Anthology*, respectively issue 2 published in 2015, issue 7 published in 2017 and issue 8 published in 2017. The cover and opening images have appeared in *Lodestars Anthology* issue 8. Some images in the Australia chapter of this book (pages 44/45, 46, 47 and 49) appeared previously in *Lodestars Anthology* issue 3 published in 2015. Some images in the Canada chapter of this book (pages 92, 98, 100 and 101) appeared previously in *Lodestars Anthology* issue 6 published in 2016. Some images in the Japan chapter of this book (pages 103 and 108/109) appeared previously in *Lodestars Anthology* issue 7 published in 2017. Some images in the New Zealand chapter of the book (pages 116, 118/119, 124/125, 127, 128/129, 131 and 132/133) appeared previously in *Lodestars Anthology* issue 8 published in 2017.

Printed and bound by Lemon Print (Estonia)

Legal deposit October 2017

ISBN 978-91-87815-874

newHeroes&Pioneers

Special thanks to Sarah Kelleher and Miranda Keymer for reading every word with such care (as always), Patrick DiMatteo and Ralph Wills of PHMedia for their patience, Jen Harrison Bunning for general wisdom and Angela and Garry – my childish parents who I hold responsible for my insatiable wanderlust.

Thank you also to our brilliant-beyond-words contributors (who venture into the unknown with such passion) and to Aosta Valley UK, Terroir Selection, Visit Sweden and JNTO's Hollie Mantle.

— Liz Schaffer